EMERGING
GLOBAL CULTURES

Second Edition

Edited by
J.A. English-Lueck
Jennifer Anderson
Sandra Cate
Soo Choi
Karen Fjelstad
Roberto Gonzalez
Patricia Lange
William Reckmeyer

San Jose State University

PEARSON

Custom
Publishing

Cover image by Mark Edwards, courtesy of Still Photography, London, England.
Interior cover map taken from CIA World Factbook.

Printed in the United States of America

10 9 8 7 6 5 4 3 2 1

ISBN 0-536-17560-8

2005500188

CS/WH

Please visit our web site at *www.pearsoncustom.com*

PEARSON CUSTOM PUBLISHING
75 Arlington Street, Suite 300, Boston, MA 02116
A Pearson Education Company

Copyright Acknowledgments

"Introduction to Transnationalism, Localization, and Fast Foods in East Asia," by James L. Watson, reprinted from *Golden Arches East: McDonald's in East Asia* (1997), by permission of Stanford University Press, www.sup.org. Copyright © 1997 by the Board of Trustees of the Leland Stanford Junior University.

"Across Space and Through Time: Tomatl Meets the Corporate Tomato," by Deborah Barndt, reprinted from *Tangled Routes: Women, Work and Globalization on the Tomato Trail* (2002), by permission of Rowman & Littlefield Publishing.

"Civilization and its Discontents," by Katharine Milton, reprinted by permission from *Natural History* (March, 1992). Copyright © 1992 Natural History Magazine, Inc.

"The Global Village: Television, Tourism and Travel," by George and Sharon Bohn Gmelch, reprinted from *The Parish Behind God's Back* (1997, reissued 2001), by permission of Waveland Press (Long Grove, IL).

"Virtually Vietnamese: Nationalism on the Internet," by Kim-An Lieberman, reprinted from *Asian America.net: Ethnicity, Nationalism, and Cyberspace*, edited by Rachel C. Lee and Sau-Ling Cynthia Wong (2003), by permission of Routledge/Taylor & Francis Group, LLC.

"Democracy and Terror in the Era of Jihad vs. McWorld," by Benjamin R. Barber, reprinted from *Worlds of Collision: Terror and the Future of Global Order* (2002), by permission of the author. Published originally in *Worlds of Collision: Terror and the Future of Global Order* (Palgrave MacMillan, 2002).

"Two Cheers for Colonialism," by Dinesh D'Souza, reprinted from *The Chronicle Review*, May 10, 2002, by permission of the author.

"What Real Globalization Would Mean," by David Graeber, reprinted from *www.progress.org*, May 2003, by permission of The Benjamin Banneker Center for Economic Justice and Progress.

Contents

Introductory remarks for each chapter by Soo Choi and J.A. English-Lueck

1. Introduction

You have booked your trip to Hong Kong using e-fares to find the most economical package. Travel to Asia is commonplace, particularly in light of the opportunities to be found there. The fare is particularly inexpensive because fears of SARS and the avian flu have made airlines desperate. Your company is heavily involved with the oil industry and you have been briefed on the political situation in Central Asia which may have bearing on any decisions that need to be made. Before you leave home, you surf the Hong Kong International Airport website and follow the links on the pop-up. Special links have been created to help you recognize SARS, and be prepared to minimize exposure. Links go to security pages informing passengers that they will be given plastic bags for their mobile phones, keys, coins and lighters to speed up the security process. The website even instructs the passengers that this will take place immediately after they leave the Immigration area and enter the security checking areas. You take the virtual tour of the airport so you will know how to proceed when you land. You do not really need to do this tour—one airport is much like another. You are going to Kowloon, to stay in the YMCA facility there. When you get off the ferry you pass the gauntlet of shops and pause at the McDonald's to grab a burger and fries, or maybe a Korean-style wrap. You may spot a bored elderly man, waiting to pose with tourists next to a rickshaw. If you wander to far into Kowloon, you may also see the equivalent of the homeless, displaced people from different parts of Asia who do not quite fit in with the skyscrapers. Welcome to the emerging global culture. Hong Kong, London, Los Angeles are much the same experience. Or are they?

If you unpack the experience outlined above and start to examine it, you will begin to discover that local cultures intertwine with the emerging global culture in ways both subtle and profound. You discover that the traveler's world is viewed quite differently by the taxi driver who takes her to her hotel. The standardization of the airports, YMCA hostels and McDonald's restaurants are not complete, but reflect the values, expectations and realities of the local consumers, as well as the tourists. Hong Kong is itself struggling with its own identity, not quite as Chinese as Beijing sees it, but not separate either. Each global organization, such as the McDonald's restaurant, is embedded in a web of economic, social and political relationships, the forerunners of which extend back into centuries. China's balance of trade is not only a 21st

1

century issue, but one that dominated relations from the 18th century onward. Globalization has been long in the making.

This book of readings is designed to provoke your thinking so that you will not be able to take that airplane trip, that burger, or even the tomato in that burger for granted again. You will reflect on the juxtaposition of historic, social and political forces that has shaped your experience. You will see that each object you hold, each bite you eat, each relationship, while shaped by global developments, intertwines with local understandings, frameworks and experiences. To unravel these linkages we need to develop a toolkit that permits us to take seemingly ordinary experiences and expose the global connections. Intrinsic to this endeavor are three perspectives.

First, we use the anthropological imagination, struggling to document and understand emerging cultures, particularly ones that challenge our own comfortable assumptions. We need to be able to grasp different points of view, which are not usually part of our experience of daily life. This includes an understanding that globalization viewed from above often looks very different from globalization as seen from below. A Wall Street banker and a woman sorting genetically-modified tomatoes will have very different perceptions and experiences with globalization; the question of power dramatically shapes attitudes, ideas and responses to global transformations. Second, we use a systems approach to track processes in time and space. Elements in a system interact and changing one part often leads to unanticipated consequences. It is necessary to understand both the whole and the part. Systems evolve; they change through time. Thus we can anticipate what may happen, at least enough to plan and apply that anthropological and systemic knowledge to the real world. This futures approach is the third perspective integral to the book. Together, the three perspectives—anthropological, systemic and anticipatory—inform how we understand globalization.

We begin the book by giving you a series of readings directly related to these three perspectives. Globalization is a current reality, but how it is experienced on the ground depends heavily on where you see it. Romantic visions of opportunity and transformation rest side by side with critiques of globalization which note that power and poverty are familiar specters. Thomas Friedman's "It's a Flat World, After All" tells a very different story than that pointed out by Roberto Gonzalez, an anthropologist, in his review, "Falling Flat." Together, this pair of articles sets up the debate about the utility and direction of globalization. Several articles, Peter Bishop's "Thinking Like a Futurist," and Victoria Razak's "Anticipatory Anthropology," take us to the next step—how to apply systems and anthropological thinking to forecasting and planning.

Outfitted with these conceptual tools you are ready to grapple with the central concept of this book—the formation and structure of globalization. Richard Robbins takes a detailed, historical look at the emergence of the global political economy in "The Rise of the Merchant, Industrialist, and Capital Controller" while anthropologist Ray Scupin examines the social and ecological consequences of "Contemporary Global Trends." The movements of populations and the interaction of States, NGO's and refugee peoples are explored in "Refugees" by Stephen Lubkemann.

However, the premise of this book is that macro-level examinations of globalization tell only part of the story. The rest of the tale lies in the experiences of people embedded in their own cultures, lives and values. To illustrate this concept we offer up the familiar world of McDonald's fast food, but as it is experienced in East Asia. The reading, "Transnationalism, Localization, and Fast Foods in East Asia," excerpted from James Watson's book, *Golden Arches East,* toys with our assumptions about the familiar and the exotic.

The political economy of the emerging global cultures is also experienced quite differently in particular settings. Several case studies illuminate the interface between economic practices and cultural experience. "Across Space and Through Time: Tomatl meets the Corporate Tomato," by Deborah Barndt takes the humble tomato through its natural and corporate history, illustrating unguessed global connections. Katherine Milton similarly illustrates the economic principles of a small-scale society in the Amazon. She contrasts the values and practices she observed with the ones these people are encountering in the wider economic sphere. "Civilization and Its Discontents" questions the assumption that such culture contact is inherently beneficial to the indigenous peoples.

Trade, travel, technology, tourism, terrorism—all of these aspects of the emerging global culture necessitate the movement of people, ideas, and material culture across the planet. George and Sharon Bohn Gmelch puts human faces on these forces in an excerpt from an ethnography on the Caribbean island of Barbados, "The Global Village: Television, Tourism and Travel." Kim-An Lieberman explores what it means to be Vietnamese after the diaspora, in cyberspace. Identity, technology and politics intertwine in the emerging global culture. In an era of worldwide interconnections, terror becomes part of that kaleidoscope. In "Democracy and Terror in the Era of Jihad vs. McWorld," Benjamin Barber, a political scientist, contrasts the reasoning behind corporate homogenization, with the worldviews of those who resist it. He sees both globalism and what he calls tribalism as intrinsic threats to democracy.

We began the book with a debate about the interpretation of globalization, and so we end it with another round. Conventional anthropological wisdom tells us that perspective matters, and that the same phenomenon can be viewed quite distinctly by people who are positioned differently within society. Dinesh D'Souza's "Two Cheers for Colonialism" looks at the legacy of colonialism quite differently than David Graeber. The latter questions "What Real Globalization Would Mean," if it were not articulated by powerful decision-makers of global economic institutions.

San Jose, California   JAEL

2. It's a Flat World, After All

Thomas Friedman

These two introductory essays frame many aspects of the current debates regarding global-ization. Globalization is often thought of as a purely economic phenomenon, so that there is almost a sense of surprise when politics and culture seem to be part of the exchange as well. Moreover, globalization is one phenomenon, a relatively simple one, when viewed from the perspective of relatively elite scholarly, business and governmental interests. It is yet another entity when viewed on the ground, when the consequences of global interdependency are expe-rienced by people whose lives are far from the experiences of the average American. Anthropology is a discipline that embraces complexity and also tries to consider phenomena from multiple perspectives—above, below, near and distant. Friedman reconsiders the old political economic model of globalization, whose descent can be directly traced to colonialism, in which "the West" is the dominant player. Has this model changed as emerging economies in Asia become significant? Using the old sports metaphor of the "level playing field" Friedman suggests that globalization is flattening the world. Anthropologist Roberto Gonzalez suggests that this posi-tion glosses over major cultural overgeneralizations, conflating economic and cultural behav-ior. He suggests that much of history is ignored or misrepresented in Friedman's argument. Gonzalez also asks us to consider the perspectives of people outside the global elite. Would farmers and factory workers so easily assert the flatness of that global playing field?

In 1492 Christopher Columbus set sail for India, going west. He had the Nina, the Pinta and the Santa Maria. He never did find India, but he called the people he met "Indians" and came home and reported to his king and queen: "The world is round." I set off for India 512 years later. I knew just which direction I was going. I went east. I had Lufthansa business class, and I came home and reported only to my wife and only in a whisper: "The world is flat."

And therein lies a tale of technology and geoeconomics that is fundamentally reshaping our lives—much, much more quickly than many people realize. It all happened while we were sleeping, or rather while we were focused on 9/11, the dot-com bust and Enron—which even prompted some to wonder whether globalization was over. Actually, just the opposite was true, which is why it's time to wake up and prepare ourselves for this flat world, because others already are, and there is no time to waste.

I wish I could say I saw it all coming. Alas, I encountered the flattening of the world quite by accident. It was in late February of last year, and I was visiting the Indian high-tech capital, Bangalore, working on a documentary for the Discovery Times channel about outsourcing. In short order, I interviewed Indian entrepreneurs who wanted to prepare my taxes from Bangalore, read my X-rays from Bangalore, trace my lost luggage from Bangalore and write my new software from Bangalore. The longer I was there, the more upset I became—upset at the realization that while I had been off covering the 9/11 wars, globalization had entered a whole new phase, and I had missed it. I guess the eureka moment came on a visit to the campus of Infosys Technologies, one of the crown jewels of the Indian outsourcing and software industry. Nandan Nilekani, the Infosys C.E.O., was showing me his global video-conference room, pointing with pride to a wall-size flat-screen TV, which he said was the biggest in Asia. Infosys, he explained, could hold a virtual meeting of the key players from its entire global supply chain for any project at any time on that supersize screen. So its American designers could be on the screen speaking with their Indian software writers and their Asian manufacturers all at once. That's what globalization is all about today, Nilekani said. Above the screen there were eight clocks that pretty well summed up the Infosys workday: 24/7/365. The clocks were labeled U.S. West, U.S. East, G.M.T., India, Singapore, Hong Kong, Japan, Australia.

"Outsourcing is just one dimension of a much more fundamental thing happening today in the world," Nilekani explained. "What happened over the last years is that there was a massive investment in technology, especially in the bubble era, when hundreds of millions of dollars were invested in putting broadband connectivity around the world, undersea cables, all those things." At the same time, he added, computers became cheaper and dispersed all over the world, and there was an explosion of e-mail software, search engines like Google and proprietary software that can chop up any piece of work and send one part to Boston, one part to Bangalore and one part to Beijing, making it easy for anyone to do remote development. When all of these things suddenly came together around 2000, Nilekani said, they "created a platform where intellectual work, intellectual capital, could be delivered from anywhere. It could be disaggregated, delivered, distributed, produced and put back together again—and this gave a whole new degree of freedom to the way we do work, especially work of an intellectual nature. And what you are seeing in Bangalore today is really the culmination of all these things coming together."

At one point, summing up the implications of all this, Nilekani uttered a phrase that rang in my ear. He said to me, "Tom, the playing field is being leveled." He meant that countries like India were now able to compete equally for global knowledge work as never before—and that America had better get ready for this. As I left the Infosys campus that evening and bounced along the potholed road back to Bangalore, I kept chewing on that phrase: "The playing field is being leveled."

"What Nandan is saying," I thought, "is that the playing field is being flattened. Flattened? Flattened? My God, he's telling me the world is flat!"

Here I was in Bangalore—more than 500 years after Columbus sailed over the horizon, looking for a shorter route to India using the rudimentary navigational technologies of his day, and returned safely to prove definitively that the world was round—and one of India's smartest engineers, trained at his country's top technical institute and backed by the most modern technologies of his day, was telling me that the world was flat, as flat as that screen on which he can host a meeting of his whole global supply chain. Even more interesting, he was citing this development as a new milestone in human progress and a great opportunity for India and the world—the fact that we had made our world flat!

This has been building for a long time. Globalization 1.0 (1492 to 1800) shrank the world from a size large to a size medium, and the dynamic force in that era was countries globalizing for resources and imperial conquest. Globalization 2.0 (1800 to 2000) shrank the world from a size medium to a size small, and it was spearheaded by companies globalizing for markets and labor. Globalization 3.0 (which started around 2000) is shrinking the world from a size small to a size tiny and flattening the playing field at the same time. And while the dynamic force in Globalization 1.0 was countries globalizing and the dynamic force in Globalization 2.0 was companies globalizing, the dynamic force in Globalization 3.0—the thing that gives it its unique character—is individuals and small groups globalizing. Individuals must, and can, now ask: where do I fit into the global competition and opportunities of the day, and how can I, on my own, collaborate with others globally? But Globalization 3.0 not only differs from the previous eras in how it is shrinking and flattening the world and in how it is empowering individuals. It is also different in that Globalization 1.0 and 2.0 were driven primarily by European and American companies and countries. But going forward, this will be less and less true. Globalization 3.0 is not only going to be driven more by individuals but also by a much more diverse—non-Western, nonwhite—group of individuals. In Globalization 3.0, you are going to see every color of the human rainbow take part.

"Today, the most profound thing to me is the fact that a 14-year-old in Romania or Bangalore or the Soviet Union or Vietnam has all the information, all the tools, all the software easily available to apply knowledge however they want," said Marc Andreessen, a co-founder of Netscape and creator of the first commercial Internet browser. "That is why I am sure the next Napster is going to come out of left field. As bioscience becomes more computational and less about wet labs and as all the genomic data becomes easily available on the Internet, at some point you will be able to design vaccines on your laptop."

Andreessen is touching on the most exciting part of Globalization 3.0 and the flattening of the world: the fact that we are now in the process of connecting all the knowledge pools in the world together. We've tasted some of the downsides of that in the way that Osama bin Laden has connected terrorist knowledge pools together through his Qaeda network, not to mention the work of teenage hackers spinning off more and more lethal computer viruses that affect us all. But the upside is that by connecting all these knowledge pools we are on the cusp of an incredible new era of innovation, an era that will be driven from left field and right field, from West and East and from North and South. Only 30 years ago, if you had a choice of being born a B student in Boston or a genius in Bangalore or Beijing, you probably would have chosen Boston, because a genius in Beijing or Bangalore could not really take advantage of his or her talent. They could not plug and play globally. Not anymore. Not when the world is flat, and anyone with smarts, access to Google and a cheap wireless laptop can join the innovation fray.

When the world is flat, you can innovate without having to emigrate. This is going to get interesting. We are about to see creative destruction on steroids.

How did the world get flattened, and how did it happen so fast?

It was a result of 10 events and forces that all came together during the 1990's and converged right around the year 2000. Let me go through them briefly. The first event was 11/9. That's right—not 9/11, but 11/9. Nov. 9, 1989, is the day the Berlin Wall came down, which was critically important because it allowed us to think of the world as a single space. "The Berlin Wall was not only a symbol of keeping people inside Germany; it was a way of preventing a kind of global view of our future," the Nobel Prize-winning economist Amartya Sen said. And the wall went down just as the windows went up—the breakthrough Microsoft Windows 3.0 operating system, which helped to flatten the playing field even more by creating a global computer interface, shipped six months after the wall fell.

The second key date was 8/9. Aug. 9, 1995, is the day Netscape went public, which did two important things. First, it brought the Internet alive by giving us the browser to display images and data stored on Web sites. Second, the Netscape stock offering triggered the dot-com boom, which triggered the dot-com bubble, which triggered the massive overinvestment of billions of dollars in fiber-optic telecommunications cable. That overinvestment, by companies like Global Crossing, resulted in the willy-nilly creation of a global undersea-underground fiber network, which in turn drove down the cost of transmitting voices, data and images to practically zero, which in turn accidentally made Boston, Bangalore and Beijing next-door neighbors overnight. In sum, what the Netscape revolution did was bring people-to-people connectivity to a whole new level. Suddenly more people could connect with more other people from more different places in more different ways than ever before.

No country accidentally benefited more from the Netscape moment than India. "India had no resources and no infrastructure," said Dinakar Singh, one of the most respected hedge-fund managers on Wall Street, whose parents earned doctoral degrees in biochemistry from the University of Delhi before emigrating to America. "It produced people with quality and by quantity. But many of them rotted on the docks of India like vegetables. Only a relative few could get on ships and get out. Not anymore, because we built this ocean crosser, called fiber-optic cable. For decades you had to leave India to be a professional. Now you can plug into the world from India. You don't have to go to Yale and go to work for Goldman Sachs." India could never have afforded to pay for the bandwidth to connect brainy India with high-tech America, so American shareholders paid for it. Yes, crazy overinvestment can be good. The overinvestment in railroads turned out to be a great boon for the American economy. "But the railroad overinvestment was confined to your own country and so, too, were the benefits," Singh said. In the case of the digital railroads, "it was the foreigners who benefited." India got a free ride.

The first time this became apparent was when thousands of Indian engineers were enlisted to fix the Y2K—the year 2000—computer bugs for companies from all over the world. (Y2K should be a national holiday in India. Call it "Indian Interdependence Day," says Michael Mandelbaum, a foreign-policy analyst at Johns Hopkins.) The fact that the Y2K work could be outsourced to Indians was made possible by the first two flatteners, along with a third, which I call "workflow." Workflow is shorthand for all the software applications, standards and electronic transmission pipes, like middleware, that connected all those computers and fiber-optic cable. To put it another way, if the Netscape moment connected people to people like never before, what the workflow revolution did was connect applications to applications so that people all over the world could work together in manipulating and shaping words, data and images on computers like never before.

Indeed, this breakthrough in people-to-people and application-to-application connectivity produced, in short order, six more flatteners—six new ways in which individuals and companies could collaborate on work and share knowledge. One was "outsourcing." When my software applications could connect seamlessly with all of your applications, it meant that all kinds of work—from accounting to software-writing—could be digitized, disaggregated and shifted to any place in the world where it could be done better and cheaper. The second was "offshoring." I send my whole factory from Canton, Ohio, to Canton, China. The third was "open-sourcing." I write the next operating system, Linux, using engineers collaborating together online and working for free. The fourth was "insourcing." I let a company like UPS come inside my company and take over my whole logistics operation—everything from filling my orders online to delivering my goods to repairing them for customers when they break. (People have no idea what UPS really does today. You'd be amazed!). The fifth was "supply-chaining." This is Wal-Mart's specialty. I create a global supply chain down to the last atom of efficiency so that if I sell an item in Arkansas, another is immediately made in China. (If Wal-Mart were a country, it would be China's eighth-largest trading partner.) The last new form of collaboration I call "informing"—this is Google, Yahoo and MSN Search, which now allow anyone to collaborate with, and mine, unlimited data all by themselves.

So the first three flatteners created the new platform for collaboration, and the next six are the new forms of collaboration that flattened the world even more. The 10th flattener I call "the steroids," and these are wireless access and voice over Internet protocol (VoIP). What the steroids do is turbocharge all these new forms of collaboration, so you can now do any one of them, from anywhere, with any device.

The world got flat when all 10 of these flatteners converged around the year 2000. This created a global, Web-enabled playing field that allows for multiple forms of collaboration on research and work in real time, without regard to geography, distance or, in the near future, even language. "It is the creation of this platform, with these unique attributes, that is the truly important sustainable breakthrough that made what you call the flattening of the world possible," said Craig Mundie, the chief technical officer of Microsoft.

No, not everyone has access yet to this platform, but it is open now to more people in more places on more days in more ways than anything like it in history. Wherever you look today—whether it is the world of journalism, with bloggers bringing down Dan Rather; the world of software, with the Linux code writers working in online forums for free to challenge Microsoft; or the world of business, where Indian and Chinese innovators are competing against and working with some of the most advanced Western multinationals—hierarchies are being flattened and value is being created less and less within vertical silos and more and more through horizontal collaboration within companies, between companies and among individuals.

Do you recall "the IT revolution" that the business press has been pushing for the last 20 years? Sorry to tell you this, but that was just the prologue. The last 20 years were about forging, sharpening and distributing all the new tools to collaborate and connect. Now the real information revolution is about to begin as all the complementarities among these collaborative tools start to converge. One of those who first called this moment by its real name was Carly Fiorina, the former Hewlett-Packard C.E.O., who in 2004 began to declare in her public speeches that the dot-com boom and bust were just "the end of the beginning." The last 25 years in technology, Fiorina said, have just been "the warm-up act." Now we are going into the main event, she said, "and by the main event, I mean an era in which technology will truly transform every aspect of business, of government, of society, of life."

As if this flattening wasn't enough, another convergence coincidentally occurred during the 1990's that was equally important. Some three billion people who were out of the game walked, and often ran, onto the playing field. I am talking about the people of China, India, Russia, Eastern Europe, Latin America and Central Asia. Their economies and political systems all opened up during the course of the 1990's so that their people were increasingly free to join the free market. And when did these three billion people converge with the new playing field and the new business processes? Right when it was being flattened, right when millions of them could compete and collaborate more equally, more horizontally and with cheaper and more readily available tools. Indeed, thanks to the flattening of the world, many of these new entrants didn't even have to leave home to participate. Thanks to the 10 flatteners, the playing field came to them!

It is this convergence—of new players, on a new playing field, developing new processes for horizontal collaboration—that I believe is the most important force shaping global economics and politics in the early 21st century. Sure, not all three billion can collaborate and compete. In fact, for most people the world is not yet flat at all. But even if we're talking about only 10 percent, that's 300 million people—about twice the size of the American work force. And be advised: the Indians and Chinese are not racing us to the bottom. They are racing us to the top. What China's leaders really want is that the next generation of underwear and airplane wings not just be "made in China" but also be "designed in China." And that is where things are heading. So in 30 years we will have gone from "sold in China" to "made in China" to "designed in China" to "dreamed up in China"—or from China as collaborator with the worldwide manufacturers on nothing to China as a low-cost, high-quality, hyperefficient collaborator with worldwide manufacturers on everything. Ditto India. Said Craig Barrett, the C.E.O. of Intel, "You don't bring three billion people into the world economy overnight without huge consequences, especially from three societies"—like India, China and Russia—"with rich educational heritages."

That is why there is nothing that guarantees that Americans or Western Europeans will continue leading the way. These new players are stepping onto the playing field legacy free, meaning that many of them were so far behind that they can leap right into the new technologies without having to worry about all the sunken costs of old systems. It means that they can move very fast to adopt new, state-of-the-art technologies, which is why there are already more cell phones in use in China today than there are people in America.

If you want to appreciate the sort of challenge we are facing, let me share with you two conversations. One was with some of the Microsoft officials who were involved in setting up

Microsoft's research center in Beijing, Microsoft Research Asia, which opened in 1998—after Microsoft sent teams to Chinese universities to administer I.Q. tests in order to recruit the best brains from China's 1.3 billion people. Out of the 2,000 top Chinese engineering and science students tested, Microsoft hired 20. They have a saying at Microsoft about their Asia center, which captures the intensity of competition it takes to win a job there and explains why it is already the most productive research team at Microsoft: "Remember, in China, when you are one in a million, there are 1,300 other people just like you."

The other is a conversation I had with Rajesh Rao, a young Indian entrepreneur who started an electronic-game company from Bangalore, which today owns the rights to Charlie Chaplin's image for mobile computer games. "We can't relax," Rao said. "I think in the case of the United States that is what happened a bit. Please look at me: I am from India. We have been at a very different level before in terms of technology and business. But once we saw we had an infrastructure that made the world a small place, we promptly tried to make the best use of it. We saw there were so many things we could do. We went ahead, and today what we are seeing is a result of that. There is no time to rest. That is gone. There are dozens of people who are doing the same thing you are doing, and they are trying to do it better. It is like water in a tray: you shake it, and it will find the path of least resistance. That is what is going to happen to so many jobs—they will go to that corner of the world where there is the least resistance and the most opportunity. If there is a skilled person in Timbuktu, he will get work if he knows how to access the rest of the world, which is quite easy today. You can make a Web site and have an e-mail address and you are up and running. And if you are able to demonstrate your work, using the same infrastructure, and if people are comfortable giving work to you and if you are diligent and clean in your transactions, then you are in business."

Instead of complaining about outsourcing, Rao said, Americans and Western Europeans would "be better off thinking about how you can raise your bar and raise yourselves into doing something better. Americans have consistently led in innovation over the last century. Americans whining—we have never seen that before."

Rao is right. And it is time we got focused. As a person who grew up during the cold war, I'll always remember driving down the highway and listening to the radio, when suddenly the music would stop and a grim-voiced announcer would come on the air and say: "This is a test. This station is conducting a test of the Emergency Broadcast System." And then there would be a 20-second high-pitched siren sound. Fortunately, we never had to live through a moment in the cold war when the announcer came on and said, "This is a not a test."

That, however, is exactly what I want to say here: "This is not a test."

The long-term opportunities and challenges that the flattening of the world puts before the United States are profound. Therefore, our ability to get by doing things the way we've been doing them—which is to say not always enriching our secret sauce—will not suffice any more. "For a country as wealthy as we are, it is amazing how little we are doing to enhance our natural competitiveness," says Dinakar Singh, the Indian-American hedge-fund manager. "We are in a world that has a system that now allows convergence among many billions of people, and we had better step back and figure out what it means. It would be a nice coincidence if all the things that were true before were still true now, but there are quite a few things you actually need to do differently. You need to have a much more thoughtful national discussion."

If this moment has any parallel in recent American history, it is the height of the cold war, around 1957, when the Soviet Union leapt ahead of America in the space race by putting up the Sputnik satellite. The main challenge then came from those who wanted to put up walls; the main challenge to America today comes from the fact that all the walls are being taken down and many other people can now compete and collaborate with us much more directly. The main challenge in that world was from those practicing extreme Communism, namely Russia, China and North Korea. The main challenge to America today is from those practicing extreme capitalism, namely China, India and South Korea. The main objective in that era was building a strong state, and the main objective in this era is building strong individuals.

Meeting the challenges of flatism requires as comprehensive, energetic and focused a response as did meeting the challenge of Communism. It requires a president who can summon the nation to work harder, get smarter, attract more young women and men to science and engineering and build the broadband infrastructure, portable pensions and health care that will help every American become more employable in an age in which no one can guarantee you lifetime employment.

We have been slow to rise to the challenge of flatism, in contrast to Communism, maybe because flatism doesn't involve ICBM missiles aimed at our cities. Indeed, the hot line, which used to connect the Kremlin with the White House, has been replaced by the help line, which connects everyone in America to call centers in Bangalore. While the other end of the hot line might have had Leonid Brezhnev threatening nuclear war, the other end of the help line just has a soft voice eager to help you sort out your AOL bill or collaborate with you on a new piece of software. No, that voice has none of the menace of Nikita Khrushchev pounding a shoe on the table at the United Nations, and it has none of the sinister snarl of the bad guys in "From Russia With Love." No, that voice on the help line just has a friendly Indian lilt that masks any sense of threat or challenge. It simply says: "Hello, my name is Rajiv. Can I help you?"

No, Rajiv, actually you can't. When it comes to responding to the challenges of the flat world, there is no help line we can call. We have to dig into ourselves. We in America have all the basic economic and educational tools to do that. But we have not been improving those tools as much as we should. That is why we are in what Shirley Ann Jackson, the 2004 president of the American Association for the Advancement of Science and president of Rensselaer Polytechnic Institute, calls a "quiet crisis"—one that is slowly eating away at America's scientific and engineering base.

"If left unchecked," said Jackson, the first African-American woman to earn a Ph.D. in physics from M.I.T., "this could challenge our pre-eminence and capacity to innovate." And it is our ability to constantly innovate new products, services and companies that has been the source of America's horn of plenty and steadily widening middle class for the last two centuries. This quiet crisis is a product of three gaps now plaguing American society. The first is an "ambition gap." Compared with the young, energetic Indians and Chinese, too many Americans have gotten too lazy. As David Rothkopf, a former official in the Clinton Commerce Department, puts it, "The real entitlement we need to get rid of is our sense of entitlement." Second, we have a serious numbers gap building. We are not producing enough engineers and scientists. We used to make up for that by importing them from India and China, but in a flat world, where people can now stay home and compete with us, and in a post-9/11 world, where we are insanely keeping out many of the first-round intellectual draft choices in the world for exaggerated security reasons, we can no longer cover the gap. That's a key reason companies are looking abroad. The numbers are not here. And finally we are developing an education gap. Here is the dirty little secret that no C.E.O. wants to tell you: they are not just outsourcing to save on salary. They are doing it because they can often get better-skilled and more productive people than their American workers.

These are some of the reasons that Bill Gates, the Microsoft chairman, warned the governors' conference in a Feb. 26 speech that American high-school education is "obsolete." As Gates put it: "When I compare our high schools to what I see when I'm traveling abroad, I am terrified for our work force of tomorrow. In math and science, our fourth graders are among the top students in the world. By eighth grade, they're in the middle of the pack. By 12th grade, U.S. students are scoring near the bottom of all industrialized nations. . . . The percentage of a population with a college degree is important, but so are sheer numbers. In 2001, India graduated almost a million more students from college than the United States did. China graduates twice as many students with bachelor's degrees as the U.S., and they have six times as many graduates majoring in engineering. In the international competition to have the biggest and best supply of knowledge workers, America is falling behind."

We need to get going immediately. It takes 15 years to train a good engineer, because, ladies and gentlemen, this really is rocket science. So parents, throw away the Game Boy, turn off the television and get your kids to work. There is no sugar-coating this: in a flat world, every individual is going to have to run a little faster if he or she wants to advance his or her standard of living. When I was growing up, my parents used to say to me, "Tom, finish your dinner—people in China are starving." But after sailing to the edges of the flat world for a year, I am now telling my own daughters, "Girls, finish your homework—people in China and India are starving for your jobs."

I repeat, this is not a test. This is the beginning of a crisis that won't remain quiet for long. And as the Stanford economist Paul Romer so rightly says, "A crisis is a terrible thing to waste."

Thomas L. Friedman is the author of "The World Is Flat: A Brief History of the Twenty-First Century."

3. Falling Flat

Roberto J. Gonzalez

Over the past 15 years, Thomas Friedman's writing has influenced presidents, policy-makers and captains of industry across the world. His New York Times columns reach millions of people daily, and he has established himself as a leading member of the American punditry.

Yet Friedman's latest book, "The World Is Flat," is culturally misinformed, historically inadequate and intellectually impoverished. It is also a runaway best-seller.

The book's main point is that the world is "flattening"—becoming more interconnected—as the result of the Internet, wireless technology, search engines and other innovations. Consequently, corporate capitalism has spread like wildfire to China, India and Russia, where factory workers, engineers and software programmers are paid a fraction of what their American counterparts are paid.

Business reporters, labor activists, historians and anthropologists have reported these trends for more than a decade, but Friedman would have us believe that he single-handedly discovered the "flat world." In fact, without a trace of irony, he compares himself to Christopher Columbus embarking upon a global journey of exploration.

To awe his readers, Friedman relies upon anecdotes and vignettes from recent trips. He breathlessly recounts visiting booming Asian cities that he portrays as landscapes littered with American logos from IBM, Goldman Sachs, Microsoft and Pizza Hut. In Bangalore (India) and Dalian (China), cheerful CEOs and young high-tech workers explain how wonderful corporate globalization has been for them. Friedman gushes about golf courses and skyscrapers built by U.S. companies around the world; he raves about handheld gadgets that send faxes, snap photos and play MP3 tunes; and he reminisces about sushi bars in Dubai and Bentonville (the Arkansas home of Wal-Mart).

Not until the final chapters does he acknowledge that most Indians and Chinese still live in poverty. He never mentions that the gap between rich and poor in both India and China is widening. Nor does he dwell on the fact that many of the companies that have laid off thousands of Bay Area employees (Santa Clara County alone lost 231,000 jobs between 2000 and 2004) have replaced them with workers in Asia.

In the second half of the book, Friedman ponders the implications of living in a "flat world." He argues that for the United States and developing countries, this is both a crisis and an opportunity. In order to succeed, the United States must produce greater numbers of specialized workers, including lawyers, accountants, brain surgeons and computer designers. Developing countries must dismantle trade barriers, privatize state industries, invite foreign companies and change their attitudes. And the "unflat world" (here Friedman really means the "Arab-Muslim world" and sub-Saharan Africa) must get over its feelings of frustration, insecurity and illness.

Toward the end of the book Friedman acknowledges that most of the global population does not live in a "flat world"—and that many have no desire to do so. To explain this, he resorts to a facile explanation: culture. He argues that cultures open to foreign ideas (he really means open to corporate capitalism and mass consumption) will blossom in the 21st century, while closed cultures will wither.

Friedman's understanding of culture is simplistic and sloppy. He relies upon analogies rather than analysis, stereotypes rather than social science, and hearsay rather than history. For example, he muses upon what the world's regions would look like if they were neighborhoods:

> "Latin America would be the fun part of town, the club district, where the workday doesn't begin until ten p.m. and everyone sleeps until midmorning. . . . The Arab street would be a dark alley where outsiders fear to tread, except for a few side streets. . . . Africa, sadly, is that part of town where the businesses are boarded up, life expectancy is declining, and the only new buildings are health-care clinics."

Friedman seems vexed by what he calls the "backwardness" of Arab and Muslim cultures. He writes, "For complicated cultural and historical reasons, many of them do not glocalize [absorb foreign ideas] well." Approvingly, he refers to economist David Landes, who argues that in the Arab Muslim world, "cultural attitudes have in many ways become a barrier to development."

This reveals a shocking ignorance of history. For seven centuries, Islam was the global civilization par excellence, and it enabled the development of many scientific, intellectual and artistic breakthroughs during that period.

Nowhere is the European (and American) colonization and occupation of the Arab and Muslim worlds over the last 200 years mentioned as a possible explanation for anger and resentment directed against the United States and Europe. Nowhere is U.S. government support of brutal dictatorships in the Middle East (from the shah to the Saudi royal family) offered as a possible reason for opposition to Western hegemony posing as "globalization" or a "flat world." In this book, history is bunk.

Friedman doesn't appear to spend much time outside of golf courses, five-star restaurants, limousines and luxury hotels. His view of the world is consistent with dozens of elites he interviews on his global journey. The chief executive officers of Fortune 500 companies,

Mexican ex-presidents, U.S. secretaries of state and military generals, Japanese financial consultants and Indian and Chinese ministers of trade inhabit Friedman's flat world. The voices of farmers, factory workers and street vendors are heard nowhere in the text, though many might tell a different story—of growing poverty, hunger and disease in the wake of World Bank, International Monetary Fund, and World Trade Organization policies.

Ultimately, Friedman's work is little more than advertising. The goal is not to sell the high-tech gadgetry described in page after page of the book, but to sell a way of life—a world view glorifying corporate capitalism and mass consumption as the only paths to progress. It is a view intolerant of lives lived outside the global marketplace. It betrays a disregard for democracy and a profound lack of imagination.

This book's lighthearted style might be amusing were it not for the fact that his subject—the global economy—is a matter of life and death for millions. Friedman's words and opinions, ill informed as they are, shape the policies of leaders around the world. Many consider him to be a sophisticated thinker and analyst—not a propagandist. It is a sobering reminder of the intellectual paralysis gripping our society today.

Roberto J. Gonzalez is professor of anthropology at San Jose State University. He is author of "Zapotec Science: Farming and Food in the Northern Sierra of Oaxaca" (2001) and editor of "Anthropologists in the Public Sphere: Speaking Out on War, Peace, and American Power."

4. Thinking Like a Futurist

Peter Bishop

Anthropologists cannot help being concerned about the future of human civilization as a whole. Globally minded, and with a long view of history, anthropologists are concerned about our future especially when conflict is upon us and we are consuming our limited sources of energy so frantically. The author helps us anticipate our future better in order to act appropriately. The article appears to be composed of standard multiple choice questions, but it asks us fundamental questions about how we think about our future. Even more importantly, Bishop points out the responsibility all of us have in determining the kind of future. Whether we ignore it or not, we will face the future in any case!

We all have assumptions about the future. Assumptions are never completely right or wrong, although some may be more useful than others under certain circumstances. The assumptions that futurists use help them anticipate the complex and sometimes surprising futures that await us.

This test consists of several questions that challenge your ability to think like a futurist. The questions are designed with no clear right answers. Instead, they probe your assumptions about the future. The discussion following the questions indicates how futurists usually answer them.

1. CAN WE KNOW THE FUTURE?

a. Yes. b. No.

Answer: a. About 50% of people usually answer Yes; about 50% say No. Your answer, of course, depends on how you define "know." If by "know" you mean that you can predict what will happen, then the answer is obviously No. Efforts to predict the exact future of human systems are so prone to error that they are futile. However, if by "know" you mean what might or could happen, then the answer is a qualified Yes. Futurists hold that we can know the majority of plausible futures, if we relax our assumptions and preconceptions of what is possible.

2. ARE THERE ONE OR MANY FUTURES?

a. One. b. Many.

Answer: b. Despite half of the respondents answering No to #1, most people say there are many futures. The future is plural, not singular—hence the term "futures." The multiplicity of the future is a blessing: It gives us the freedom to influence what the future will be. If there were only one future, it would be completely determined and our influence would be either negligible or preordained.

3. WHAT IS THE FARTHEST AHEAD THAT WE CAN USEFULLY FORECAST?

a. 1–2 years.
b. 3–5 years.
c. 5–10 years.
d. 10–25 years.
e. More than 25 years.

Answer: All answers are correct. The answer depends on the subject of the forecast. Actuaries and futurists prefer the long term (more than 10 years); politicians and investors must be prepared for radical change in the short term (next week). Contrary to what most business people think, the future beyond five years (the standard business-planning horizon) can be useful, particularly when long-term investments or decisions are involved. Both individuals and companies have more influence in the long term than in the short because short-term outcomes are already determined, for the most part. Consistent effort toward a goal over long periods can produce amazing results, even when one's power or influence at any one time is small. Rock holds water in the short run, but water erodes rock in the long.

4. WHICH IS BETTER FOR UNDERSTANDING THE LONG-TERM FUTURE?

a. Single, clear predictions.
b. Multiple possible futures.
c. Neither.
d. Both.

Answer: b. Would that we could have single, clear predictions that are useful! The problem is that predictions give a false sense of certainty and precision. Multiple possible futures are the best we can do and are therefore better for understanding the future. Unfortunately, some people prefer single, clear predictions. Futurists believe that basing a decision on a single prediction is like putting all your eggs in one basket. The purpose of forecasting is not to be right, but to avoid being surprised. If decision makers are prepared for the range of plausible futures, then they can be successful no matter what occurs, as long as it occurs in that range.

5. WHICH IS THE MOST IMPORTANT CHARACTERISTIC FOR A GOOD FORECAST?

a. Accuracy.
b. Precision.
c. Utility.
d. Clarity.

Answer: c. Accuracy and precision are supposed to make the best forecasts, particularly quantitative ones. People even ask futurists how often they are correct—i.e., what their batting average is. The question indicates a misunderstanding of applied futurism. The best long-term forecasts are not necessarily accurate or precise, but useful to decision makers. They point out the most likely future as one possibility in a range of alternative plausible futures. Useful forecasts can even be inaccurate, as when the forecast of impending doom promotes action that averts the doom.

6. IS THE FUTURE ALREADY DETERMINED?

a. Yes.
b. No.

Answer: b. People who answer Yes are likely those who only learned about forecasting from well-behaved mechanical systems rather than from complex human systems. We learned to predict where a pendulum would be, how much ice would melt, when a lunar eclipse would occur. These kinds of phenomena are "determined" (and therefore predictable). Similar predictions are impossible, however, in the economic, social, or political systems in which individuals acting with incomplete knowledge and free will have yet to exert their influence. Fortunately, the indeterminacy of the future also gives us the time and opportunity to exert our own influence.

7. WHICH INFLUENCES THE LONG-TERM FUTURE THE MOST?

a. Trends.
b. Events.
c. Choices.
d. All influence the future equally.

Answer: d. Each of the three specific factors—trends, events, and choices—represents a theory of how the future develops. Those who emphasize Trends believe that the future will be like the present, differing only in certain measurable quantities. Those who select Events see a turbulent future, full of uncertainty and unpredictability. Those who emphasize Choice believe they and others control the future. In fact, each influences the future somewhat, but differently in various domains—trends in demographics, events and choices in politics, for instance. The future is a combination of them all; leaving out any one truncates the range of plausible futures.

8. WHICH TYPE OF FUTURE IS MOST USEFUL?

a. The most-probable future.
b. Plausible futures other than the most probable.
c. The future we prefer.
d. All are equally useful.

Answer: d. All is a good answer, for probable, plausible, and preferable futures are all useful in specific ways. The Probable Future is what most people believe a forecast should be; it is what will happen if nothing really surprising happens. Plausible Futures are useful for indicating the variations around the Probable Future. Possibilities that represent critical assumptions about the future prepare decision makers for a wider range of contingencies than the Probable Future alone. The Preferable Future is valuable both for forecasting (things preferred are more likely to occur because people work toward making them happen) and for action (mobilizing action toward a consensus goal).

9. WHICH INFLUENCES THE LONG-TERM FUTURE THE MOST?

a. Demographics.
b. Physical environment.
c. Technology.
d. Economics.
e. Government.
f. Culture.
g. All influence the future equally.

Answer: g. All influence the future equally. Some people think certain influences are more powerful than others: Americans generally see technology as more powerful than do people from other cultures; rulers and politicians believe that government is in charge; environmentalists believe that the physical environment will have the last word; economists say the economy, and so on. Futurists are careful to weigh all the influences appropriately and realize that in the long run all of these forces will have their impacts. Rather than specializing in any one field, futurists specialize in the interaction of all fields.

10. WHICH IS THE MOST SERIOUS CAUSE OF FORECASTING ERRORS?

a. Lack of information.
b. The forecaster's assumptions.
c. External events.

Answer: b. Most people respond that Assumptions are the most serious error, but significant numbers choose Lack of Information and External Events as well. It is easier to blame

Information and Events because we are not responsible for them. Our Assumptions, on the other hand, are our own making. A reading of history shows that the most serious errors are the result of mistaken assumptions: A patent official forecast a decline in invention around the turn of the century; a physicist said heavier-than-air flight was impossible; an office equipment executive saw no need for more than six computers worldwide. Forecasters had all the information in front of them. Their interpretation of what the information meant caused the error.

11. WHICH ATTITUDE TOWARD THE FUTURE IS MOST OFTEN CORRECT?

a. Optimism.
b. Pessimism.
c. Transformationalism.
d. Fatalism.
e. All are equally correct.

Answer: e. All are equally correct because the future is plural—there are optimistic, pessimistic, transformational, and fatalistic futures out there. Which one is most often correct depends on the domain and the time frame. For example, major change is easier to effect over a long period of time than a short one, so a transformational attitude is more appropriate for the long term, and a fatalistic attitude for the short. People tend to be more optimistic about their immediate individual future and more pessimistic about more distant societal or global issues. The point is that all views need to be considered to get a full, well-rounded view of the real future.

12. TELLING STORIES ABOUT POSSIBLE BUT UNLIKELY FUTURES IS USEFUL.

a. True.
b. False.

Answer: a. Science-fiction stories ranging from *The Time Machine* to *The Terminator* have told highly implausible but highly engaging visions of the future.
Stories capture the essence of the future without claiming to know the details. Futurists borrow the techniques of storytellers in developing scenarios to enliven a plausible future. The best response to a scenario is, "Yes, you're right; that could happen."

13. WHO SETS THE VISION FOR THE ORGANIZATION?

a. The leader.
b. The top management.
c. The strategic-planning team.
d. Managers in general.
e. Everyone.
f. None of the above.

Answer: f. Most people answer The Leader. A sizable group of people also say Everyone. Both are correct. Vision is a tool of the futurist or leader who wants to create transformational change. A vision is an attractive future that motivates people to work beyond themselves (and beyond what they're getting paid for) and synchronizes their effort with those of others working for the same vision. It appears as though the leader sets the vision, but a more accurate view holds that the leader articulates the vision in everyone's heart. The leader is the spokesperson for the vision, but he or she can only know what to speak after listening to the visions of everyone involved.

14. WHICH ARE THE THREE MOST IMPORTANT CHARACTERISTICS OF AN EFFECTIVE STRATEGIC PLAN?

    a. Commitment to carry it out.
    b. Coverage of everything the organization does.
    c. General direction for fundamental chance.
    d. Detailed implementation plans.
    e. Understanding by everyone.
    f. Valid planning methodology.

Answer: a, c, and e. Strategic planning is the most often used and the most poorly practiced technique in the futurist's toolkit. We have all had the experience—end less forms. pointless meetings, large three-ring binders stuffed with details. The "plan" is supposed to contain everything the organization is going to do for the next five years. What it really contains is what everyone is currently doing, put there to protect their position. The best strategic plans are short. They set the Direction, not every detail of carrying it out. Details more than a year out are impossible anyway. Everyone must Understand the plan. Who can understand 350 pages of dense outlines? And everyone must be Committed to it. Aha, there's the rub! The plan is approved, but serious disagreements remain. What happens to the implementation? Strategic planning is often so painful that the last thing people want to do is ever see the plan again, much less implement it. Direction, Understanding, Commitment—those are the essentials. Leave the details to the annual plan.

15. WHICH IS THE MOST FREQUENTLY OVERLOOKED CHARACTERISTIC OF SUCCESSFUL CHANGE?

    a. Communication.
    b. Trust.
    c. Vision.
    d. Commitment.

Answer: b. Every one of us has one or two golden projects in our background—a group of people who worked together for a worthy goal and maybe even made a difference. A staff group, reflecting on the projects in their past, developed these four attributes of successful projects: Communication, Trust, Vision, Commitment. They are clearly all important, even necessary. The leadership of that same organization went through the same exercise and came up with exactly three of the characteristics. Which characteristic of a successful project did not occur to them? Trust. All are necessary, but trust is the most often overlooked.

Trust among project members reinforces the belief that everyone is working for the good of the project, not using the project to advance themselves or their interests. Even more importantly, trust between managers and workers prevents the cynicism that often accompanies the announcement of significant change. People have been burned too many times before. Leaders announce change, people get on board—only to see the leaders "change their minds." The goal is harder to achieve, more expensive, more time-consuming than once thought. Trust is everyone's belief that their colleagues and leaders will do what it takes to achieve the goal.

These questions have no "right" answers, to be sure; but a host of common-sense insights can help us understand, anticipate, and influence the future more effectively. Understanding our assumptions about the future can increase our ability to conceive alternative plausible futures, understand the implications of those futures for ourselves and others, and begin to work with others to increase the chances of the preferred future occurring.

5. Anticipatory Anthropology

Victoria M. Razak

Along with Bishop, Razak introduces how forecasters think. In her case, she describes the onset of futures thinking in anthropology, anticipatory anthropology. Anthropologists can offer a distinctive perspective to forecasters, thinking about culture holistically but also conscientiously considering the details of life. Coupled with the creation of the field of applied anthropology, anticipatory anthropologists dig deeply into the way people in different cultures think about their own futures and turn plans into action. This article provides a basic framework for integrating the anthropological, systems and futures perspectives in order to understand the emerging global cultures.

1. INTRODUCTION

Anticipatory Anthropology is that area of anthropology that uses the perspective, theories, models, and methods of anthropology in an anticipatory manner, so that individuals, citizens, leaders, and governments will be better able to make informed policy decisions, thereby improving the community's or society's chances for realizing preferred futures and avoiding undesired ones [1].

From the perspective of the World Future Society, the largest such gathering, futurists "try to suggest things that might happen in the future, so that people can decide what they want to make happen. By looking at current trends, for example, it is possible to make a projection of what might be the case in the future" [2]. The society cites a successful anticipation of the future, President Kennedy's dream of placing a man on the moon and predicting it would occur before 1970. This dream was embraced by America, and supported by an aggressive funding of research and development, and the implementation of a time factored plan. The vision—the dream, the scenario—was realized in 1969 when *homo sapiens* took his first step onto the moon's pristine dusty surface—"an achievement that awed the world" [3]. This sequence—the 'dreaming' followed by the 'planning' of actions to be implemented in pursuit of the dream—comprise the nature of, not only a combination of futures studies and planning, but reflects human nature itself.

Anthropologists have been actively involved in the art of anticipation from a cultural perspective for well over 30 years. Anthropologists are very good at thinking about 'culture', it is their key concept, defined broadly as the shared, socially learned knowledge and patterns of behavior of a group (ethnic, societal, or para- [sub] cultural), transmitted through enculturation to each new generation.[1] Sharing a pattern, or system, of culture enables people to communicate and interact with one another appropriately and efficiently. We need culture—it is essential for our survival because it bestows upon each new generation the skills and techniques needed to adapt to the natural environment. It provides each individual with norms, values, expectations, common understandings, classifications of reality and world views, needed to live with others in groups. As a discipline, anthropology is divided into four major fields: archaeology, which studies material remains from the past to describe and explain human behavior; biological/physical anthropology, which studies humans as biological organisms throughout their evolution; sociocultural anthropology, which studies humans as social beings; and anthropological linguistics, which studies the relationship between language and culture. Where these fields address practical problems, we find applied anthropology.

2. PLANNING AND APPLIED ANTHROPOLOGY

Applied anthropology employs anthropological data, methods, theory and perspectives to identify, assess, and solve social problems [4]. About half of all anthropologists call themselves applied, or practicing anthropologists, and work for non-academic clients such as planning agencies, major corporations, mental health centers, international development agencies, tribal and ethnic organizations, advocacy and public interest groups, governmental social services, and education agencies, for example.[2] One of the first opportunities for anthropologists to become involved in anticipation was in social impact assessment research, often associated with the environmental paradigm. These studies assessed the social gains and losses that might be expected to accompany a program of planned change in order for development projects to proceed with a minimum of societal disruption. In the United States, requirements for social impact assessment developed from public and Congressional concern with the preservation of resources, including the social well-being and cultural vitality of people—and a concern for the 'possible disruptions to community identity and sense of place' [5]. Many of these studies involved genuinely interdisciplinary research efforts in which anthropologists became involved not only in domestic ethnographic field work, but also in the administration of foreign development projects, where they demonstrated a greater sensitivity to social and cultural issues than their predecessors [6].

Applied research projects are concerned not only with assessing the future impacts of present policies, but also with projecting people's future needs and expectations. Here anthropology's ethnographic approach takes researchers into people's cultural living spaces to understand their future visions of their built and natured environments, that these may become a part of a properly inclusive strategic planning process.[3]

3. ANTICIPATORY ANTHROPOLOGY

The term 'anticipatory anthropology' was introduced by anthropologist Marion Lundy Dobbert in 1984 [7], and subsumes various terminologies used by anthropologists in preceding years, such as futurology, futuristics, anthropology of the future, and speculative anthropology [8], cultural futures, and so on. As later defined by Robert B. Textor, anticipatory anthropology is not a separate subfield but a *mode* of enquiry that might be practiced by virtually any anthropologist. The approach pays serious attention to anticipating what a future version of an existing local, regional, national, or global sociocultural system could or should look like in the middle-range future, by focusing on what the group visualizes as a possible, probable, or preferable future for themselves.

In the mid-1970s we began to see the emergence of a true futures-orientation within anthropology as ideas began to flow between that discipline and futures studies and strategic planning. In her 1979 essay, *Why anthropology and futures* [9], Dobbert asserts that "applied anthropology is in reality a futurist discipline concerned with the design and development of the short term and intermediate futures. In this sense, anthropologists have been futurists for more than a century and from long experience can make a number of contributions to the development of futures studies". She notes that anthropology has studied culture as a system which "consists minimally of a set of closely interrelated and practically inseparable ideological, social and techno-economic subsystems . . . critical for both the design and exploration of alternative human futures". Morever, she continues, ethnographic research has provided "a wide variety of social designs and theories about group living" from non-Western cultures that have already been tested by human beings, and that these "form a set of natural experiments which may be analyzed from different theoretical, and practical values and perspectives for their advantages and disadvantages to those living in them." Moreover, citing Mead (1971) she suggests that through the use of archaeological data we can supply cultural data for very long runs on some human societies [10].

In addition to Textor and Dobbert, a number of scholars—both inside and outside of anthropology—may be credited with establishing futures research as a legitimate area of interest within anthropology: by seeking to organize and institutionalize interest in the future through the application and development of anthropological methods, through their applied contributions, and through their teaching. These include: Misha Adams, Paul Bohannan, Philip DeVita, Jan English-Lueck, Ben Finney, James Funaro, George M. Guilmet, Beth Hagens, Joel Hagens, David Hakken, Arthur Harkins, Barbara Joans, Morton Klass, Rod Kirk, Ruthanne Kurth-Schai, Timothy McKeown, Magoroh Maruyama, Margaret Mead, Beatrice D. Miller, Robert J. Miller, Doug Raybeck, Reed Riner, Devayani Smith, Sol Tax, Darlene Thomas, Steven I. Thompson, Robert N. Tyzzer, Charles Urbanowicz, Alvin W. Wolfe, Markus Young Owl, and others.

According to Reed Riner, anthropologists' professional interest in the future began with some unchronicled discussions in the later 1960s, in which Margaret Mead was a conspicuous participant. Subsequently a series of symposia on 'Cultural Futurology/Futuristics', organized by Magoroh Maruyama and Arthur Harkins, were presented at annual meetings of the American Anthropological Association between 1970 and 1974. These sessions motivated a community of scholars, whose interests had traditionally been in the past and the ethnographic present, to turn their attention to the study of the future [11]. Selected papers from the 1974 symposium were published as *Cultures beyond earth* [12], then a much larger invited collection, *Cultures of the future* [13] was published. Interest in the topic continued, leading to the organization of three futures research committees within anthropology: the Cultural and Educational Futures Committee of the Council on Anthropology and Education, and the Cultural Futures Research Committee of the Society for Applied Anthropology (both organized by Dobbert and Textor); and the Futurology Commission of the International Union of Anthropological and Ethnographic Sciences.

The journal *Cultural Futures Research* (CFR) was created as a forum for the collective interests of the three futures committees, and featured themes such as the future of the world system, human settlement in space, the future of communication and cognition, and the possible use of anthropological methods and case studies in anticipating the future.[4] CFR was also explicitly established to contribute to a resolution of some of the problems that anthropologists saw as inherent in the then current approaches in futures studies. A 1983 editorial argued that anthropology possessed a unique perspective characterized by it's extended time depth, its cross-cultural bases, and its holism. From the perspective of these tenets, the non-anthropological futurist's extrapolations tended to be too shallow in time depth, failed to encompass longer biological and cultural evolutionary trends and dynamics, and were constructed in terms of the assumptions, norms, and values of late 20th century urban-industrial society which were space-bound (ethnocentric) and time-bound (tempocentric), and failed to include holistically and integrally all aspects of human community, language, biology and history [14]. However, although the then current anthropology was good at "predicting the past", it did not provide anthropologists "with the methods and fundamental ideas of foresight" [15].

In 1983, another area of interest in the future emerged in anthropology, with a unique interdisciplinary conference organized by anthropologist Jim Funaro, and artist-anthropologist, Joel Hagen, which brought together anthropologists and other social scientists, science fiction writers and artists, futurists, and NASA research scientists to collaborate in the discussion and exploration of longer-range futures for humanity [16]. CONTACT, as the collaboration became known, has continued successfully into the new millennium, and today "constitutes a sort of 'Leftcoast Futures Society', in complement to the World Future Society, in that it emphasizes the participants' active and self-critical involvement in building and critiquing images of alternative, scientifically plausible futures" [17].

4. ETHICS AND ADVOCACY

The ways in which different peoples anticipate the future are bound by their native cultural categories of time and potentiality, and their particular relationship to nature and the cosmos. So when Westerners speak of 'anticipation;', and 'dreaming', and 'planning' towards the deliberate realization of something they call the 'future', they risk speaking from a peculiarly Western frame of reference—a particular sequential patterning of thoughts and actions, and a set of categories coined in Western terms. Ideas about the meaning of 'the future', and the possibilities for shaping the future are far from globally shared. Different histories, different experiences, and different worldviews potentially produce varying perceptions of the present, and for most (some languages carry no word for the future), myriad possible and dreamed-of futures.

Futurist and sociologist Eleonora Masini, highly cognizant of the ethical and ethnocentric traps we all face, says that "sometimes futurists reflect their culture without knowing it; they think they are speaking for the world and forget that it is their cultural biases, their disciplinary education and their social character that is being expressed—and that these are only partial aspects of the world. Futurists, more than any other scientists, need to acknowledge the existence and the value of cultures, attitudes and objectives that are different from their own. . . . [Projects] for, and of, the future, must be many, reflecting different values and appreciated for their diversity" [18]. She adds, however, that increasingly non-Western countries *are* futuring in their own terms, for example, Morocco, Egypt, Kenya, Tanzania, India, Sri-Lanka, Japan, Mexico, Venezuela, and Brazil.

For anthropologists, studying the way people dream about and approach the time ahead, and perceive their power to shape the future, reminds us not only how much we humans are both alike and different, but also how inappropriate it is to encompassingly apply our own etic system of values and beliefs to someone else's future, and expect them to willingly participate in the way of life that we would create for them. (Among the worst offenders in this regard are the IMF and the World Bank.)

Anthropology itself is not an innocent in this regard, and has sometimes lent its skills in the interests of the outsider over the insider. Some early anthropologists occasionally worked unwittingly (and in some cases, even wittingly), in the interests of the nations or organizations that funded their research, by producing detailed information about a people through ethnographic fieldwork. Sometimes the information thus acquired, during colonial times in particular, was used to the detriment of the 'natives under study'. However, for the most part, we are very proud of our philosophical and ethical approach, and of our research methods which privilege local knowledge over our own, as well as our strong, often urgent, advocacy for the needs and desires of the peoples we study and work beside. Knowledge about the traditions and beliefs of groups and subgroups within nations is a critical precursor to the process of planning design and implementation of programs that directly affect those groups. When people *want* the change, and when the new structures proposed fit well with their lifestyles, worldview, and traditions, then their adoption of the change will be more successful, beneficial, and cost-effective [19].

5. SEEING THROUGH ANTHROPOLOGICAL LENSES

For educators, the most important continuing contribution of anthropology has been its role (however small) in reducing ethnocentrism in every nation where anthropology is taught, by sensitizing people to ways of life, values and worldviews very different from their own, and by bringing about an appreciation for the potentiality of cultural diversity [20]. A second major contribution to the research and understanding of the human condition (and to a synergistic partnership with futures studies), is anthropology's unique ethnographic fieldwork approach, which involves direct, first hand observation of, and participation in, the daily behavior of the group under study for a prolonged period of time (over one year) in which the myriad details of everyday life, seasonal and unusual events and happenings may be experienced. Facts about the visions, expectations and preferences held by members of a given group can be obtained, analyzed, and interpreted, and combined meaningfully with facts derived from data bases on the group's demography, technology, and economy. Specifically, anthropology can contribute much information and analysis needed for discussion and decision making by citizens, activists, leaders and governments of a given society, community or organization, especially where serious attention is paid to the means whereby preferable futures may be achieved, and undesirable ones avoided. In gathering such information, we are not totally impartial and detached observers; we engage in 'deep conversations' with our well-informed native mentors, informants, and teachers (*not* as 'subjects' or as 'objects for observation') and *listen carefully* to their beliefs, values, perceptions, and fears and desires for their future. If possible, an ethnographic project will be extended to study the processes of adaptation and change over a period of several decades [21]. The method and practice of ethnography remains as vital today as it was a century ago, and has become increasingly sophisticated and intellectually challenging [22]. With its experience-near engaged relativism, it has the ability to come closer to detailing the reality of motivated, intentional human life, than any other method in the social sciences.

A major contribution to a futures methodology was developed in the 1970s based on the ethnographic approach described above. Robert B. Textor surveyed the futures studies literature with the purpose of developing some practical methods through which anthropologists could contribute to the study of the future. He developed, and continues to develop, a qualitative methodology called ethnographic futures research (EFR) which is used for building culturally and emically based (from the insider's point of view) scenarios of the future. Through intensive interviewing, informants are asked to provide a variety of scenarios focusing on what they want for their future. The method has been used for whole nations, as well as for a variety of decision-making situations at the local or community level.[5] In response to the increasing demand that anthropology become more relevant to important issues of policy and practice, Textor believes that EFR and/or approaches like it, can provide practical tools for anthropologists and others who want to become involved in cultural futures research [23].

It is my hope that a truly collaborative emic/etic futures studies approach to the visioning and crafting of the future will become a standard approach used in the practice of foresight planning—collaborative because an interface with theory, hindsight, practice and cool objectivity provides a necessary broader context to the visioning process. Anthropologists have much to offer to such anticipatory fields as technological forecasting, social and educational planning, regional and city planning, environmental impact assessment, and land-use planning, as well as the broad field of futures studies. The ethnographic approach used in conjunction with necessary quantitative data gathering and analysis, can straddle the divide between an etic (outsider point of view) based approach and an emic-centered approach to anticipatory planning.

ACKNOWLEDGEMENTS

I am most grateful for the support and encouragement of Bob Textor and Reed Riner in bringing forth this collection of essays and for their thoughtful inputs to earlier drafts. Thanks also to Sam Cole for reading and discussing with me the many essays received from his perspective as a futurist and planner.

REFERENCES

[1.] Adapted from Robert B. Textor. Prospectus for a Robert B. Textor and family prize for excellence in anticipatory anthropology (unpublished document), 1999.

[2.] World Future Society. The art of forecasting: a brief introduction to thinking about the future, 1996.

[3.] World Future Society, 1996.

[4.] C.P. Kottak. *Mirror for humanity,* McGraw Hill (1996) 235.

[5.] E. Chambers. *Applied anthropology: a practical guide,* Prentice Hall, New Jersey (1985) 167–179.

[6.] G. Cochrane. *The cultural appraisal of development projects,* Praeger, New York (1979) 172.

[7.] Dobbert ML. Anticipatory anthropology; Cultural Futures Research 1984 (1986) 8(3):33–35. And, Textor RB. Anticipatory anthropology and the telemicroelectronic revolution: a preliminary report from Silicon Valley. Anthropology and Education Quarterly 1985;16(1):3–30.

[8.] R.W. Wescott, The anthropology of the future as an academic discipline. *Cultural futurists* (1971) 205.

[9.] M.L. Dobbert, Why anthropology and futures?. *Journal of Cultural and Educational Futures* **1** 1 (1979), p. 0.

[10.] M. Mead, A note on contributions of anthropology to the science of the future. In: M. Maruyama and J. Dator, Editors, *Human Futuristics* (Social Science Research Institute ed.),, University of Hawaii, Honolulu (1971), p. 3.

[11.] Riner R. The future as sociocultural problem in American Behavioral Scientist. 42(3):347–364, Nov/Dec 1998.

[12.] M. Maruyama and A. Harkins, Editors, *Cultures beyond earth,* Vintage Books, New York (1975).

[13.] M. Maruyama and A. Harkins, Editors, *Cultures of the future,* Mouton Press, New York (1978).

[14.] Editorial, in Cultural Futures Research 1983;7(4):3.

[15.] Riner 1987:312.

[16.] James Funaro. The evolution of COTI: a personal memoir. Electronic publication: <http:www.cabrillo.cc.ca.us/contact/history.html>.

[17.] Riner 1998.

[18.] E. Masini. In: Z. Sardar, Editor, *Rescuing all our futures: the future of futures studies,* Westport, Connecticut: Praeger (1999), p. 45.

[19.] Kottak 1996:235.

[20.] Razak V, Cole S, editors. Editors introduction: anthropological perspectives on the future of culture and society. Futures (special issue) 27(4) May 1995.

[21.] Kottak 1996:6–7.

[22.] G.E. Marcus and M.M.J. Fischer. *ANTHROPOLOGY AS CULTURAL CRITIQUE,* University of Chicago Press (1986) 165-168.

[23.] R.B. Textor, The ethnographic futures research method: an application to Thailand. *Futures* 27 4 (1995), pp. 461–471.

NOTES

1. Edward Burnett Tylor (under the influence of Matthew Arnold) adopted the word anthropology and 'culture' from the German. Tylor applied the word anthropology to the study of both the human animal and human culture. He defined culture as "That complex whole which includes knowledge, belief, art, morals, law, custom, and any other capabilities and habits acquired by man as a member of society" (Tylor E. B. Primitive culture: researches into the development of mythology, philosophy, religion, art and custom. London: John Murray Publishers. 1871).

2. The National Association for the Practice of Anthropology (NAPA) of the American Anthropological Association was founded in 1983 to promote the practice of anthropology and the interests of practicing anthropologists, and to further the practice of anthropology as a profession. Members receive NAPA Bulletins, technical reports and discounts on training workshops organized by NAPA.

3. Observation research has been used extensively outside anthropology for a long time, but what makes open-ended interviewing, and on-site information gathering different from the ethnographic method is "the essential anthropological concern for cultural context" and on discovering new bases for understanding. (Walcott, Harry 1980. In Erve Chambers. Applied anthropology: a practical guide. New Jersey: Prentice Hall. 1985:175).

4. Reed Riner. Doing futures research—anthropologically. Futures 19(3) June 1987. Note also that Cultural Futures Research subsumed the journal, Anthro-Tech when that journal merged with Cultural and Educational Futures (begins with Vol VII(1), Autumn 1982, and continues through Vol VIII(3), dated Spring 1984 but not issued until sometime in the 1984/5 academic year). In an informal meeting of the founding and current editors of Anthro-Tech: a Journal of Speculative Anthropology (Darlene Thomas), and Cultural and Educational Futures (CEF) (Marion Lundy Dobbert); and the three interlocking members of the Contributing Editorial Boards, Anthro-Tech was asked to accept the CEF journal in merger. Since its inception CEF had served as the official publication of the two futures committees. It was agreed that the merged publication would be edited by Reed Riner and published as Cultural Futures Research. It would become the official publication of the two committees, that the editorial boards would be merged. And, Thomas and Dobbert would assume positions as founding editors.

5. Robert B. Textor. A handbook on Ethnographic Futures Research. Third edition. Version A. Stanford: Stanford University School of Education and Department of Anthropology. 1980. For an applied example of the method, see Sippanondha Ketudat, with the ethnographic and editorial collaboration of Robert B. Textor. The middle path for the future of Thailand: technology in harmony with culture and environment. Institute of Culture and Communication, East-West Center, Honolulu, Hawaii; and, Faculty of Social Sciences, Chiang Mai University, Thailand. 1990.

6. The Rise of the Merchant, Industrialist, and Capital Controller

Richard Robbins

This article discusses how, when, where, by whom globalization really started. Anthropologists are interested in the socioeconomic, political, and religious factors that influence historical change. Robbins writes about the role of merchants in connecting historic landmasses into a global network. It was the merchants who initiated and sustained navigation in order to find products that could be sold in largely European markets for profit. These merchants were a major force toward historic globalization. Nowadays, we call them businessmen. This article also illustrates the roles of non-Western cultures, such as China, in shaping international trading. Robbins provides a foundation for understanding the birth of the corporation and the backdrop for contemporary economic globalization.

From the fifteenth century on, European soldiers and sailors carried the flags of their rulers to the four corners of the globe, and European merchants established their storehouses from Vera Cruz to Nagasaki. Dominating the sea-lanes of the world, these merchants invaded existing networks of exchange and linked one to the other. In the service of "God and profit" they located sources of products desired in Europe and developed coercive systems for their delivery. In response, European craft shops, either singly or aggregated into manufactories, began to produce goods to provision the wide-ranging military and naval efforts and to furnish commodities to overseas suppliers in exchange for goods to be sold as commodities at home. The outcome was the creation of a commercial network of global scale.

—Eric Wolf, People Without History

When I think of Indonesia—a country on the Equator with 180 million people, a median age of 18, and a Moslem ban on alcohol—I feel I know what heaven looks like.

—Donald R. Keough, President of Coca Cola

At no other time in human history has the world been a better place for capitalists. We live in a world full of investment opportunities—companies, banks, funds, bonds, securities, and even countries—into which we can put money and from which we can get more back. These money-making machines, such as the Nike Corporation, have a ready supply of cheap labor, capital, raw materials, and advanced technology to assist in making products that people all over the world clamor to buy. Moreover, governments compete for their presence,

Fifteenth-century merchants in Paris display their wares and services.

passing laws and making treaties to open markets, while maintaining infrastructures (roads, airports, power utilities, monetary systems, communication networks, etc.) that enable them to manufacture products or provide services cheaply and charge prices that remain competitive with other investments. Nation-states maintain armies to protect investments and see that markets remain open. Educational institutions devote themselves to producing knowledgeable, skilled, and disciplined workers, while researchers at colleges and universities develop new technologies to make even better and cheaper products. Our governments, educational institutions and mass media encourage people to consume more and more commodities. Citizens order their economic and social lives to accommodate work in the investment machines and to gain access to the commodities they produce. In return the investment machines churn out profits that are reinvested to manufacture more of their particular products or that can be invested in other enterprises, producing yet more goods and services.

But there are economic, environmental, and social consequences of doing business and making money. We live in a world in which the gap between the rich and poor is growing, a world that contains many wealthy and comfortable people but also contains almost one billion hungry people, one-fifth of its population. Then there are the environmental consequences of doing business: Production uses up the earth's energy resources and produces damaged environments in return. There are health consequences as well, not only from damaged environments but also because those too poor to afford health care often do without it. Finally there are the political consequences of governments' using their armed force to maintain conditions that they believe are favorable for business and investors.

In the long view of human history these conditions are very recent ones. For most of human history human beings have lived in small, relatively isolated settlements that rarely exceeded three or four hundred individuals. And until some ten thousand years ago virtually all of these people lived by gathering and hunting. Then in some areas of the world, instead of depending on the natural growth of plant foods and the natural growth and movements of animals, people began to plant and harvest crops and raise animals themselves. This was not necessarily an advance in human societies—in fact, in terms of labor, it required human beings to do the work that had been done largely by nature. The sole advantage of working harder was that the additional labor supported denser populations. Settlements grew in size until thousands rather than hundreds lived together in towns and cities. Occupational specialization developed, necessitating trade and communication between villages, towns, cities, and regions. Political complexity increased; chiefs became kings, and kings became emperors ruling over vast regions.

Then, approximately four or five hundred years ago, patterns of travel and communication contributed to the globalization of trade dominated by "a small peninsula off the landmass of Asia," as Eric Wolf called Europe. The domination by one region over others was not new in the world. There had existed prior to this time civilizations whose influence had spread to influence those around them—the Mayan civilization in Central America, Greek civilization of the fourth millennium B.C., Rome of the first and second centuries A.D., and Islamic civilization of the eighth and ninth centuries. But there was an important difference. The building of these empires was largely a political process of conquest and military domination, whereas the expansion of Europe, while certainly involving its share of militarism, was largely accomplished by economic means, by the expansion and control of trade.

Now let's shift our focus to the development of the *capitalist*—the merchant, industrialist, and financier—the person who controls the capital, employs the laborers, and profits from the consumption of commodities. This will be a long-term, historical look at this development, particularly because if we are to understand the global distribution of power and money that exists today and the origins of the culture of capitalism, knowledge of its history is crucial.

Assume for a time the role of a businessperson, a global merchant, or merchant adventurer, as they used to be called,[1] passing through the world of the last six hundred years. We'll begin searching the globe for ways to make money in the year 1400 and end our search in the year 2000, taking stock of the changes in the organization and distribution of capital that have occurred in that time. Because we are looking at the world through the eyes of a merchant, there is much that we will miss—many political developments, religious wars, revolutions, natural catastrophes, and the like. Because we overlook these events does not mean they did not affect how business was conducted—in many cases they had profound effects. But our prime concern is with the events that most directly influenced the way in which business was conducted on a day to day basis and how the pursuit of profit by merchant adventurers influenced the lives of people all over the world.

Our historical tour will concentrate on three areas:

1. An understanding of how capital came to be concentrated in so few hands and how the world came to be divided into rich and poor. There were certainly rich people and poor people in 1400, but today's vast global disparity between core and periphery did not exist then. *How did the distribution of wealth change, and how did one area of the world come to dominate the others economically?*

2. An understanding of the changes in business organizations and the organization of capital, that is, who controlled the money? In 1400, most business enterprises were small, generally family-organized institutions. Capital was controlled by these groups and state organizations. Today we live in an era of multinational corporations, many whose wealth exceeds that of most countries. We need to trace the evolution of the power of capital over our lives and the transformation of the merchant of 1400 into the industrialist of the eighteenth and nineteenth centuries then into the investor and capital controller of the late twentieth century. *How and why did these transformations in the organization of capital come about?*

3. The increase in the level of global economic integration. From your perspective as a merchant adventurer, you obviously want the fewest restraints possible on your ability to trade from one area of the world to another; the fewer restrictions, the greater the opportunity for profit. Such things as a global currency, agreement among nations on import and export regulations, ease of passage of money and goods from area to area, freedom to employ who you want and to pay the lowest possible wage are all to your advantage; furthermore, you want few or no government restrictions regarding the consequences of your business activities. *How did the level of global economic integration increase, and what were the consequences for the merchant adventurer, as well as others?*

With these questions in mind, let's go back to the world of 1400 and start trading.

THE ERA OF THE GLOBAL TRADER

A Trader's Tour of the World in 1400

If, as global merchants in 1400, we were searching for ways to make money, the best opportunities would be in long-distance trade, buying goods in one area of the world and selling them in another (see Braudel 1982:68). If we could choose which among the great cities of the world—Cairo, Malacca, Samarkand, Venice—to begin trading, our choice would probably be Hangchow, China. China in 1400 had a population of 100 million and was the most technologically developed country in the world. Paper was invented in China probably as early as A.D. 700 and block printing as early as 1050. China of 1400 had a thriving iron industry; enormous amounts of coal were burned to fuel the iron furnaces, equal in northern China alone to 70 percent of what metal workers in Great Britain used at the beginning of the eighteenth century. The explosive power of gunpowder was harnessed around 650 A.D. and by 1000 was used by Chinese armies for simple bombs and grenades. Cannons were in use by 1300, some mounted on the ships of the Chinese navy, and by the fourteenth century the Chinese were using a metaled-barreled gun that shot explosive pellets (Abu-Lughod 1989:322ff).

If you were to tour the Chinese countryside you would have been struck by the networks of canals and irrigation ditches that criss-crossed the landscape, maintained by wealthy landowners or the state. China was governed by a royal elite and administered largely by mandarins, people selected from the wealthy classes and who were exempt from paying taxes. State bureaucrats were also selected and promoted through civil service examinations open to all but those of the lowest rank of society (e.g., executioners, slaves, beggars, boatpeople, actors, laborers) (Hanson 1993:186). China produced some of the most desired trade goods in the world, particularly silk, spices, and porcelain.

The economic conditions in China also favored traders. There were guilds and associations of merchants such as jewelers, gilders, antique dealers, dealers in honey, ginger, and boots, money-changers, and doctors. China had its own currency system. In the Middle East and Europe governments issued money in the form of coins of precious metals whose value depended on their weight. In China there was not only copper coin, but paper money (cotton paper stamped with a government seal) to provide merchants with a convenient means of exchange. Paper money also allowed the state to control the flow of money in and out of the country. Precious metals, such as gold and silver, could not be used by foreigners in trade, so foreign traders were forced to exchange their gold or silver for paper money, which they then exchanged for gold and silver when they left. Since they had usually purchased Chinese commodities to sell elsewhere, they usually left with less gold and silver than when they arrived (Abu-Lughod 1989:334).

China was also politically stable. The rulers, members of the Ming Dynasty, had successfully rebelled against the Mongols 25 years earlier. The Mongols, no-madic horsemen who roamed the vast steppes of Central Asia, conquered China in 1276 and set up their own dynasty, the Yuan. The Mongols, eager to establish trade with the rest of the world, had established relatively safe trade routes to the rest of Asia, the Middle East, and Europe. At least at first, the Ming appeared to want to maintain that trade, sending its impressive navy as emissaries to ports along the Indian Ocean.

The splendor and wealth of fifteenth- and sixteenth-century China is portrayed in this engraving of a Mandarin's terrace and garden.

The city of Hangchow was situated between the banks of the Che River leading to the sea and the shore of an enormous artificial lake. According to Ibn Battuta, an Arab trader who visited the city in the 1340s, the city extended over six to seven square miles and was surrounded by walls with five gateways through which canals passed. Thirteen monumental gates at which its great thoroughfares terminated, provided entry to the city. Situated on the hills overlooking the city were the imperial palace and homes of the wealthy state bureaucrats and merchants; at the opposite end of the city were the houses of the poor—crowded, narrow-fronted, three- to five-story houses with workshops on the ground floors. The main thoroughfare, the Imperial Way, was three miles long and 180 feet wide, crowded with carriages drawn by men or tiny horses.

The city was a trader's paradise. Inside the city were ten markets as well as tea houses and restaurants where traders could meet and arrange their business. Outside the city were a fish market and wholesale markets. Ibn Battuta said it was "the largest city on the face of the earth." Sections of the cities contained concentrations of merchants from all over the world. Jewish and Christian traders from Europe in one; Muslim traders in another, with bazaars and mosques, and muezzins calling Muslims to noon prayer. The bazaars of Chinese merchants and artisans were in yet another section. In brief, Hangchow would have been an ideal place to sell merchandise from Europe, the Middle East, or other parts of Asia and to purchase goods, such as spices and silks, that were in demand in other parts of the world.

Silk was particularly desired by foreign traders because its light weight and compactness made it easy to transport, and because China had a virtual monopoly in the silk trade. Syrian traders had smuggled silk worms out of China in the thirteenth century, and in 1400 one could purchase silk in India and Italy; but the quality of Chinese silk was superior. Since the production of silk was likely in the hands of Chinese merchants, you would have purchased it directly from them. You might also purchase Chinese porcelain, especially if you planned to travel by ship, since porcelain could be used as ballast by ships returning to the Middle East or Europe (see Figure 6.1).

Your next task would be to arrange to transport your goods to where you planned to sell them. Let's assume you had orders from merchants in cities such as Venice, Cairo, and Bruges, where Chinese goods were in demand. Your first task is to get your goods to the Mediterranean. You could go overland through China, through central Asia to Northern India, or to ports on the Black Sea, then travel to European ports such as Venice and Naples. The trip overland through Asia to Europe would take you at least 275 days using pack trains—camels over the deserts, mules through the mountains, ox carts where roads existed, human carriers, and boats. The overland route was popular in the thirteenth and fourteenth centuries, when the Mongols had through their conquests unified Central Asia and issued safe conduct passes to traders. In 1400, however, with the Empire fragmented, you may have risked raiding by nomadic bands of Mongol horsemen.

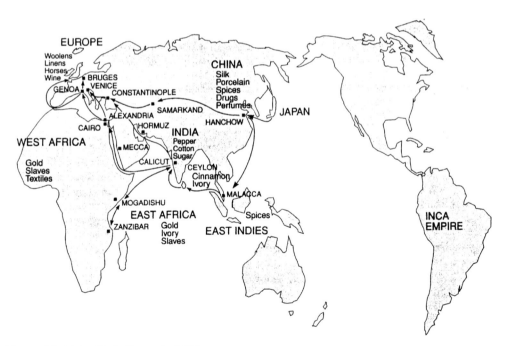

Figure 6.1 Major Trade Routes in 1400

A safer route in 1400 would have been the sea route, down the East Coast of China, through the Strait of Malacca to Southern India, and then either through the Persian Gulf to Iran and overland, through Baghdad to the Mediterranean, or through the Red Sea to Cairo, and finally by ship to Italy.

Traveling through the Strait of Malacca and into Southeast Asia, you would have found powerful elites ruling states from their royal palaces, surrounded by armed retainers, kin, artisans, and specialists. Beyond this was a peasantry producing rice to support themselves and the elites. These were the civilizations that built Angkor Thom and Angkor Wat in Cambodia. You would likely have been more at home, however, in the seaports that dotted the Strait of Malacca which owed their existence to trade. Occasionally these ports would merge with inland kingdoms such as Madjapahit in Java. The main city of the area in 1400 was Malacca, founded by pirates led in rebellion twenty years earlier by a prince from Madjapahit. The prince converted to Islam, attracting to Malacca wealthy Muslim merchants, and by 1400 Malacca was a city of forty to fifty thousand people with sixty-one nations represented in trade. The Portuguese Tomé Pires, writing a century later, said "Whoever is lord of Malacca has his hands on the throat of Venice" (cited Wolf 1982:58). While in Malacca, you likely would have obtained additional trade goods to take West. Spices, particularly cinnamon (at one time in Egypt considered more valuable than gold), were highly valued because they were easy to transport and brought high profits in the Middle East and Europe.

From Malacca you probably would have traveled along the coast of Southeast Asia and on to India, whose wealth in 1400 rivaled that of China. Southeast India had a thriving textile industry. Farmers grew cotton and passed it on to spinners, who made thread for the weavers. There is some evidence that merchants provided cotton and thread to spinners and weavers and paid the artisans for what they produced. There was a sophisticated technology: a vertical loom, block printing, and the spinning wheel, probably introduced from Turkey. But cotton and textiles were not the only items you might have obtained in India for trade; there were also dyes, tannins, spices, oil seed, narcotics, lumber, honey, and ivory (see Wolf 1982).

From India you might travel to East Africa, where from Bantu-speaking peoples you might have obtained slaves, ivory, leopard skins, gold from Zimbabwe, and rhinoceros horns (still believed in some parts of the world to be an aphrodisiac).

Leaving East Africa you would have journeyed up the coast through the Red Sea to Cairo or through the Persian Gulf, through Iraq to Baghdad, and on to Constantinople and the Eastern Mediterranean. You would have found the Islamic countries of the Middle East favorable to business, with a sophisticated body of law regulating trade, including rules for the formation of trading partnerships and the extension of credit. One law allowed people to pay for merchandise at a later date at a higher price, a convenient way around the Islamic prohibition of lending money at interest. Bags of gold coin whose value was printed on the outside, and whose contents were apparently never checked, served as money. There were bankers who changed money, took deposits, and issued promissory notes, another way of extending credit and making loans. Merchants kept their accounts by listing credits and debits. Thus all the rudiments of a sophisticated economy—capital, credit, banking, money, and account keeping—were present in Islamic trade (Abu-Lughod 1989:216ff).

From Cairo you could join a caravan to go south through the Sahara to West Africa, where textile goods were in demand and where you might obtain slaves or gold. Virtually two-thirds of the gold circulating in Europe and the Middle East came from West Africa. Or you might travel a short way to Alexandria, still a major city. From there you would travel by ship on the Mediterranean to one of the city-states of Italy, such as Venice or Genoa. Italy was the center of European and Mediterranean trade. At European fairs Italian traders would set up a bench (*banco,* from which *bank* is derived) with their scales and coins, enabling traders to exchange currency from one area of the world for another. Italian bankers monopolized the international exchange of money and credit, and it was they who pioneered the *bill of exchange.* This was a document in which a buyer agreed to deliver payment to a seller at another time and place in the seller's home currency. In the absence of any widely recognized currency, the bill of exchange greatly facilitated foreign trade (Abu-Lughod 1989:93).

You might then join other merchants from Genoa, Pisa, and Milan who formed caravans to take goods such as silks and spices from the Orient or the Middle East, alum, wax, leather, and fur from Africa, dates, figs, and honey from Spain, and pepper, feathers, and brazilwood from the Middle East, over the Alps to the fairs and markets of Western and Northern Europe, a trip taking five weeks. Or you could send your goods by ship, through the Mediterranean and the North Sea to trading centers such as Bruges.

Once you reached Northern or Western Europe, you had already left the wealthiest part of the world. After the decline of the Roman Empire Western Europe was a backward area, exploited for its iron, lumber, and slaves. Urban areas had declined and artisan activity retreated to rural areas. Moreover, Europe had been devastated in the fourteenth century by bubonic plague: In the mid-fourteenth century Europe's population was about eighty million (Abu-Lughod 1989:94). By 1400 plague had reduced it by 45 percent, to between forty and fifty million. The plague likely originated in Central Asia or China. It traveled the trade routes, stricking Chinese cities as early as 1320 and first striking Europe in Caffa, on the Black Sea, in 1346. It arrived in Alexandria in 1347, probably from Italian ports on the Black Sea. At its height in Alexandria it killed 10,000 people a day, finally killing 200,000 of the city's half million people. It struck Italy in 1348, appeared in France and Britain the same year, and reached Germany and Scandinavia a year later.

Feudalism was still the main form of political and economic organization in Europe. Kings bestowed lands, or fiefs, to subjects in return for their loyalty and service. Lords "rented" land to peasants, generally for a share of the produce, which they used to pay tribute to the kings and to finance their own expenses.

Woolen textiles were the most important products of Northern and Western Europe in 1400. Flanders (Western Belgium and Northwest France), the textile center of Northern Europe, had virtually monopolized the purchase of raw wool from England, and woolen textiles from Flanders were in demand throughout Europe and in other parts of the world.

Let's assume you have sold the commodities you brought from China and realized a handsome profit. The question is *what to do with your capital and profits?* You might buy Flemish textiles in Bruges or, depending on the political circumstances, travel to England to buy textiles. You might buy land or finance other traders in return for a share of their profits. If, however, you decided to undergo another trade circuit, returning east would be your likely alternative. The Americas were probably unknown, and certainly unreachable. You might have traveled down the European coast to West Africa, where European textiles were in great demand and where you could obtain slaves and gold. But while the wind patterns of the Eastern

Atlantic would have carried your ship to West Africa, they made it impossible, given the sailing technology, to return by sea, and you would be forced to return overland across Northern Africa. Your likely trade route, then, would have been back to Italy and east through the Mediterranean to India, the East Indies, and China.

What if you had been able to cross the sea to the Americas? What would you have found in 1400? No one left a written record of life in the New World just prior to the arrival of Europeans. Archaeologists, however, have created a record from what was left behind. You would have discovered elaborate trade routes extending from South America into North America and the remains of great civilizations in Central Mexico and the Yucatan Peninsula.

The Inca were just beginning their expansion which would produce the Andean Empire confronted by Pizarro in 1532. Inca society in 1400 was dominated by the Inca dynasty, an aristocracy consisting of relatives of the ruling group, local rulers who submitted to Inca rule. Men of local rank headed endogamous patrilineal clans, or ayllus, groups who traced descent to a common male ancestor and who were required to marry within their clan. These groups paid tribute to the Inca aristocracy by working on public projects or in military service. Women spent much of their time weaving cloth that was used to repay faithful subjects and was imbued with extraordinary ritual and ceremonial value. The state expanded by colonizing new agricultural lands to grow maize. It maintained irrigation systems, roads, and a postal service in which runners carried information from one end of the empire to another. Groups that rebelled against Inca rule were usually relocated far from their homeland (Wolf 1982:62–63).

If you had traveled into the Brazilian rainforests you might have encountered peoples such as the Tupinambá, who lived on small garden plots while gathering and hunting in the forests. Sixteenth-century traveler Calvinist pastor Jean de Léry concluded that the Tupinambá lived more comfortably than ordinary people in France (cited Maybury-Lewis 1997:13).

In Mexico in 1400 the Aztecs were twenty years from establishing their vast empire with its capital at Tenochtitlán. In the Caribbean there were complex chieftainships with linkages to the civilizations of Mesoamerica and the Andes. A merchant of 1400 would have been able to follow trade routes that spread from Mexico into the southeastern and northeastern United States, encountering descendants of those who archaeologists called the Mississippians. In this society goods and commodities were used to indicate status and rank. A trader would have encountered towns or ceremonial centers focused on great terraced, earthen platforms. The Mississippians relied on the cultivation of maize, beans, and squash, called "the three sisters" by the Iroquois. You might have met the Iroquois at the headwaters of the Ohio River, the Cherokee in the southern Appalachians, the Natchez on the lower Mississippi River, and the Pawnee and the Mandan on the Missouri River. On the surrounding prairies your would have encountered the peoples of the Northwest, the buffalo hunters of the plains (the horse, often associated with the Plains Indians, wouldn't arrive for another century), and the Inuit hunters of the Arctic and subarctic. These civilizations and cultures might in later centuries have provided a lucrative market for the sale and purchase of goods, had not other events led to their devastation.

As we complete our global tour, the barriers to commerce are striking. For example, most political rulers were not yet committed to encouraging trade. While states might value trade for the taxes, tolls, and rents they could extract from traders, merchants were still looked down upon. Rulers generally viewed trade only as a way to gain profit from traders and merchants, and some states even attempted to control some trade themselves. In China, for example, trade in salt was monopolized by the government. Religious authorities in Europe, the Middle East, and China discouraged trade by extracting high taxes or forbidding loans at interest.

Geography was obviously a major barrier: trade circuits might take years to complete. Roads were few and ships relatively small and at the mercy of winds and tides. Security was a problem: a merchants' goods were liable to be seized or stolen, or merchants might be forced to pay tribute to rulers along the way.

Economically there were various restrictions. We were a long way in 1400 from anything resembling a consumer economy. Most of the world's population lived on a subsistence economy, that is, produced themselves whatever they needed to exist. In Europe, for example, where 90 percent of the population was rural, people might buy an iron plow, some pots, and textile products, but that was all. Consumers tended to be the urban dwellers, largely the clergy, aristocracy, and the small middle class consisting of artisans, merchants, and bureaucrats. Furthermore, if people wanted to buy more, there was virtually no currency with which to do it; even if all the gold and silver of Europe had been in circulation, it would have amounted to only about two dollars per person (Weatherford 1988:14).

Thus, overall the world of 1400 seemed little affected by trade. China and India were probably the richest countries in the world, and there is little doubt that royal rulers controlled most of the wealth, largely through the extraction of tribute from peasants, artisans, and traders. Much of this they redistributed in the form of gifts, feasts, and charity. Moreover, the people who worked the soil, as those who re-mained gathering and hunting at the fringes and outside the world system, had ready access to food. Though there is evidence of periodic famine in which thousands perished, it is unlikely that, as now, one-fifth of the world's population in 1400 was hungry. Thus while a growing system of trade was beginning to link more of the world's people together, there had yet to develop the worldwide inequities that exist today. This, however, would rapidly begin to change over the next one hundred years.

The Economic Rise of Europe and Its Impact on Africa and the Americas

Two events dominate the story of the expansion of trade after 1400: the increased withdrawal of China from world trade networks, and the voyage of Vasco da Gama around the southern tip of Africa. These events resulted in a shift in the balance of economic dominance from a country of one hundred million occupying most of Asia to a country of one million occupying an area just slightly larger than the state of Maine.

The reason for China's withdrawal from its position of commercial dominance is something of a mystery. The ruling dynasty moved the capital of China inland and allowed its powerful navy gradually to disintegrate. Regardless of the reasons for these actions, they resulted in a diminished role for China in global trade and Portugal, with the most powerful navy in the world, was quick to fill the vacuum left by China in the East Indies. Portugal used its navy to dominate trade and supplemented trading activities with raiding (Abu-Lughod 1989:243).

Japan also took the opportunity after China's withdrawal to expand its trading activity in Southeast Asia. Japan, like England, was in the fifteenth century a feudal society divided into an upper nobility, the *daimyo*, or great lords; and the *samurai*, vassals of the *daimyo*; and the *chonin*, or merchants, who were looked down on by the nobility. There was contact between Japan and Europe by the mid-sixteenth century, and Christian missionaries soon established themselves in Japan. But around 1500 Japan was involved in heavy trade with China, trading refined copper, sulfur, folding fans, painted scrolls, and, most important, swords. One trade expedition carried ten thousand swords to China and returned with strings of cash, raw silk, porcelains, paintings, medicines, and books. Thus in the fifteenth century, Japan was beginning economic expansion to areas vacated by China (San-derson 1995:154).

Technological advances in boat building were partially responsible for Portugal's power. Around 1400 European boat builders combined the European square rigger with the lateen rig of the Arabs, the square rig giving ships speed when running and the lateen rig allowing the boat to sail closer to the wind. They also equipped their ships with cannons on the main deck and upper decks by cutting holes in the hull. The result was a speedy and maneuverable galleon, half warship and half merchantman (Wolf 1982:235).

Equally important for Portugal was location. Prior to the fifteenth century, Portugal was at the edge of the world system. The Mediterranean was controlled by the city-states of Italy and by Islamic powers. The Americas were seemingly out of reach, even if traders were aware of them. The west coast of Africa was inaccessible by boat unless one sailed south down the coast and returned overland. But once the route east to India and China was restricted, action shifted to the Atlantic, and as Africa and the Americas became readily accessible, Portugal was suddenly at the center of world trade.

It was the era of discovery and conquest, of the voyages of Columbus, of efforts to find alternative routes to China and the East Indies. Columbus believed he had discovered China or Ciangu (Japan), and as late as 1638 the fur trader Jean Nicolet, on meeting Winnebago Indians in the shores of Lake Michigan, wore a Chinese robe he brought to wear when meeting the Great Kahn of China (Wolf 1982:232).

Much is made in popular culture and history books of the spirit of adventure of early "explorers" such as Marco Polo, Vasco da Gama, and Christopher Columbus. But they were less explorers than merchant sailors. Their motivation was largely economic; they were seeking alternative ways to the riches of China and the East Indies. One might say that European economic domination, to the extent it was fueled by the wealth of the Americas, was due to the accidental discovery of two continents that happened to be in the way of their attempts to find alternative routes to China, Japan, and India.

If you were a global trader in the sixteenth century and if your starting point was Lisbon, Portugal, you had a choice of trade routes. You could go east to the Middle East, India, or Southeast Asia, all kept open to Portuguese traders by Portugal's navy. You could go south along the African coast, or follow Columbus's route to the New World. Or you could simply trade into the rest of Europe. All routes could prove profitable. In our reincarnation as a Portuguese trader, let's first go south to Africa.

Let's assume you have the capital to hire a ship to carry yourself and your goods to Africa. You would probably be carrying Mediterranean wine, iron weapons, perhaps horses, much in demand in Africa, and a consignment of textiles consisting perhaps of Egyptian linen and cotton. *What sort of commodities would you acquire in Africa for trade in Europe?*

Africans were already producing the same things as Europeans—iron and steel (possibly the best in the world at the time), elaborate textiles, and other goods. As a trader, you would have been interested in the textiles made in Africa, which were in demand in Europe. You would also have been anxious to trade in gold mined in West Africa, the source until that time of most of the gold in Europe and the Middle East. But your real interest would likely have been slaves.

The institution of slavery goes back well into antiquity. The ancient Greeks kept slaves, and slave labor was used throughout the Middle East and Europe in 1500. Moslems enslaved Christians, Christians enslaved Muslims, and Europeans enslaved Slavs and Greeks. Coal miners in Scotland were enslaved into the seventeenth and eighteenth centuries, and indentured servitude was widespread in Europe. However, there was about to be a huge surge in the demand for slave labor from the new colonies being established in the Americas.

The nature of the slave trade has long been a contentious issue among historians. Many believe the slave trade was forced on Africa, if not by direct military intervention then by economic extortion, Europeans offering guns and horses needed by rulers to maintain their authority in exchange for slaves. But there is increasing evidence that the slave trade was largely an African institution that Europeans and others were only too happy to tap into. Slavery in Africa was different from slavery in Europe, however, and different from what it was to become in the Americas.

Slaves were regarded traditionally in Africa as subordinate family members, as they were in Europe going back to Aristotle's time. Thus slaves in Africa could be found doing any duties a subordinate family member might do. To understand the African institution of slavery it is also necessary to understand that among people in African states there was little notion of private property; for example, land was owned by "corporate kinship groups," networks of related individuals who together owned land in common. People were given the right to use land but not to own it. Slaves comprised the only form of private, revenue-producing property recognized in African law. Slaves could produce revenue because if you had the labor in the form of family members, wives, or slaves, you could claim the use of more land. African conceptions of property are reflected also in the fact that, whereas in Europe taxes were paid on land, in Africa taxes were paid on people, "by the head" (Thornton 1992).

The size of African states may have reflected the lack of concern with land as property. John Thornton (1992:106) estimated that only 30 percent of Atlantic Africa contained states larger than fifty thousand square kilometers (roughly the size of New York State), and more than half the total area contained states of five hundred to one thousand square kilometers. Africans went to war generally not to acquire land, as in Europe, but to acquire slaves, with which more land could be worked.

Given these attitudes toward land and toward labor, there existed in Africa at the time of European arrival a large slave population and a thriving slave market. Slaves were a major form of investment; a wealthy African could not buy land but could acquire slaves and, as long as land was available, claim more land to use. Moreover, slaves, since they were property, could be inherited by individuals, whereas land, since it belonged to the corporate kin group, could not. Investing in slaves would have been the wealthy African's equivalent of a European investing in land, and if you were not using slaves you could sell them (Thornton 1992:87). Thus European traders found ready sources of slaves, not because Africans were inveterate slave traders but because in Africa the legal basis for wealth revolved around the idea of transferring ownership of people (Thornton 1992:95).

Once you obtained the slaves, you might have obtained a special ship to transport them back to Europe or to one of the Atlantic islands, where they were in demand as workers on the expanding sugar plantations. Sugar in the sixteenth century was still a luxury item, used by the wealthy to decorate food or as medicine. The primary areas of supply were around the Mediterranean—Egypt, Italy, Spain, and Greece. But with the opening of the Atlantic, sugar plantations were established first on the Canary Islands and the Azores and later in the Caribbean. Sugar production was a labor-intensive activity, and slaves from Africa supplied much of that labor. From 1451 to 1600 some 275,000 slaves were sent from West Africa to America and Europe. In the seventeenth and eighteenth centuries sugar would begin to play a major role in the world economy, but in the sixteenth century its possibilities were only beginning to be recognized.

Let's assume that after buying slaves in Africa and selling them in the new sugar plantations of the Azores, you resume your journey and go west to the Americas. The opening of the Americas brought into Portugal and Spain vast amounts of gold and silver plundered from the Inca and Aztec Empires and extracted from mines by slave and indentured labor. When Pizarro invaded Peru and seized Atahualpa in 1532, he demanded and received a ransom of a roomful of gold and killed the emperor anyway. When Cortes conquered the Aztec he demanded gold; after the Aztec's counterattack Cortes's fleeing men carried so much loot that one-quarter drowned as they fell from a causeway into a lake, so burdened down were they by their cargo (Weatherford 1988:7).

At the time of the conquest of the Americas, there was approximately $200 million worth of gold and silver in Europe; by 1600 that had increased eight times. Some 180–200 tons of gold, with a contemporary value of $2.8 billion, flowed into Europe, much of it still visible in the robes, statuary, and sacred objects of European churches (Weatherford 1988:14).

Most of the silver came from San Luis Potosí. Cerro Rico ("rich hill" in Spanish), the mountain above Potosí in Bolivia, is the richest mountain ever discovered, virtually a mountain of silver. In 1545 slaves and indentured laborers recruited from the indigenous population began digging silver out of the mountain, forming it into bars and coins, and sending it to Spain. By 1603 there were 58,800 Indian workers in Potosí, 43,200 free day laborers, 10,500 contract laborers, and 5,100 labor draftees. By 1650, Potosí rivaled London and Paris in size, with a population of 160,000 (Wolf 1982:136).

The amount of currency in circulation worldwide increased enormously, enriching Europe but eroding the wealth of other areas, and helping Europe expand into an international market system. China reopened its trading links to Europe and took in so much silver that by the mid-eighteenth century its value had declined to one-fifth what it had been prior to the discovery of America. The gold from the Americas also had the effect of destroying the African gold trade (Weatherford 1988).

Gold and silver were not the only wealth extracted from the New World. Spain imported cochineal, a red dye made from insects (it took 70,000 dried insects to produce one pound of cochineal), indigo (blue dye), and cocoa. Portuguese traders established sugar plantations on the Northeast coast of Brazil.

The cost of the European expansion of trade to the Americas, at least to the people of the Americas, was enormous. It resulted in the demographic collapse of the New World, what Eric Wolf called "the great dying" (1982:133).

There is broad disagreement about the population of the Americas at the time of the European conquest. In 1939 Alfred E. Kroeber, one of the founders of American anthropology, estimated that the total population of the Americas was about 8.4 million of which 900,000 were in North America. Harold Herbert Spinden, relying on archeological evidence, suggested there were 50–75 million people in the Americas in a.d. 1200. Henry F. Dobyns, working with archeological evidence, estimates of the carrying capacity of given environments, and historical documents, estimated 90–112 million in the hemisphere and 12.5 million in the area north of Mexico. The disagreement reflected in these numbers is not unimportant, for it involves an important legal question: *Did the "discovery" of the New World permit Europeans to move on to unoccupied wilderness, or did they displace and destroy a settled indigenous population?* If the latter is the case, then European claims of legal ownership of the land based on the doctrine of *terra nullius*—land belonging to no one—would be legally invalid.

There is little doubt, we think, that the higher estimates are closer to the actual population of the Americas. In 1500, Europe, a fraction the size of the Americas, had a population of 45 million; France alone had a population of 20 million, and tiny Portugal 1 million. And this was after the bubonic plague epidemics. There seems little doubt that the environment and societies of the Americas were capable of supporting large populations. The peoples of the Americas built empires, palisaded settlements, temples, great pyramids, and irrigation complexes. There was certainly an adequate supply of foodstuffs to support a large population; most of our diet today comes from plants domesticated first in the New World, including corn, potatoes, yams, sweet potatoes, tomatoes, squash, pumpkins, most varieties of beans, pepper (except black), amaranth, manioc, mustard, some types of rice, pecans, pineapples, bread fruit, passion fruit, melons, cranberries, blueberries, blackberries, coffee, vanilla, chocolate, and cocoa.

In 1496 Bartolomé Colón, Christopher's brother, authorized a headcount of adults of Española, the present-day Haiti and Dominican Republic, then the most populous of the Caribbean Islands. The people of the island, the Tainos, created a culture that extended over most of the Caribbean. Colón arrived at a count of 1.1 million working adults; if we add children and the elderly, and consider that disease and murder had already diminished the population, there must have been at least 2 million and as many as 8 million on that island alone (Sale 1991:160–161). Thus it is hardly unreasonable to suppose that the population of the Americas as a whole was upwards of 50–100 million people.

The scale of death after the arrival of the Europeans is difficult to conceive and rivals any estimate made for the demographic consequences of a nuclear holocaust today. When the Spanish surveyed Española in 1508, 1510, 1514, and 1518, they found a population of under one hundred thousand. The most detailed of the surveys, taken in 1514, listed just 22,000 adults, which anthropologists Sherburne Cook and Woodrow Borah estimated to represent a

In the early 1600s an epidemic (possibly smallpox) killed some 90 percent of the Wampanoags of Massachusetts.

total population of 27,800 (Cook and Borah, 1960). Thus in just over twenty years there was a decline from at least 2 million to 27,800 people. Bartolomé de Las Casas, the major chronicler of the effects of the Spanish invasion, said that by 1542 there were just two hundred indigenous Tainos left, and within a decade they were extinct. Cook and Borah concluded that in Central America an estimated population of 25.3 million was reduced by 97 percent in a little over a century. In all, it is estimated that 95–98 percent of the indigenous population of the Americas died as a consequence of European contact.

Many died in battles with the invaders; others were murdered by European occupiers desperate to maintain control over a threatening population; and still others died as a result of slavery and forced labor. But the vast majority died of diseases introduced by Europeans to which the indigenous peoples had no immunity.

The most deadly of the diseases was smallpox. It arrived sometime between 1520 and 1524 with a European soldier or sailor and quickly spread across the continent, ahead of the advancing Europeans. When Pizarro reached the Inca in 1532, his defeat of a divided Empire was made possible by the death from smallpox of the ruler and the crown prince. When a Spanish expedition set out from Florida for the Pacific in 1535, they found evidence of the epidemic in West Texas. Dobyns (1983) assumed that virtually all the inhabitants of the hemisphere were exposed to smallpox during that one epidemic. *What would the mortality rate have been from this one pathogen alone?*

Dobyns (1983:13–14; see also Stiffarm and Lane 1992) estimated that in the epidemic of 1520–1524 virtually all indigenous peoples—certainly those in large population areas—would have been exposed to smallpox, and since there would have been no immunity the death rate, judging by known death rates among other Native American populations, must have been at least 60–70 percent. Spanish reports of the time that half of the native population died, said Dobyns, most certainly were underestimates.

And this was not the only smallpox epidemic. Dobyns calculated that there were forty-one smallpox epidemics in North America from 1520 to 1899, seventeen measles epidemics from 1531 to 1892, ten major influenza epidemics from 1559 to 1918, and four plague epidemics from 1545 to 1707, to name a few. In all, he said, a serious epidemic invaded indigenous populations on average every four years and two and half months during the years 1520–1900.

Dobyns estimated that the population of Florida at the time of European contact was over 700,000. There was a smallpox epidemic in 1519, gastrointestinal infection in 1528, measles from 1528 to 1533 and an epidemic in 1535–1538, bubonic plague in 1545–1548, typhus in 1549, mumps in 1550, influenza in 1559, unidentified epidemics from 1564 to 1570 and 1585, Cape Verde fever in 1586, measles in 1596, and Bubonic plague from 1613 to 1617. During that time, the population declined from 700,000 to 36,450. The remainder perished in the centuries that followed, marking the disappearance of all populations that inhabited Florida at the time of the first Spanish voyage.

Thus the occupation of the New World by Europeans was not so much an act of conquest as it was an act of replacing a population ravaged by pathogens that Europeans carried with them. Depopulation was not the only consequence of the economic expansion of Europe into the Americas. The deaths of indigenous peoples proved a boon to the slave trade, as Europeans transported millions of Africans to the plantations and mines to replace the dying indigenous laborers. Much of the remaining native population gathered around mining communities and Spanish agricultural estates, providing a surplus labor supply, producing cheap crafts and agricultural products, and paying tribute and taxes to the colonizers (Wolf 1982:149). Their descendants today still suffer economic and social discrimination at the hands of descendants of European and indigenous unions.

The environment did not escape the consequences of the expansion of trade in the sixteenth century. Columbus imported to the New World the livestock-raising ranchero system from Castile, complete with what was to become our own "cowboy" tradition—roundups, lassos, open ranges, branding, and cowboys on horseback. The stock depleted native grasses, compacted the tropical soil, and stripped the ground cover that had prevented soil erosion, implanting the system, said historian Kirkpatrick Sale, of a red meat-dependent society that ensured future environmental destruction (Sale 1991:164).

In 1776, Adam Smith, in *Wealth of Nations,* which was to become the bible of capitalism, wrote, "The discovery of America, and that of a passage to the East Indies by the Cape of Good Hope, are the two greatest and most important events recorded in the history of mankind" (cited Crosby 1986 vii).

A decade later there was a debate among the savants of France over whether the discovery of the New World was a blessing or a curse. Abbé Guillaume Reynal, author of a four-volume study of trade between Europe and the East and West Indies, wrote a paper to answer this question. In it he listed the gains that Europe had received and discussed the costs to the peoples of Asia and the Americas. He concluded:

> Let us stop here, and consider ourselves as existing at the time when America and India were unknown. Let me suppose that I address myself to the most cruel of the Europeans in the following terms. There exist regions which will furnish you with rich metals, agreeable clothing, and delicious food. But read this history, and behold at what price the discovery is promised to you. Do you wish or not that it should be made? Is it to be imagined that there exists a being infernal enough to answer this question in the affirmative! Let it be remembered that there will not be a single instant in futurity when my question will not have the same force. (cited Sale 1991:366–367)

THE RISE OF THE TRADING COMPANIES

The expansion of trade into the Americas marked an important development in the control of global trade and commerce: states began to take a much more direct interest in commerce within their borders. For example, states controlled much of the trade with the Americas. Each year two fleets of the Spanish Crown would leave from Cadiz or Seville carrying European goods, one landing at Vera Cruz and the other, with goods bound for Peru, landing at Cartagena or Portobelo in Panama. From there mules carried the goods into the Andes, returning with silver and American goods for shipment home. The two fleets converged in Havana before returning to Spain (Wolf 1982:149).

The seventeenth century marked the era of what economists call *mercantilism,* as European states did all they could to protect, encourage, and expand industry and trade, not for its own sake but to prevent wealth, largely in the form of gold and silver, from leaving their countries. States enacted protective legislation to keep out foreign goods and to prevent gold and silver from leaving, and they subsidized the growth of selected industries by ensuring the existence of a cheap labor supply. Also during the seventeenth-century the so-called trading or joint stock company evolved, a joining of trade and armed force designed to ensure the continued extraction of wealth from areas around the world.

As a global merchant in 1700 your best chance of making profits would have been to join a trading company, by far the most sophisticated instrument of state-sponsored trade. The companies consisted of groups of traders, each of whom invested a certain amount of capital and were given charters by the state and presented with monopolistic trade privileges in a particular area of the world. Since other countries also gave monopolistic trading privileges to their companies, there was often armed conflict between them. For example, in 1600 the British crown issued a royal charter to the Governor and the Company of Merchants of London trading with the East Indies, later known simply as the British East India Company. The company was formed to share in the East Indian spice trade but met with resistance from the Dutch, who in 1602 formed the Dutch East India Company to monopolize Asian trade.

East India House, the corporate headquarters of the East India Company in Amsterdam, included offices, warehouses, and an arsenal for its fleet. Spices filled its cellars, and, in the rear, herds of cattle were slaughtered and the meat salted for ship provisions.

The Dutch maintained political control over its posts in India with an army of ten to twelve thousand troops and a navy of forty to sixty ships. The company brought 10–12 million florins worth of goods to Europe each year, producing a profit of 25–30 percent (Braudel 1982). In 1623 the Dutch authorities in what is now Ambon, Indonesia, executed ten Englishmen, ten Japanese, and one Portuguese, believing that the English planned to attack the Dutch garrison when their ships arrived. In India, however, the British East India Company defeated Portuguese troops and gained trading concessions from the Mughal Empire. The British East India Company gradually extended its trade into Southeast Asia. In 1757 it defeated Indian troops and took control of all of Bengal, looting the Bengal treasury of some £5 million. Eventually its control expanded to most of India, and it became the managing agency for the British colonization of India.

Other trading companies granted charters by the British state include the Virginia Company in 1606, the English Amazon Company in 1619, the Massachusetts Company in 1629, the Royal Adventurers into Africa in 1660, and the Hudson's Bay Company in 1670.

The Dutch were initially best able to exploit the new developments in trade, largely because of their large merchant fleet and the development of the fluitschip, a light and slender vessel that carried heavy cargoes. The availability of funds in financial centers such as Antwerp and Amsterdam, much of it originating in the gold and silver of the Americas, allowed builders to get the best woods and best craftsmen and employ foreign sailors. Gradually, however, England and its navy gained, and the English trading companies soon dominated world trade.

As a merchant adventurer in the first part of the eighteenth century you may have joined the Virginia Company and established a trading post, or "factory," in southern Appalachia, probably in a Cherokee village. The Cherokee were necessary to supply the commodities you would want to acquire for trade, items such as deerskins, ginseng and other herbs in demand in Europe as aphrodisiacs and cures for venereal disease, and war captives that you could sell as slaves. In exchange, you would supply the Cherokee with European goods such as guns, ammunition, iron utensils, and European clothing. Your normal business practice would be to advance these goods to the Cherokee, thus obligating them to repay you. But to succeed in making a profit, you would need the cooperation of the Cherokee. This is where the British government came in.

Prior to European contact the Cherokee lived in large towns in which land was owned communally, and subsistence activities consisted of hunting, fishing, gathering, and agriculture. The Cherokee population had been decimated by disease by the early eighteenth century, but they still retained most of their traditional culture. For example, Cherokee villages were relatively independent from each other, each having its own leaders and each relatively self-sufficient in food and production of necessities such as clothing, weapons, and cooking utensils. The independence of village leaders, however, made it difficult for the British government and traders to deal with the Cherokee. If there were overall leaders who could make agreements binding on large groups, with whom government and merchants could deal, it would be far easier to make treaties, collect trade debts, and engineer political alliances (Dunaway 1996:31). Consequently, using their military power and the threat of withdrawing trade, the British government appointed chiefs who they recognized as having the power to make agreements binding on the entire Cherokee nation whether or not their authority was recognized by other Cherokee. The British government also encouraged conflict between indigenous groups, reasoning, as the South Carolina governor reported in the 1730s, ". . . for in that consists our safety, being at War with one another prevents them from uniting against us"(Dunaway 1996:28).

Thus merchants, such as yourself, along with the Cherokee, became integrated into a global trade network in which slaves and deerskins were sent through Charleston, Virginia, to England, the northern colonies, and the West Indies. In return, Charleston received sugar and tobacco from the West Indies and rum from the northern colonies that was manufactured from molasses from the West Indies which the Northern colonies acquired in exchange for lumber and other provisions. In exchange for the deerskins sent to England, Charleston received goods manufactured in England, such as woolens, clothing, guns, and iron tools. The deerskins were converted in England into leather goods, which merchants in England traded for raw materials, luxury goods, and meat provisions from all over the world (Dunaway 1996:34).

For traders, these arrangements worked very well: by 1710 as many as 12,000 Indians had been exported as slaves and by 1730 some 255,000 deerskins were being shipped annually from British trading posts to England and other parts of the world (Dunaway 1996:32). Furthermore, with the help of the British military strength and diplomacy, traders were making a 500–600 percent profit on goods advanced to the Cherokee in exchange for deerskins, slaves, and herbs.

In this early nineteenth-century engraving, rival fur trading companies are competing with each other to secure trade with indigenous peoples in Canada.

But what of the Cherokee? By becoming integrated into the global economy on terms dictated by British government officials and traders, the Cherokee economy was transformed from self-sufficient agricultural production to a "putting-out" system in which they were given the tools for production (e.g., guns) along with an advance of goods in exchange for their labor—an arrangement that destroyed traditional activities and stimulated debt peonage. To pay off debts accumulated to acquire European goods, communal Cherokee land was sold by chiefs appointed by the British: in little more than fifty years the British extinguished title to about 57 percent of the Cherokee traditional land (some 43.9 million acres).

In addition, the new economy brought profound changes in Cherokee social life. Trade was male-oriented, men being responsible for acquiring the items—slaves and deer—desired by the British. This removed men from traditional agricultural activities as well as incapacitating them with rum (Dunaway 1996:37). By the mid-1700s, British observers noted that "women alone do all the laborious tasks of agriculture," freeing men to hunt or go to war.

Furthermore, traditional crafts deteriorated with the increased consumption of European goods such as guns, axes, knives, beads, pottery, clothing and cooking utensils. By the mid-1700s the British could report that "the Indians by reason of our supplying them so cheap with every sort of goods, have forgotten the chief part of their ancient mechanical skill, so as not to be able now, at least for some years, to live independent from us" (Dunaway 1996:38). In 1751, the Cherokee chief Skiagonota would observe that "the clothes we wear we cannot make ourselves. They are made for us. We use their ammunition with which to kill deer. We cannot make our guns. Every necessity of life we have from the white people" (cited Dunaway 1996:39).

THE ERA OF THE INDUSTRIALIST

By 1800, England had militarily, politically, and economically subdued her closest rivals of the early eighteenth century—France and Holland. British commerce thrived, fueled largely by the growth of industry, particularly textiles, and the related increase in the availability of cheap labor. And while the British lost her American colonies—politically if not economically—she gained in many ways a wealthier prize—India.

But the big news was the industrial development of England. From 1730 to 1760 iron production increased 50 percent; the first iron bridge was built in 1779 and the first iron boat in 1787. In 1783 Watt produced the double-effect steam engine. From 1740 to 1770 consumption of cotton rose 117 percent, and by 1800 mechanized factories were producing textiles at an unprecedented rate.

Social scientists often pose the related questions, *what made England take off?* and *why was there an industrial revolution at all?* These are more than academic questions. As planners in so-called economically undeveloped countries attempt to improve peoples' lives through economic development, they often look to the history of Great Britain to discover the key ingredients to economic success. England became, to a great extent, the model for economic development, the epitome of progress, so it was believed, particularly in Great Britain.

The reasons for the industrial revolution in England and the emergence of the capitalist economy are varied, and while analysts disagree on which were the most important, there is general agreement on those that played some part. They include the following (see Wallerstein 1989:22ff).

1. An increase in demand for goods. This demand may have been foreign or domestic, supplemented by increased demands for largely military products from the state. The textile industry was revolutionary also in its organization of labor and its relationship to the foreign market, on which it depended for both raw materials (in the case of cotton) and markets. Historian Eric Hobsbawm argued that there was room for only one world supplier, and that ended up being England.

2. The increase in the supply of capital. An increase in trade resulted in greater profits and more money, and these profits supplied the capital for investment in new technologies and businesses.

3. A growth in population. Population increased dramatically in England and Europe in the eighteenth century. From 1550 to 1680 the population of Western Europe grew by 18 percent and from 1680 to 1820 by 62 percent. From 1750 to 1850 England's population increased from 5.7 million to 16.5 million. Population increase was important because it increased the potential labor force and the number of potential consumers of commodities. But there is disagreement as to why population increased and the effects it had on industrialization.

    Some account for the increase with lower mortality rates attributable to small-pox inoculation and an improved diet related to the introduction of new food-stuffs, such as the potato. Life expectancy at birth went from thirty-five to forty years (M. Guttmann 1988:130). Others attribute the rise in population to an increase in fertility. Indeed, families were larger in the eighteenth century. In England between 1680 and 1820 the gross reproduction rate (number of females born to each woman) went from two to nearly three and the average number of children per family from four to almost six. Later we will need to examine the relationship of population growth to industrialization because it is key to understanding the rapid growth of population today.

4. An expansion of agriculture. There was an expansion of agricultural production in England in the eighteenth century that some attribute to enclosure laws. These laws drove squatters and peasants from common lands and forests from which they had drawn a livelihood. The rationale was to turn those lands over to the gentry to make them more productive, but this also had the effect of producing a larger landless and propertyless population, dependent on whatever wage labor they might find. Regardless, some argue that the increased agricultural yields allowed the maintenance of a larger urban workforce.

5. A unique English culture or spirit. Some, notably sociologist Max Weber, attribute the rise of England to the development of an entrepreneurial spirit, such as the Protestant ethic, that motivated people to business success in the belief that it would reveal to them that they were among God's elect.

6. State support for trade. Some claim that a more liberal state structure imposed fewer taxes and regulations on businesses, thus allowing them to thrive. The state did take action to support trade and industry. There was continued political and military support for extending Britain's economy overseas, along with domestic legislation to protect merchants from labor protest. A law of 1769 made the destruction of machines and the buildings that housed them a capital crime. Troops were sent to put down labor riots in Lancaster in 1779 and in Yorkshire in 1796, and a law passed in 1799 outlawed worker associations that sought wage increases, reduction in the working day, "or any other improvement in the conditions of employment or work" (Beaud 1983:67).

7. The ascendence of the merchant class. Stephen Sanderson (1995) attributed the development of capitalism to an increase in the power of the merchant class.

There has always been, he suggested, competition between merchants and the ruling elites, and while elites needed merchants to supply desired goods and services, they nevertheless looked down on them. But gradually the economic power of the merchant class grew until, in the seventeenth and eighteenth centuries, the merchant emerged as the most powerful member of Western, capitalist society. Capitalism, said Sanderson (1995:175–176), "was born of a class struggle. However, it was not, as the Marxists would have it, a struggle between landlords and peasants. Rather, it was a struggle between the landlord class and the merchants that was fundamental in the rise of capitalism."

8. A revolution in consumption. Finally, some attribute the rapid economic growth in England to a revolution in the patterns of retailing and consumption. There was a growth in the number of stores and shops and the beginning of a marketing revolution, led by the pottery industry and the entrepreneurial genius of Josiah Wedgewood, who named his pottery styles after members of the Royal Family to appeal to the fashion consciousness of the rising middle class.

Regardless of the reasons for England's rise and the so-called industrial revolution, there is little doubt that in addition to the traditional means of accumulating wealth—mercantile trade, extracting the surplus from peasant labor, pillage, forced labor, slavery, and taxes—a new form of capital formation increased in importance. It involved purchasing and combining the means of production and labor power to produce commodities, the form of wealth formation called capitalism that we diagramed earlier as follows: $M \rightarrow C \rightarrow {}_{IP}-^{MP} \rightarrow C'$ Æ $\rightarrow M'$ [Money is converted to commodities (capital goods) that are combined with the means of production and labor power to produce other commodities (consumer goods), that are then sold for a sum greater than the initial investment]. *How did this mode of production differ from what went before?*

Eric Wolf offered one of the more concise views. For capitalism to exist, he said, wealth or money must be able to purchase labor power. But as long as people have access to the means of production—land, raw materials, tools (e.g., weaving looms, mills)—there is no reason for them to sell their labor. They can still sell the product of their labor. For the capitalistic mode of production to exist, the tie between producers and the means of production must be cut; peasants must lose control of their land, artisans control of their tools. These people once denied access to the means of production must negotiate with those who control the means of production for permission to use the land and tools and receive a wage in return. Those who control the means of production also control the goods that are produced, and so those who labor to produce them must buy them back from those with the means of production. Thus the severing of persons from the means of production turns them not only into laborers, but into consumers of the product of their labor as well. Here is how Wolf (1982:78–79) summarized it:

> Wealth in the hands of holders of wealth is not capital until it controls means of production, buys labor power, and puts it to work continuously expanding surpluses by intensifying production through an ever-rising curve of technological inputs. To this end capitalism must lay hold of production, must invade

the productive process and ceaselessly alter the conditions of production themselves . . . Only where wealth has laid hold of the conditions of production in ways specified can we speak of the existence or dominance of a capitalistic mode. There is no such thing as mercantile of merchant capitalism, therefore. There is only mercantile wealth. Capitalism, to be capitalism, must be capitalism-in-production.

Wolf (1982:100) added that the state is central in developing the capitalist mode of production because it must use its power to maintain and guarantee the ownership of the means of production by capitalists both at home and abroad and must support the organization and discipline of work. The state also has to provide the infrastructure, such as transportation, communication, judicial system, and education, required by capitalist production. Finally, the state must regulate conflicts between competing capitalists both at home and abroad, by diplomacy if possible, by war if necessary.

The major questions are *how did this industrially driven, capitalist mode of production evolve, and what consequences did it have in England, Europe, and the rest of the world?*

Textiles and the Rise of the Factory System

Assume once again your role as a textile merchant; let's examine the opportunities and problems confronting you as you conduct business. Typical textile merchants of the early eighteenth century purchased their wares from specialized weavers or part-time producers of cloth or from *drapers*, persons who organized the production of cloth but did not trade in it. The merchant then sold the cloth to a consumer or another merchant who sold it in other areas of Europe or elsewhere. The profit came from the difference between what the merchant paid the artisan or draper and what the customer paid. This is not a bad arrangement. It does not require a large capital outlay for the merchant, since the artisan has the tools and material he or she needs, and as long as there is a demand for the cloth there is someone who will buy it.

But as a merchant you face a couple of problems. First, the people who make the cloth you buy may not produce the quantity or quality that you need, especially as an expanding population begins to require more textiles. Moreover, the artisan may have trouble acquiring raw materials, such as wool or cotton, further disrupting the supply. What can you do?

One thing to do is to increase control over what is produced by "putting out"—supplying the drapers or weavers with the raw materials to produce the cloth—or, if you have the capital, buy tools—looms, spinning wheels, and so on—and give them to people to make the cloth, paying them for what they produce. Cottage industry of this sort was widespread throughout Europe as merchants began to take advantage of the cheaper labor in rural areas, rather than purchasing products from artisans in towns and cities. In England of the mid-eighteenth century there was probably plenty of labor, especially in rural areas, supplied by people who had been put off their land by enclosure legislation or because of failure to pay taxes or repay loans. In the land market of the eighteenth century, there were far more sellers than buyers (M. Guttmann 1988).

Another problem English textile merchants faced in the mid-eighteenth century was that the textile business, especially in cotton, faced stiff competition from India, whose calico cloth was extremely popular in England. *How do you meet this competition?* The first thing England did was to ban the import of Indian cloth and develop its own cotton industry to satisfy domestic demand. This not only helped protect the British textile industry, it virtually destroyed the Indian cotton industry, and before long India was buying British cotton textiles. The result was summed up in 1830 in testimony before the House of Commons by Charles Marjoribanks (cited Wallerstein 1989:150):

> We have excluded the manufactures of India from England by high prohibitive duties and given every encouragement to the introduction of our own manufactures to India. By our selfish (I use the word invidiously) policy we have beat down the native manufactures of Dacca and other places and inundated their country with our goods.

And in 1840, the chairman of Britain's East India and China association boasted that

> [t]his Company has, in various ways, encouraged and assisted by our great manufacturing ingenuity and skill, succeeded in converting India from a manufacturing country into a country exporting raw materials (cited Wallerstein 1989:150).

The next, and to some extent inevitable, stage in textile production was to bring together in one place as many of the production phases of textiles as possible: preparing the raw wool or cotton, spinning the cotton yarn and wool, weaving the cloth, and applying the finishing touches. This allowed the merchant or industrialist to control the quantity and quality of the product and control the use of materials and tools. The only drawback to the factory system is that it is capital-intensive; the merchant was now responsible for financing the entire process, while the workers supplied only their labor. Most of the increase in cost was a consequence of increased mechanization.

Mechanization of the textile industry began with the invention by John Kay in 1733 of the flying shuttle, a device that allowed the weaver to strike the shuttle carrying the thread from one side of the loom to the other, rather than weaving it through by hand. This greatly speeded up the weaving process. However, when demand for textiles, particularly cotton, increased, the spinning of thread, still done on spinning wheels or spindles, could not keep up with weavers, and bottlenecks developed in production. To meet this need James Hargreaves introduced the spinning jenny in 1770. Later, Arkwright introduced the water frame, and in 1779 Crompton introduced his "mule" that allowed a single operator to work more than 1,000 spindles at once. In 1790 steam power was supplied. These technological developments increased textiles production enormously: the mechanical advantage of the earliest spinning jennies to hand spinning was twenty-four to one. The spinning wheel had become an antique in a decade (Landes 1969:85). The increase in the supply of yarn—twelve times as much cotton was consumed in 1800 than in 1770—required improvements in weaving, which then required more yarn, and so on.

But the revolution in production produced other problems. *Who was going to buy all the goods that were being produced, and where was the raw material for production to come from?*

Power loom weaving in a cotton textile factory in 1834. Note that virtually all the workers are women.

The Age of Imperialism

The results of the industrial revolution in Europe were impressive. The period from 1800 to 1900 was perhaps one of the most dynamic in human history and, certainly until that time, the most favorable for accumulation of vast fortunes through trade and manufacture. Developments in transportation such as railroads and steamships revolutionized the transport of raw materials and finished commodities. The combination of new sources of power in water and steam, a disarmed and plentiful labor force, and control of the production and markets of much of the rest of the world resulted in dramatic increases in the level of production and wealth. These advances were most dramatic in England and later in the United States, France, and Germany. In England, for example, spun cotton increased from 250 million pounds in 1830 to 1,101 million pounds in 1870; coal production increased from 10 million tons in 1800 to 110 million tons in 1870. World steam power production went from 4 million horsepower in 1850 to 18.5 million horsepower twenty years later; coal production went from 15 million tons in 1800 to 132 million tons in 1860, and 701 million tons in 1900. The consumption of inanimate energy from coal, lignite, petroleum, natural gasoline, natural gas, and water power increased sixfold from 1860 to 1900; railway trackage went from 332 kilometers in 1831 to 300,000 kilometers in 1876. The Krupp iron works in Germany employed 72 workers in 1848; there were 12,000 by 1873.

There was also a revolution in shipping as ocean freight costs fell, first with the advent of the narrow-beamed American clipper ship and later with the introduction of the steamship. A clipper ship could carry 1,000 tons of freight and make the journey from the south coast of China to London in 120–130 days; in 1865 a steamship from the Blue Funnel Line with a capacity of 3,000 tons made the journey in 77 days. The construction of the Suez Canal, completed in 1869 with the labor of 20,000 conscripted Egyptian *fellaheen,* or peasants, cut the travel time from England to eastern Asia in half—although it bankrupted the Egyptian treasury and put the country under Anglo-French receivership. These events initiated a military revolt that the British stepped in to put down, consequently cementing the British hold on Egypt and much of the Middle East. Politically, the United States emerged as a world power, and Japan was building its economy and would be ready to challenge Russia. The Ottoman Empire was on its way to disintegrating as France, England, and Russia sought to gain control over the remnants.

But it was not all good news for the capitalist economy. There was organized worker resistance to low wages and impoverished conditions, resistance and rebellion in the periphery, and the development of capitalist business cycles that led to worldwide economic depressions. Thus while business thrived in much of the nineteenth century, it had also entered a world of great uncertainty. First, with the expansion of the scope of production, capital investments had increased enormously. It was no longer possible, as it had been in 1800 when a forty-spindle jenny cost £6, to invest in the factory production of textiles at fairly modest levels. Furthermore, there was increased competition, with factory production expanding dramatically in Holland, France, Germany, and the United States. There was the constant problem of overproduction, when supply outstripped demand and resulted in idle factories and unemployed workers. Unlike agricultural production—there seemed always to be a market for food—industrial production depends on the revolution in demand or, as Anne-Robert-Jacque Turgot put it, "a transformation of desires" (cited in Braudel 1982:183). Until the eighteenth century manufacturers launched their enterprises only when profit was guaranteed by subsidies, interest-free loans, and previously guaranteed monopolies. Now manufacturers just had to hope people would buy their products.

The Great Global Depression of 1873 that lasted essentially until 1895 was the first great manifestation of the capitalist business crisis. The depression was not the first economic crisis: For thousands of years there had been economic declines because of famine, war, and disease. But the financial collapse of 1873 revealed the degree of global economic integration, and how economic events in one part of the globe could reverberate in others. The economic depression began when banks failed in Germany and Austria because of the collapse of real estate speculation. At the same time, the price of cast iron in England fell by 27 percent because of a drop in demand. The drop in iron prices increased British unemployment, while European investors, needing to cover their losses from real estate, withdrew their money from American banks. This led to bank collapses in the United States. In England from 1872 to 1875, exports fell by 25 percent, the number of bankruptcies increased, and rail prices fell by 60 percent. In France, the Lyon stock market crashed in 1882; bank failures and rising unemployment followed. Competition among railroads decreased profits and led to the collapse of railroad securities in the United States (Beaud 1983:119–120; see also R. Guttmann 1994).

The Depression of 1873 revealed another big problem with capitalist expansion and perpetual growth: it can continue only as long as there is a ready supply of raw materials and an increasing demand for goods, along with ways to invest profits and capital. Given this situation, *if you were an American or European investor in 1873, where would you look for economic expansion?*

The obvious answer was to expand European and American power overseas, particularly into areas that remained relatively untouched by capitalist expansion—Africa, Asia, and the Pacific. Colonialism had become, in fact, a recognized solution to the need to expand markets, increase opportunities for investors, and ensure the supply of raw material. Cecil Rhodes, one of the great figures of England's colonization of Africa, recognized also the importance of overseas expansion for maintaining peace at home. In 1895 Rhodes said:

> I was in the East End of London yesterday and attended a meeting of the unemployed. I listened to the wild speeches, which were just a cry for "bread," "bread," and on my way home I pondered over the scene and I became more than ever convinced of the importance of imperialism. . . . My cherished idea is a solution for the social problem, i.e., in order to save the 40,000,000 inhabitants of the United Kingdom from a bloody civil war, we colonial statesmen must acquire new lands for settling the surplus population, to provide new markets for the goods produced in the factories and mines. The Empire, as I have always said, is a bread and butter question. If you want to avoid civil war, you must become imperialists. (cited Beaud 1983:139–140)

P. Leroy-Beaulieu voiced the same sentiments in France when, to justify the conquest of foreign nations, he said:

> It is neither natural nor just that the civilized people of the West should be indefinitely crowded together and stifled in the restricted spaces that were their first homes, that they should accumulate there the wonders of science, art, and civilization, *that they should see, for lack of profitable jobs, the interest rate of capital fall further every day for them,* and that they should leave perhaps half the world to small groups of ignorant men, who are powerless, who are truly retarded children dispersed over boundless territories, or else to decrepit populations without energy and without direction, truly old men incapable of any effort, of any organized and far-seeing action. (cited Beaud 1983: 140)

As a result of this cry for imperialist expansion, people all over the world were converted into producers of export crops as millions of subsistence farmers were forced to become wage laborers producing for the market and required to purchase from European and American merchants and industrialists, rather than supply for themselves, their basic needs. Nineteenth century British economist William Stanley Jevons (cited Kennedy 1993:9) summed up the situation when he boasted:

> The plains of North America and Russia are our cornfields; Chicago and Odessa our granaries; Canada and the Baltic are our timber forests; Australasia contains our sheep farms, and in Argentina and on the western prairies of

> North America are our herds of oxen; Peru sends her silver, and the gold of
> South Africa and Australia flows to London; the Hindus and the Chinese grow
> tea for us, and our coffee, sugar, and spice plantations are all in the Indies.
> Spain and France are our vineyards and the Mediterranean our fruit garden,
> and our cotton grounds, which for long have occupied the Southern United
> States are now being extended everywhere in the warm regions of the earth.

Wheat became the great export crop of Russia, Argentina, and the United States, much of it produced in the United States on lands taken from the Native Americans. Rice became the great export of Southeast Asia, spurred by Great Britain's seizure of lower Burma in 1855 and its increase in rice production from one million to nine million acres. Argentina and Australia joined the United States as the major supplier of meat as cattle ranchers in Australia and the United States turned indigenous peoples into hired hands or hunted them to extermination, as did the ranchers in California into the late nineteenth century (see Meggitt 1962).

In 1871 a railroad promoter from the United States built a railroad in Costa Rica and experimented in banana production; out of this emerged in 1889 the United Fruit Company that within thirty-five years was producing two billion bunches of bananas. The company reduced its risk by expanding into different countries and different environments and by acquiring far more land than it could use at any one time as a reserve against the future.

The demand for rubber that followed the discovery of vulcanization in 1839 led to foreign investments in areas such as Brazil, where one major supplier in-creased production from 27 tons in 1827 to an average of 20,000 tons per year at the end of the nineteenth century. The laborers who collected the rubber were workers who had lost their jobs with the decline in the sugar industries and Indians, who were sometimes held captive or tortured or killed if they didn't collect their quota of rubber, or whose wives and children would be killed if they didn't return (Taussig 1987).

In the nineteenth century palm oil became a substitute for tallow for making soap and a lubricant for machinery, resulting in European military expansion into West Africa and the conquest of the kingdoms of Asante, Dahomey, Oyo, and Benin.

Vast territories were turned over to the production of stimulants and drugs such as sugar, tea, coffee, tobacco, opium, and cocoa. In the Mexican state of Chiapas and in Guatemala legislation abolished communal ownership of land. Land could now be privately owned and subject to purchase, sale, and pawning, allowing non-Indians to buy unregistered land and foreclose mortgages on Indian borrowers (Wolf 1982:337). These lands were then turned to coffee production and, later, cattle ranching. In Ceylon, common land was turned into royal land and sold to tea planters. In 1866 diamonds and gold were discovered in the Orange Free State of West Africa. By 1874, 10,000 Africans were working in the European-owned diamond mines and by 1884 almost 100,000 were working in the gold mines. By 1910, 255,000 were working the mines, and by 1940 there were 444,000.

Colonization was not restricted to overseas areas; it occurred also within the borders of core states. In 1887 the U.S. Congress passed the General Allotment Act (the "Dawes Act") to break up the collective ownership of land on Indian reservations by assigning each family its own parcel, then opening unallotted land to non-Indian homesteaders, corporations, and the federal government. As a consequence, from 1887 to 1934 some 100 million acres of land assigned by treaty to Indian groups was appropriated by private interests or the government (Jaimes 1992:126).

At first glance it may seem that the growth in development of export goods such as coffee, cotton, sugar, and lumber, would be beneficial to the exporting country, since it brings in revenue. In fact, it represents a type of exploitation called unequal exchange. A country that exports raw or unprocessed materials may gain currency for their sale, but they then lose it if they import processed goods. The reason is that processed goods—goods that require additional labor—are more costly. Thus a country that exports lumber but does not have the capacity to process it must then re-import it in the form of finished lumber products, at a cost that is greater than the price it received for the raw product. The country that processes the materials gets the added revenue contributed by its laborers.

Then there is the story of tea and opium and trade in China. China, of course, was a huge prize, but the British and Western European nations had a problem with trade into China: Chinese products, notably tea, were in high demand, but there was little produced in England or the rest of Europe that the Chinese wanted or needed. However, there was a market in China for opium, virtually all of which was produced and controlled by the British East India Company. Opium was illegal in China, but the government seemed incapable of stopping the smuggling that was hugely profitable for British, American, and French merchants. When in 1839 the Chinese government tried to enforce laws against opium sales by seizing opium held by British merchants in warehouses in Canton, the British government sent in troops and effectively forced the Chinese government to stop enforcing opium laws. An analogy today might be the Colombian government sending troops to the United States to force acceptance of Colombian cocaine shipments. Moreover, using its military superiority, the British demanded and received additional trading rights into China, opening a market not only for opium but for British textiles as well.

The British-led opium trade from India to China had three consequences. First, it reversed the flow of money between China and the rest of the world; during the first decade of the nineteenth century, China still took in a surplus of $26 million dollars; by the third decade $34 million dollars left China to pay for opium. Second, it is estimated that by the end of the nineteenth century one out of every ten Chinese had become an opium addict. Finally, cotton exports to India and China had increased from 6 percent of total British exports in 1815 to 22 percent in 1840, 31 percent in 1850, and more than 50 percent after 1873 (Wolf 1982:255ff).

Thus as a merchant adventurer your economic fortune has been assured by your government's control over foreign economies. Not only could you make more money investing in foreign enterprises, but the wealth you accumulated through trade and manufacturing gained you entry into a new elite, one with increasing power in the core countries. Power was no longer evidenced solely in the ownership of land, but in the control of capital. In England, for example, the great families of high finance and international trade, businessmen, manufacturers, ship owners, bankers, parliamentarians, jurists, families of the aristocracy and gentry, all crisscrossed by ties of marriage and kinship, became the new ruling class. This new elite depended for their economic power on business and industry to a great extent: in the eighteenth century landed inheritance accounted for 63.7 percent of national wealth in Great Britain; toward the end of the nineteenth century that figure had decreased to 23.3 percent. Meanwhile, during the same period, wealth linked to capitalist development increased from 20.8 percent to almost 50.0 percent (Beaud 1983:93).

In the United States a new capitalist elite emerged during and after the Civil War, as people such as J. P. Morgan, Jay Gould, Jim Fisk, Cornelius Vanderbilt, and John D. Rockefeller—most of whom made their fortunes in dealings with the U.S. government—emerged as a new bourgeoisie. More important, they were the driving force behind the emergence of a relatively new form of capital organization—the multinational corporation.

THE ERA OF THE CORPORATION, THE MULTILATERAL INSTITUTION, AND THE CAPITAL CONTROLLER

While the imperialist activities of the core powers allowed their economies to grow, they also created international conflict on a scale never before imagined. In 1900, each of the great powers sought to carve out a sphere of domination in Asia, Africa, and South and Central America that with the help of nationalism, racism, and xenophobia turned economic competition into political and military conflict. These conflicts fed on myths of national or racial superiority—British, French, American, White, and so on—and the supposed civilizing mission of the West (Beaud 1983:144). At the Berlin Conference of 1885, great European powers met to carve up zones of influence and domination in Africa, laying the groundwork for levels of colonialization from which Africa still has not recovered.

Attempts to extend or defend these zones of economic influence triggered what was until then the bloodiest war ever fought—World War I. Eight million people were killed. Britain lost 32 percent of its national wealth, France 30 percent, Germany 20 percent, and the United States 9 percent. Germany was forced to pay $33 billion in reparations. Industrial production fell in all countries except the United States. Then the Russian Revolution cut off huge markets for European and American products, while colonized countries demanded independence.

The United States emerged from World War I as the world's leading economic power: its national income doubled and coal, oil, and steel production soared. However, workers' real wages and the power of labor unions declined; new forms of factory organization led to greater fatigue—there were 20,000 fatal industrial accidents per year in the 1920s; and the courts blocked the formation of new unions and the application of social laws such as those prohibiting child labor. It was an era of the rise of a new, great economic power—the corporation.

The Rise of the Corporation

From your perspective as a merchant adventurer, the most important development of the early twentieth century was the merger frenzy in the United States that led to the concentration of wealth in fewer hands. Companies such as Ford, General Motors, and Chrysler in automobiles, General Electric and Westinghouse in electric, Dupont in chemicals, and Standard Oil in petroleum dominated the market. In 1929, the two hundred largest companies owned half of the country's non-banking wealth. Since then, of course, corporations have become one of the dominant governance units in the world. By 1992 there were 37,000 transnational corporations controlling one-third of the world's private wealth. From their foreign operations alone they generated about $5.5 trillion in sales. The largest corporations exceed in size, power, and wealth most of the world's nation-states and, directly or indirectly, define policy agendas of states and international bodies (Korten 1995:54). Since, as a merchant adventurer, you have now entered the corporate age, *what kind of institution is the corporation and how did it come to accumulate so much wealth and power?*

Technically a corporation is a social invention of the state; the corporate charter, granted by the state, ideally permits private financial resources to be used for a public purpose. At another level, it allows one or more individuals to apply massive economic and political power to accumulate private wealth while protected from legal liability for the public consequences. As a merchant adventurer, clearly you want to create an institution in which you can increase and protect your own profits from market uncertainties (Korten 1995:53–54).

The corporate charter goes back to the sixteenth century, when any debts accumulated by an individual were inherited by his or her descendants. Consequently, someone could be jailed for the debts of a father, mother, brother, or sister. If you, in your role as merchant adventurer, invested in a trading voyage and the goods were lost at sea, you and your descendants were responsible for the losses incurred. The law, as written, inhibited risky investments. The corporate charter solved this problem because it represented a grant from the crown that limited an investor's liability for losses to the amount of the investment, a right not accorded to individual citizens.

The early trading companies, such as the East India Company and the Hudson's Bay Company, were such corporations, and some of the American colonies themselves were founded as corporations—groups of investors granted monopoly powers over territory and industries. Consequently corporations gained enormous power and were able to influence trade policy. For example, in the eighteenth century the English parliament, composed of wealthy landowners, merchants, and manufacturers, passed laws requiring all goods sold in or from the colonies to go through England and be shipped on English ships with British crews. Furthermore, colonists were forbidden to produce their own caps, hats, and woolen or iron goods.

But suspicion of the power of corporations developed soon after their establishment. Even eighteenth century philosopher and economist Adam Smith, in *Wealth of Nations,* condemned corporations. He claimed corporations operated to evade the laws of the market by artificially inflating prices and controlling trade. American colonists shared Smith's suspicion of corporations and limited corporate charters to a specific number of years. If the charter was not renewed, the corporation was dissolved. But gradually American courts began to remove restrictions on corporations' operation. The U.S. Civil War was a turning point: corporations used their huge profits from the war, along with the subsequent political confusion and corruption, to buy legislation that gave them huge grants of land and money, much of which they used to build railroads. Abraham Lincoln (cited Korten 1995:58) saw what was happening, and just before his death observed:

> Corporations have been enthroned. . . . An era of corruption in high places will follow and the money power will endeavor to prolong its reign by working on the prejudices of the people . . . until wealth is aggregated in a few hands . . . and the Republic is destroyed.

Gradually corporations gained control of state legislatures, such as those in Delaware and New Jersey, lobbying for (and buying) legislation that granted charters in perpetuity, limited the liabilities of corporate owners and managers, and gained the right of corporations to operate in any way not specifically prohibited by the law. For example, courts limited corporate liability for accidents to workers, an important development in the nineteenth century when fatal industrial accidents from 1888 to 1908 killed 700,000 workers, or roughly one hundred per day. Other favorable court rulings and legislation prohibited the state from setting minimum wage laws, limiting the number of hours a person could work, or setting minimum age requirements for workers.

But it was a Supreme Court ruling in 1886 that arguably set the stage for the full-scale development of the culture of capitalism, by handing to corporations the right to use their economic power in a way they never before had. Relying on the Fourteenth Amendment, added to the Constitution in 1868 to protect the rights of freed slaves, the Court ruled that a private corporation is a *natural person* under the U.S. Constitution, and consequently has the same rights and protection extended to persons by the Bill of Rights, including the right of free speech. Thus corporations were given the same "rights" to influence the government in their own interest as were extended to individual citizens, paving the way for corporations to use their wealth to dominate public thought and discourse. The debates in the United States in the 1990s over campaign finance reform, in which corporate bodies can "donate" millions of dollars to political candidates, stem from this ruling, although rarely if ever is that mentioned. Thus corporations, as "persons," were free to lobby legislatures, use the mass media, establish educational institutions such as the many business schools founded by corporate leaders in the early twentieth century, found charitable organizations to convince the public of their lofty intent, and in general construct an image that they believed would be in their best interests. All of this in the interest of "free speech."

Corporations used this power, of course, to create conditions in which they could make more money. But in a larger sense they used this power to define the ideology or ethos of the emerging culture of capitalism. This cultural and economic ideology is known as *neoclassical, neoliberal,* or *libertarian economics, market capitalism,* or *market liberalism* and is advocated in society primarily by three groups of spokespersons: economic rationalists, market liberals, and members of the corporate class. Their advocacy of these principles created what David Korten called *corporate libertarianism,* which places the rights and freedoms of corporations above the rights and freedoms of individuals—the corporation comes to exist as a separate entity with its own internal logic and rules. Some of the principles and assumptions of this ideology include the following.

1. Sustained *economic growth,* as measured by gross national product (GNP), is the path to human progress.

2. *Free markets,* unrestrained by government, generally result in the most efficient and socially optimal allocation of resources.

3. *Economic globalization,* achieved by removing barriers to the free flow of goods and money anywhere in the world, spurs competition, increases economic efficiency, creates jobs, lowers consumer prices, increases consumer choice, increases economic growth, and is generally beneficial to almost everyone.

Painter Diego Rivera's depiction of the symbols of corporate wealth, as John D. Rockefeller (rear left), J. P. Morgan (rear right), Henry Ford (to Morgan's left), and others read a ticker tape while dining.
Courtesy of The Granger Collection, New York.

4. *Privatization,* which moves functions and assets from governments to the private sector, improves efficiency.
5. The primary responsibility of government is to provide the infrastructure necessary to advance commerce and enforce the rule of law with respect to *property rights and contracts.*

However, hidden in these principles, said Korten, are a number of questionable assumptions. First, there is the assumption that humans are motivated by self-interest, which is expressed primarily through the quest for financial gain (or, people are by nature motivated primarily by greed). Second, there is the assumption that the action that yields the greatest financial return to the individual or firm is the one that is most beneficial to society (or, the drive to acquire is the highest expression of what it means to be human). Third, is the assumption that competitive behavior is more rational for the individual and the firm than cooperative behavior; consequently, societies should be built around the competitive motive (or, the relentless pursuit of greed and acquisition leads to socially optimal outcomes). Finally, there is the assumption that human progress is best measured by increases in the value of what the members of society consume, and ever-higher levels of consumer spending advance the well-being of society by stimulating greater economic output (or, it is in the best interest of human societies to encourage, honor, and reward the above values).

While corporate libertarianism has its detractors, from the standpoint of overall economic growth few can argue with its success on a global scale. World economic output has increased from $3.8 trillion in 1950 to $18.9 trillion in 1992 (constant 1987 dollars); economic growth in *each decade* of the last half of the twentieth century was greater than the economic output in all of human history up to 1950. World trade has increased from total exports of $308 billion in 1950 to $3,554 billion (1990 dollars) (Korten 1995:18).

However, there were still some problems for the merchant adventurer in the early twentieth century. As corporations rose to power in the 1920s and 1930s, political and business leaders were aware that corporations, by themselves, could not ensure the smooth running of the global economy. The worldwide economic depression of the 1930s and the economic disruptions caused by World War II illustrated that. That every country had its own currency and that it could rapidly rise or fall in value relative to others created barriers to trade. Tariffs and import or export laws inhibited the free flow of goods and capital. More important, there was the problem of bringing the ideology of corporate libertarianism, and the culture of capitalism in general, to the periphery, especially given the challenge of socialism and the increasing demands of colonized countries for independence. The solution to these problems was to emerge from a meeting in 1944 at a New Hampshire resort hotel.

Bretton Woods and the World Debt

In 1944 President Franklin D. Roosevelt gathered the government financial leaders of forty-four nations to a meeting at the Mt. Washington Hotel in Bretton Woods, New Hampshire. From your perspective as a merchant adventurer it was to be one of the most far-reaching events of the twentieth century. The meeting was called ostensibly to rebuild war-ravaged economies and to outline a global economic agenda for the last half of the twentieth century. Out of that meeting came the plan for the International Bank for Reconstruction and Development (The World Bank), the International Monetary Fund (IMF) to control currency exchange, and the framework for a worldwide trade organization that would lead to the establishment in 1948 of the General Agreement on Tariffs and Trade (GATT) to regulate trade between member countries. While GATT was not as comprehensive an agreement as many traders would have liked, its scope was widely enlarged on January 1, 1995, with the establishment of the World

Trade Organization (WTO). The functions of these agencies are summarized in Table 6.1.

The IMF constituted an agreement by the major nations to allow their currency to be exchanged for other currencies with a minimum of restriction, to inform representatives of the IMF of changes in monetary and financial policies, and to adjust these policies to accommodate to other member nations when possible. The IMF also has funds that it can lend to member nations if they face a debt crisis. For example, if a member country finds it is importing goods at a much higher rate than it is exporting them, and if it doesn't have the money to make up the difference, the IMF will arrange a short-term loan (Driscoll 1992:5).

The World Bank was created to finance the reconstruction of Europe after the devastation of World War II, but the only European country to receive a loan was Holland, then engaged in trying to put down a rebellion of its Southeast Asian colonies. The World Bank then began to focus its attention on the periphery, lending funds to countries to foster economic development, with, as we shall see, mixed results.

The GATT has served as a forum for participating countries to negotiate trade policy. The goal was to establish a multilateral agency with the power to regulate and promote free trade among nations. However, since legislators and government officials in many countries, particularly the United States, objected to the idea of an international trade agency with the power to dictate government trade policy, the creation of such an agency did not occur until the WTO was finally established on January 1, 1995. In essence, the agency can react to claims by member nations that other nations are using unfair trade policies in order to give businesses in their country an unfair advantage (see Low 1993:42). There are also ongoing negotiations among the twenty-seven largest industrialized countries to formulate a Multilateral Investment Agreement (MIA) that would grant transnational investors the unrestricted right to invest their assets and buy, sell, and move businesses wherever and whenever they like.

The year 1994 marked the fiftieth anniversary of the Bretton Woods institutions, prompting a worldwide review of their successes and failures. Generally the reviews were not favorable, and even the World Bank's own evaluations were highly critical of its performance. In spite of lending some quarter of a trillion dollars to peripheral countries, one billion people in the world are desperately poor; furthermore, the disparity of wealth in the world between the core and periphery has doubled in the last thirty years. The richest 20 percent of the world's

Table 6.1 The Bretton Woods Institutions

Institution or Agency	Function
International Monetary Fund **(IMF)**	To make funds available for countries to meet short-term financial needs and to stabilize currency exchanges between countries
International Bank for Reconstruction and Development **(World Bank)**	To make loans for various development projects
General Agreement on Tariffs and Trade **(GATT)**	To ensure the free trade of commodities among countries

people now consume 150 times more of the world's goods than the poorest 20 percent (United Nations 1993:11).

One of the most profound consequences of the Bretton Woods meeting is the accumulation of the debt of peripheral countries; some consider this "debt crisis" the gravest one facing the world. The reasons for the debt crisis, and the possible impact it can have on everyone's lives, is complex but essential to understand. Overwhelming debt of peripheral countries is one of the major factors in many global problems that we will explore, including poverty, hunger, environmental devastation, the spread of disease, and political unrest.

Three things were particularly important in creating the debt crisis: the change over the last third of this century in the meaning of money; the amount of money lent by the World Bank to peripheral countries; and the oil boom of the early 1970s and the pressure for financial institutions to invest that money.

Money constitutes the focal point of capitalism. It is through money that we assign value to objects, behaviors, and even people. The fact that one item can, in various quantities, represent virtually any item or service, from a soft drink to an entire forest, is one of the most remarkable features of our lives. But it is not without its problems. The facts that different countries have different currencies and that currencies can rise or fall in value relative to the goods they can purchase has always been a barrier to unrestricted foreign trade and global economic integration. Furthermore, there have always been disputes concerning how to measure the value of money itself. Historically money has been tied to a specific valuable metal, generally gold. Thus money in any country could always be redeemed for a certain amount of gold, although the amount could vary according to the value of a specific country's currency.

While the meeting at Bretton Woods would not lead to the establishment of a global currency, the countries did agree to exchange their currency for U.S. dollars at a fixed rate, while the United States guaranteed that it would exchange money for gold stored at Fort Knox at thirty-five dollars per ounce. But in the 1960s, during the Vietnam War and the increase in U.S. government spending on health, education, and welfare programs, the United States was creating dollars far in excess of its gold supply, while at the same time guaranteeing all the rest of the money in the world. As a result, in 1971 the United States declared it would no longer re-deem dollars on demand for gold. This totally divorced the American dollar and, effectively, all the other currencies in the world, from anything of value other than the expectation that people would accept dollars for things of value. Money became simply unsecured credit (see R. Guttmann 1994).

But since countries no longer needed to have a certain amount of gold in order to print money, money became more plentiful; the increase in the amount of money in circulation also meant there was more to lend, and this led banks and other lending institutions to lower their interest rates to attract borrowers. This proved to be a boon, not only for individual borrowers but also for peripheral countries seeking to develop their economies. The problems were that the interest on most loans was adjustable (could go up or down depending on economic circumstances) and that debts began to accumulate beyond what countries could repay.

The second factor that led to the debt crisis was the operation of the World Bank. The Bank itself had a problem. European countries, whose economies it was to help rebuild, didn't need the help. *With a lack of demand for their services, what could they do? How could the institution survive?* The Bank's solution was to lend money to peripheral countries to develop their economies. The plan was to help them industrialize by funding things such as large-scale hydro-electric projects, roads, and industrial parks. Furthermore, the bigger the project, the more the Bank could lend; thus in the 1950s and 1960s money suddenly poured into India, Mexico, Brazil, and Indonesia, the Bank's four largest borrowers. From 1950 to 1970, the Bank lent some $953 million. We should not overlook the fact that these loans also benefited wealthy core countries, who largely supplied the construction companies, engineers, equipment, and advisors needed to develop these projects.

But the success of the Bank in lending money created another problem—what economists call net negative transfers; borrowing nations collectively were soon paying more money into the Bank than the Bank was lending out. Put another way, the poor or peripheral nations were paying more money to the rich core nations than they were receiving from them. Aside from the consequences for poor countries, this would lead ultimately to the bank going out of business—its only purpose would be to collect the money it had already lent out. This is not a problem for regular banks because they can always recruit new customers, but the World Bank has a limited number of clients to which to lend money. Now what do you do? The Bank's solution was to lend still more. Robert McNamara, past chief of the Ford Motor Company and Secretary of Defense during the John F. Kennedy and Lyndon B. Johnson administrations, more than any one person, made the World Bank into what it is today. During his tenure from 1968 to 1981, the Bank increased lending from $953 million to $12.4 billion and increased staff from 1,574 to 5,201. The result was to leave many peripheral countries with a stagger-ing debt burden. But there were other problems as well.

The third source of the debt crisis was the oil boom of the early 1970s. Oil producers were making huge profits ("petrodollars"). The problem was that this money needed to be invested, particularly by the banks into which it went and from which depositors expected interest pay-ments. But banks and other investment agents had a problem finding investments. One of their solutions was to lend even more money to peripheral countries. The source of the debt crisis is illustrated in Figure 6.2.

Thus, by the late 1970s peripheral countries had borrowed huge sums of money and, with this infusion, were doing generally well. But then financial policies in the wealthy countries precipitated an economic collapse. With their own economies in recession because of the increase in oil prices in the 1970s, core governments reacted by raising interest rates. Countries such as Brazil, Mexico, and Indonesia that had borrowed large sums of money at adjustable, rather than fixed, interest rates suddenly found that they could no longer pay back what they owed. Many couldn't even pay back the interest on the loans. Furthermore, an economic recession in the core nations decreased the demand for whatever commodities peripheral countries had for sale, further undermining their economies.

This all sounds largely like an economic problem that would have little effect on people such as you or me, or on a peasant farmer in Mexico, craftsperson in Africa, or small mer-chant in Indonesia. But, in fact, it has had an enormous impact, and it illustrates how global problems are tied closely to today's merchant adventurers. It is estimated that the amount of money owed by peripheral countries increased from $100 billion in 1971 to $600 billion by 1981 (Caufield 1996:134). And the problem hasn't improved: the total owed by countries in the periphery increased in 1994 to well over $2 trillion (see World Development Report 1996:222). Table 6.2 on the next page shows the increases in external debt for a few selected

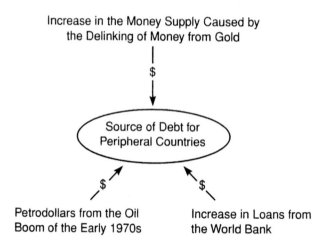

Figure 6.2 The source of the Global Debt Crisis

countries, along with the percentage of their yearly GNP (total of goods and services produced) that the debt represents. For example, Rwanda in 1980 owed $190 million, representing 16.3 percent of its GNP; by 1994 it owed $954 million, or 164.8 percent of its GNP. India in 1980 had an external debt of $20,582 million, or 11.9 percent of its GNP; by 1994 it owed $98,990 million, or 34.2 percent of its annual GNP.

This debt has not only created problems for the debtor countries; it has created a major problem for lending institutions and investors. There is an old joke that says that when an individual can't pay his or her bank debts, he or she is in trouble, but when a big borrower, such as a corporation or country, can't repay its debts, the bank is in trouble. This, in brief, was the dilemma posed by the global debt crisis for private lending institutions and the World Bank.

The World Bank and the IMF responded to the debt crisis by trying to reschedule the repayment of debts or extending short-term loans to debtor countries to help them meet the financial crises. However, to qualify for a rescheduling of a debt or loan payment a government had to agree to alter its fiscal policies to improve its balance-of-payments problems; that is, it had to try to take in more money and spend less. But how do you do that? There are various ways, all creating, in one way or another, serious problems. For example, countries had to promise to manage tax collecting better, sell government property, increase revenues by increasing exports, reduce government spending on social programs such as welfare, health, and education, promise to refrain from printing more money, and take steps to devalue their currency, thus making their goods cheaper for consumers in other countries but making them more expensive for their own citizens.

While these measures are rarely popular with their citizens, governments rarely refuse IMF requests to implement them because not only might they not receive a short-term loan, but agencies such as the World Bank and private capital controllers such as banks and foundations would also then refuse to make funds available. Yet structural adjustment programs (SAPs),

TABLE 6.2 External Debt of Selected Countries, 1980 and 1994

Country	Total External Debt (millions $)		External Debt as % of GNP	
	1980	1994	1980	1994
Bangladesh	4,327	16,569	33.4%	63.4%
Brazil	72,920	151,104	31.8%	27.9%
China	4,504	100,536	2.2%	19.3%
Ecuador	5,997	14,955	53.8%	96.6%
Egypt	19,131	33,358	89.2%	78.3%
India	20,582	98,990	11.9%	34.2%
Indonesia	20,944	96,500	28.0%	94.7%
Mexico	57,378	128,302	30.5%	35.2%
Nigeria	8,921	33,485	10.1%	102.5%
Pakistan	9,930	29,579	42.4%	56.6%
Peru	9,386	22,623	47.6%	46.2%
Philippines	17,417	39,302	53.7%	59.7%
Russian Federation	4,477	94,232	—	25.4%
Rwanda	190	954	16.3%	164.8%
Tanzania	2,616	7,441	—	229.5%

From World Development Report 1996:220–221.

as they are called, can have very detrimental effects on people in the country. Structural adjustment usually increases unemployment and increases the plight of the poor. In Zambia the number of children suffering from malnutrition increased after structural adjustment from one in twenty to one in five. In Brazil, the need to raise funds to pay back World Bank loans resulted in increased cutting of the rainforests, not only for lumber but to produce commodities, such as cattle, in high demand in the core nations. In Mexico, Guatemala, and other Central American countries, the need to produce crops for export resulted in the consolidation of peasant landholdings into large, capital-intensive farms.

Furthermore, structural adjustment and the need to repay loans and attract foreign capital forces countries to seek money from outside investors by persuading banks, corporations, mutual fund managers, and others who control capital that they will receive a higher rate of return if they invest money in their country rather than other countries. This competition for investors, as we shall see, has greatly increased the power of capital.

Finally there is the question, *where did all the money that was lent to peripheral countries go?* Since "capital flight"—money leaving the periphery—increased dramatically during the period of rising debt, the prevailing view is that loans were siphoned off by the elites in the periphery and invested back in the core. The World Bank estimates that between 1976 and 1984 capital flight from Latin America was equal to the area's whole external debt (Caufield 1996:132). Capital flight from Mexico alone from 1974 to 1982, invested in everything from condominiums to car dealerships, amounted to at least $35 billion. "The problem," joked one member of the U.S. Federal Reserve Board, "is not that Latin Americans don't have assets. They do. The problem is they are all in Miami"(Caufield 1996:133).

The Power of Capital Controllers

One of the enduring tensions in the culture of capitalism is the separation between political power and economic power; in a democracy, people grant the government power to act on their behalf. However, in capitalism, there are, in addition to elected leaders, capital controllers, individuals or groups who control economic resources that everyone depends on but who are accountable to virtually no one, except perhaps a few investors or stockholders. Their goals often conflict with state goals. As a merchant, industrialist, or investor your goals are simple: you want to attain the highest possible profit on your investment, you want to be certain your right to private property is protected, and you want to keep your financial risks to a minimum. As Jeffrey A. Winters (1996:x) suggested, if capital controllers, who are unelected, unappointed, and unaccountable, were all to wear yellow suits and meet weekly in huge halls to decide where, when, and how much of their capital (money) to invest, there would be little mystery in their power. But, of course, they don't. Collectively they make private decisions on where, when, and how to distribute their investments. Furthermore, under this system of private property, capital controllers are free to do whatever they wish with their capital: they can invest it, they can sit on it, or they can destroy it. States are virtually helpless to insist that private capital be used for anything other than what capital controllers want to do with it.

The anonymity of investors and the hidden power they hold (or that is hidden from us) present problems for political leaders: while the actions of capital controllers can greatly influence our lives, it is political leaders that we often hold responsible for the rise and fall of a country's financial fortunes. When unemployment increases, when prices rise, when taxes are raised or important services discontinued or decreased, we can fire our governmental representatives at the next election. However, we do not have the power to "fire" the board of General Motors or the investment counselors at Smith, Barney's or Chase Manhattan.

Though investors may not consciously coordinate their actions, their choices have enormous consequences for societies and state leaders. The reasons for this are obvious. States depend on revenue for their operation and maintenance. This revenue can come from various sources, including income taxes, corporate taxes, tariffs on imported goods, revenue from state-run enterprises (e.g., oil revenue), charges for state services (e.g., tolls), foreign aid, and credit, loans, or grants from abroad. In the case of peripheral countries, much of this money comes from international lending agencies. But money from international lending agencies represents only a small percentage of the money that flows into peripheral countries. Far more comes from capital controllers, those who control vast amounts of money that must be invested to ensure investors a competitive return. As a final stop on our historical tour as merchant adventurers, let's assume the role of capital controller. *You have substantial sums of money to invest; what do you do with it?*

During the last half of the twentieth century there has been enormous growth in the number of people with capital to invest. Many are the very wealthy, the elite 1 or 2 percent who control vast resources, such as the major corporations of the world. Others, as mentioned above, are responsible for deciding where to invest public moneys from multilateral organizations or state agencies. In addition, there are the less wealthy who save in banks and have pension funds or insurance policies. Investment capital from these different sources and held by capital controllers represents enormous power. Furthermore, with modern methods of communication most of this money is now extremely mobile: billions of dollars can be transferred from one place to another with the touch of a computer key. Capital was not always so mobile. For example, if you had money to invest fifty years ago in a textile plant, you might be constrained by import laws to build your factory in the country in which you wanted to sell your merchandise. In today's free trade environment, however, you can build your factory wherever you can get the cheapest labor.

Global investors and capital controllers remain virtually anonymous as they drive the worldwide flow of capital in such arenas as the Hong Kong Stock Exchange.
Courtesy of David McIntyre/Stockphoto.com.

With an increase in free trade, standardized currencies, and economic globalization in general, capital can move freely all over the world. This can greatly increase the power of the capital controller, because if more regions or countries compete to attract capital investment, you, as a capital controller, are more able to demand conditions that guarantee profits and minimize risk. If you could build a textile factory in a country with strong labor unions or one with weak ones, which would you choose? If one country had strong environmental laws that required you to control toxic waste, while another had few such regulations, where would you build? If one country had a high minimum wage, while another had none, where would you likely realize the highest profit? These issues have become subsumed under the term "competitiveness"; that is, to be competitive in a global economy, a country must institute policies that allow it to compete successfully for mobile capital with other countries.

This fact determines social, economic, and political policy in countries and regions all over the world, and it affects your life as well. The mobility of capital means that social systems that produce profitable investment climates will attract the most investment capital. *What constitutes a favorable investment climate? Investment climate* refers to the constellation of policies within a given jurisdiction (city, state, region, country) that either advance or inhibit the key goals of investors (profit, property guarantees, and low risk). A bad climate might involve the risk of the expropriation of private property, political instability, high taxes, strong worker's unions, strong environmental regulations, and social laws regarding minimum wage and child labor. A favorable climate can be created by low tax rates, tax holidays and other special incentives, weak unions, little environmental regulation, and few social regulations. Furthermore, capital (money) will flow away from locations (e.g., countries) that do not create profitable investment climates. This capital, constantly flowing in and out of communities, regions, or countries, represents what Winters (1996:x) calls "power in motion."

The amount of power in motion is difficult to measure; by 1992 the amount of direct foreign investment—money invested in such things as factories, equipment, and research facilities—reached $2 trillion. Furthermore, the amount being invested in peripheral countries has almost doubled since 1987 (Winters 1996:27). Thus, on an average day the volume of money transacted around the world amounted to close to $1 trillion. But the amount that flows into any given area can vary enormously; in 1995, for example, Africa received just 1.5 percent of the world's total.

The case of Indonesia offers a good example of what countries need to do to attract capital (Winters 1996). Indonesia fought for and gained independence from the Dutch in 1949. After a period of intense regional competition President Sukarno, the victor in this competition, instituted a policy to free the country from foreign influence, carefully trying to balance power between the army and a strong Communist Party. Among his actions, he began nationalizing foreign firms. With their property at risk, and no longer guaranteed by the state, companies and investors began to pull their money out of the country. Consequently, the economy collapsed. Then in 1965 the military, under General Suharto, put down an alleged coup by the PKI, the Indonesian communist party. The subsequent blood bath led to the slaughter of hundreds of thousands of Indonesians believed to be sympathetic to or members of the Communist Party and removal of Sukarno from power.

With little money, the new ruler, President Suharto, faced the problem of rebuilding an economy in ruins. To solve the problem Suharto turned to economics professors at the University of Jakarta and assigned them the task of designing a policy to attract foreign investors. The first thing they did was to send signals through the press that they were changing economic policies and appointing people to government offices known to be friendly to foreign investors. Next, they applied for loans from multilateral institutions such as the World Bank and the IMF, hoping their approval would build the confidence of foreign investors in their country. Then, to assure capital controllers that their country was politically stable, the government suppressed all political dissent and limited the power of workers to mobilize unions. Finally, the government modified their tax structure to favor foreign investors. The result was that foreign capital began to flow into the country, and in the late 1960s and early 1970s the Indonesian economy began to thrive.

But the story did not end there; what happened next illustrates how the power of capital controllers to create conditions favorable to investment is not absolute. Indonesia has large oil reserves, and when in the early 1970s oil revenue increased, Indonesia's need for foreign investment decreased. Since it had another source of money, the country became less friendly to foreign investors: taxes increased, preference was shown to domestic industries, and bureaucratic procedures became more cumbersome for foreigners wanting to do business in Indonesia. As a result, foreign investments decreased dramatically. As long as oil revenues were stable, Indonesia had no problem. But in the early 1980s, oil prices plunged, and once again the Indonesian economy was close to ruin. Once again, in response to domestic political pressure from those who were suffering from economic decline, the government, still under the control of President Suharto, found itself instituting the measures outlined above to attract capital investors once again.

Foreign investment did return to Indonesia, particularly in the growth of assembly plants; thus until late 1997, the economy was doing well. However the collapse of the value of Asian cur1rencies in late 1997 left the Indonesian economy once again in ruin, its currency plummeting in value, unemployment spreading, and social unrest increasing. The government responded with greater social and political repression but ultimately Suharto resigned.

Nigeria offers an interesting counterexample to Indonesia; it illustrates that the conditions in which capital controllers operate can differ enormously in spite of similar needs (Winters 1996). Nigeria in the 1960s had as great a need for capital investors as did Indonesia, but because of internal conditions it was far less able to create a climate conducive to attracting capital controllers. One of the problems was the cultural and linguistic heterogeneity of Nigeria as opposed to Indonesia. Early in the process of decolonalization, Indonesia decided to adopt the neutral trade language of Malay-Indonesian. In Nigeria, on the other hand, there are hundreds of tribal languages. In addition, Indonesia gained its independence after a long military struggle with the Dutch, a struggle that served to unite the population and establish an effective military presence, one that evidences great solidarity. Nigeria, formed as a British colony in 1914, was "given" its independence in 1960 by Great Britain with little struggle, but in a way that heightened regional divisions which the British had created to ease the process of colonial governance. As a consequence of the lack of political centralization, there were, between 1960 and 1993, five successful military coups, at least four attempted coups, six different military leaders, and only nine years without soldiers in authority. Because of the cultural heterogeneity and political unrest it was virtually impossible for Nigeria to respond as did Indonesia to the demands of mobile capital controllers. As a result, it has been unable to attract needed capital investment.

In fact, virtually all countries today, core nations as well as those in the periphery, seek to create conditions to attract or keep capital investment, to create or keep jobs for the millions of people dependent on wage labor. To this end they work to maintain and promote the confidence of foreign banks and investors in the viability of their economy and the stability of their political regimes.

The major lesson of this analysis is that the economic goals of capital controllers—profit, a guarantee for private property, and little risk—can often conflict with larger societal goals, such as relative economic equality, environmental safety, equal access to medical care, and equal access to food. In other words, making the world safe for capital sometimes means making it unsafe for people. Many of the global problems that we will examine in later chapters—population growth, poverty, hunger, environmental devastation, disease, ethnic conflict, and the oppression of indigenous peoples—all, in one way or another, find their origins in the drive of capital to profit, to keep the profit, and to minimize the risks of capital investment. Having said that, we must also recognize that no other large-scale economic system has been able to do as well for so many, and that many of the vast gains in areas such as food production, technology and science, and medicine are directly attributable to the same economic drives. The important thing is to understand the dynamics of the system so that we can understand what we may need to give up and what we are able to maintain if we ever hope to solve global problems.

CONCLUSION

We began this chapter with the goal of trying to understand three historical developments that have had a profound influence on today's world and in the development of the culture of capitalism—the increase in the division of world wealth, changes in the organization of capital, and the increase in the level of economic globalization. We found that the division of wealth has grown enormously, between both countries and areas of the world. In 1995, over 1 billion people lived in absolute poverty, earning the equivalent of less than one dollar per day, while, according to the Maryland-based Bread for the World Institute, 358 billionaires listed by Forbes Magazine had a combined net worth equal to the combined income of the bottom 45 percent of the world's population (Dayal and Lobe, 1995).

The organization of capital has changed dramatically. We began our journey with capital largely in the hands of individual merchants, family groups, or limited partnerships and ended with the era of capital controllers, such as transnational corporations, multilateral institutions, and investment firms. In 1400, it might take a global merchant a year's journey from one area of the world to another to complete an investment cycle of buying and selling goods; today a capital controller can transfer billions from one area of the world to another without ever leaving the computer.

Finally, we have seen global economic integration increase to the extent that global trade is easier today than trade between adjacent towns was in 1400, as trade treaties dissolve regional and country boundaries, freeing capital to migrate where it is most likely to accumulate.

NOTE

1. The name is taken from a sixteenth century English trading company, The Merchant Adventurers, cloth wholesalers trading to Holland and Germany with bases of operation in Antwerp and Bergen-op-Zoom, and, later, Hamburg. The company survived until 1809.

7. Contemporary Global Trends

Raymond Scupin

Anthropology is a discipline of studying human cultures and culture changes. Scupin considers the consequences of the enormous changes that are upon us. Using an anthropologist's eye, he takes the broad view of human adaptation to the environment. Industrial adaptations have displaced other forms of human interaction with the environment. Even if peo- not be permitted. *themselves to have mastery over the environment, they are not free from its* ____ *in collectivized economies, privatization, and mechanized* ____ *ense populations, increased consump-* ____ *sions. Economic and political changes* ____ *and the poor. Ethnic unrest and major* ____ *lace. Holistic approaches that take the* ____ *at are now needed to navigate this new* ____ *xity of globalization as it is experienced*

dependence, or what we have called *global-* ntemporary world. This process began after ies were either absorbed into larger states or Industrial Revolution, the trend toward global gh the process of colonialism. As the world and, interconnections are developing among global village has been described as a world in er through the mass media, instantaneous communications political networks. This chapter reviews some opment of this global village.

ENVIRONMENTAL TRENDS

Hunting-gathering, horticulturalist, pastoralist, and intensive agriculture societies survived by extracting natural resources from a particular biome. In these societies, people were directly linked with nature and the environment, and they lived in relative harmony with the natural environment. This is not to suggest that humans in preindustrial societies did not harm their environments in any manner. Slash-and-burn horticulture, intensive agriculture, pastoralism, and sometimes even foraging caused some environmental damage. Overgrazing, soil erosion, and the depletion of certain species have always been part of humankind's evolution.

With the development of globalization, however, the negative consequences for the environment have multiplied rapidly. Ironically, many people in industrial societies came to believe that they had gained mastery over the natural environment and were therefore free from its constraints. But in recent decades, people have become more aware that they are as dependent on the natural environment as were preindustrial peoples. It has become evident that the pollution created by global industrialization is threatening the ecological balance of the planet and the health of plant and animal species, including the human species.

Mechanized Agriculture and Pollution

One major source of pollution is commercialized, mechanized agriculture, known as **agribusiness.** *Mechanized agriculture,* or *agribusiness,* depends on the use of fossil fuels, chemical fertilizers, large tracts of land, and toxic poisons such as herbicides and pesticides to increase agricultural yields. This form of agriculture is not only prevalent in the industrialized world; it is also becoming common in developing countries. For example, some farmers in societies such as Mexico, India, and Indonesia have adopted mechanized agriculture. The spread of mechanized agriculture has been labeled the **Green Revolution** (Schusky, 1990). Through biotechnology research, sometimes known as *genetic engineering,* and other methods, scientists have produced hybrid species of wheat and rice seeds that generate higher agricultural yields. To take advantage of these yields, however, farmers must use expensive, capital-intensive technology for irrigation and cultivation; nonrenewable fossil fuels such as gasoline and oil; synthetic chemical fertilizers; and toxic weed killers, or herbicides, and pesticides.

The use of capital-intensive agriculture, however, can have negative consequences for the global environment. One of the most tragic cases resulting from the Green Revolution occurred in 1984 in Bhopal, India, where toxic fumes leaking from a chemical-fertilizer plant killed or injured thousands of people. Many of the consequences of mechanized agriculture, however, are much less dramatic (and therefore less publicized), although perhaps just as dangerous. For example, research has shown that much of the food produced in both industrialized and developing countries contains traces of pesticides and other poisons. Even when governments ban the use of chemicals, the residues may remain in the food chain for many years. Because many new synthetic chemicals are being produced for agribusiness every year, the danger to the environment continues to increase.

Air Pollution

Air pollution, especially from the emissions of motor vehicles, power generators, and waste incinerators, continues to be a major problem for industrializing societies. As less developed countries industrialize, the degree of global air pollution steadily multiplies. It appears that atmospheric pollution is depleting the earth's ozone layer, which absorbs 99 percent of the ultraviolet radiation from the sun. These pollutants could irreversibly alter the earth's ability to support life. Satellite data show that during the period from 1978 to 1984, the ozone layer eroded at an average annual rate of 0.5 percent. In addition, acid rain produced by the burning of fossil fuels such as coal and gasoline has become a global problem, spreading across national boundaries and wreaking havoc on forests, lakes, and various species of aquatic life.

Scientific data suggest that the increased levels of carbon dioxide produced primarily by the burning of fossil fuels and tropical rain forests, methane, and nitrous oxide will create a **greenhouse effect,** or *global warming.* According to this hypothesis, after solar rays reach the earth's surface, the carbon dioxide (CO_2) in the atmosphere traps the heat and prevents it from radiating back into space. This process could eventually melt the polar ice caps, which would raise sea levels, flood major coastal cities, create violent weather patterns, and turn the tropics into deserts. An enormous amount of scientific data has accumulated that confirms the greenhouse effect hypothesis and global warming. Emissions of these greenhouse gases are likely to increase in the future. Predictions based on present-day estimates suggest that CO_2 emissions from industrialized countries will reach levels of 50 to 70 percent above 1990 levels by 2020. However, as more countries such as China begin to emit more greenhouse gases, global warming could proceed more quickly. China accounts for 13 percent of the CO_2 emissions today. At this level, it is becoming the world's second largest emitter of CO_2 after the United States, which generates 23 percent (Wang, 1999). Stabilizing atmospheric concentrations of greenhouse gases will require reversing current emission trends.

Population Trends

With industrialization, new demographic trends have arisen. A recent model used to measure population trends is based on the **demographic-transition theory,** which assumes a close connection between fertility and mortality rates and socioeconomic development (Figure 7.1). According to the demographic-transition model, societies pass through three major phases of population change. During Phase 1, a high fertility rate is counterbalanced by a high mortality rate, resulting in minimal population growth. Phase 1 describes preindustrial societies. At first, societies used various methods of population regulation, such as self-induced abortions, postpartum abstinence, infanticide, or migration to limit population growth. As preindustrial societies developed intensive agriculture, population began to increase, but disease, famine, and natural disasters kept mortality rates fairly high, thus limiting growth.

In Phase 2, population tends to increase rapidly because of continued high fertility rates coupled with lower mortality rates. Mortality rates decline because of increases in the food supply, the development of scientifically based medical practices, and improved public sanitation and health care. Improvements in nutrition and health care enable people to control certain diseases, thus diminishing infant mortality rates and increasing life expectancy. Consequently,

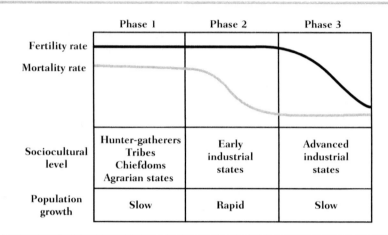

Figure 7.1 The demographic-transition model.

during Phase 2, population growth is dramatic. Growth of this magnitude was associated with the early phases of industrialization in Western Europe and North America, but it is also visible in many Third World societies that are now in the early stages of industrialization.

Phase 3 of the demographic-transition model represents the stage in which fertility rates begin to fall along with mortality rates. According to the model, as industrialization proceeds, family planning is introduced, and traditional institutions and religious beliefs supporting high birth rates are undermined. Values stressing individualism and upward mobility lead couples to reduce the size of their families. Phase 3 describes the stage of advanced industrial societies such as Western Europe, the United States, and Japan. Other trends, such as geographic mobility and the increased expense of rearing children, also affect reproductive decisions in industrial societies. Hence, in advanced industrial societies, as the birth rate, or fertility rate, falls, population growth begins to decline.

The Demographic-Transition Model Applied

The demographic-transition model seems to have some validity when applied to global population trends. World population during the Paleolithic period (Phase 1) is estimated to have been about 10 million (Hassan, 1981). Following the agricultural revolution, around the year a.d. 1, global population was approximately 300 million. But after the early stages of industrialization (Phase 2), from 1650 to 1900, world population tripled from 510 million to 1.6 billion. By 1950, the global population had risen to 2.5 billion, and by 1970, another billion people had been added. By 1990, the world population was approximately 5.4 billion, with 150 babies being born every minute (Figure 7.2). By the year 2000, world population exceeded 6 billion, and by 2050, global population will reach 10.2 billion.

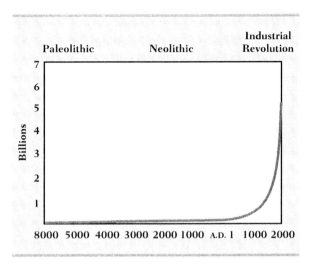

Figure 7.2 Global population growth. From about ten million people in the Paleolithic period, world population reached one billion by 1850. Following the Industrial Revolution and decreases in mortality rates, world population has increased to over five billion people.

Thomas Robert Malthus (1766–1834), a British clergyman and economist, is known as the father of demography. Malthus predicted that human populations would increase at a rapid, or exponential, rate, but the production of food and other vital resources would increase at a lower rate. Thus, populations would always grow more quickly than the food supply to support them. As a result, human societies would constantly experience hunger, increases in warfare, resource scarcities, and poverty.

To measure the exponential growth rate, demographers use the concept of **doubling time,** the period it takes for a population to double. For example, a population growing at 1 percent will double in 70 years; one growing at 2 percent will take 35 years to double; and one growing at 3 percent will double in 23 years.

The industrial nations of Western Europe, the United States, and Japan have reached Phase 3 of the demographic-transition model. The U.S. population is growing at only 0.7 percent. Countries such as Germany, Hungary, and Japan actually have negative growth rates, which means that they are not replacing the number of people dying with new births. For a society to maintain a given level of population, each woman must give birth to an average of 2.1 children. At this point, the society has achieved **zero population growth (ZPG),** meaning that the population is simply replacing itself. When the average number of births falls below 2.1, a society experiences negative growth. Thus, Japan, with an average of 1.8 births, is actually experiencing a population decline (Martin, 1989). Decreased growth rates in industrialized nations have helped lower the global growth rate from 2 to 1.7 percent.

The demographic-transition model provides a conceptual scheme for evaluating global population trends, especially for the core industrial societies, yet it must be used carefully

Globalization creates dense traffic problems in major cities such as Bangkok.
COURTESY OF LINDSAY HEBBERD/WOODFIN CAMP & ASSOCIATES.

as a hypothesis. Although the industrial societies of North America, Western Europe, and Japan have reached Phase 3, the vast majority of the world's people reside in societies that are in Phase 2, with exponential growth rates. Population growth in African countries such as Kenya is almost 4 percent (doubling every 15 years), and Mexico's growth rate is 2.6 percent (doubling every 27 years). Thus, the demographic-transition hypothesis explains population trends in industrial societies, but it may not accurately predict population growth elsewhere for Phase 3. Suggesting that all societies will follow the path of development of the advanced industrial societies is somewhat naive. It took at least 500 years of historical experience for these countries to become fully industrialized societies and reach Phase 3 of the demographic model.

Most peripheral societies maintain high birth rates related to their agricultural lifestyles. As these societies become industrialized, however, death rates fall, leading to dramatic population increases. These societies have not had an extended time period to adjust to the demographic trends related to industrialization. Consequently, predicting a movement to Phase 3 is problematic. Most underdeveloped countries can attain population decline only through changes in technology, political economy, and social and cultural practices.

The One-Child Policy in China

One developing country that has taken steps to drastically reduce its population growth is China. In the 1950s Mao Zedong perceived China's revolution as being based on peasant production and small-scale, labor-intensive technology. For this reason, he encouraged population growth among the peasantry. After Mao's death, however, a new leadership group emerged that reversed his policies regarding population growth.

In 1979, a demographic study was presented at the Second Session of the Fifth National People's Congress that indicated that if the existing average of three children per couple were maintained, China's population would reach 1.4 billion by the year 2000 and 4.3 billion by the year 2080. Alarmed by the implications of these statistics, the government introduced a one-child policy designed to achieve zero population growth (ZPG), with a target of 1.6 children per couple by the year 2000. Families that restricted their family size to one child were given free health care and free plots of land. In addition, their children would receive free education and preferential employment treatment. Families that had more than one child would be penalized through higher taxes and nonpreferential treatment. The one-child policy was enforced by neighborhood committees at the local level, and contraceptives, sterilization, and abortion services were provided free of charge. Neighborhood committees monitored every woman's reproductive cycle to determine when she was eligible to have her one child.

With some exceptions, the one-child policy has been remarkably effective. Between 1980 and 1990, the birth rate in China was reduced, and the annual growth rate fell from 2.0 percent to 1.4 percent, a record unmatched by any developing nation. This rate is similar to those of the most advanced industrial societies (World Population Data Sheet, 1991). Incentives, propaganda campaigns, and government enforcement combined to produce a new image of the Chinese family, one that had only a single child. Billboards and TV ads throughout China showed radiant mothers nurturing their one child.

Because the one-child policy is an attempt to reverse Chinese family patterns that have existed for thousands of years, it created controversies and problems. In the agricultural areas, it generated a great deal of resentment. Many Chinese prefer sons to daughters—a long-established Confucian tradition. In some cases, couples that have a daughter may practice female infanticide so that they may have a son to assume family responsibilities. Although infanticide is a criminal offense in China, it appears to be increasing in rural areas. Moreover, anthropologist Steven Mosher (1983) has reported that government officials sometimes forced women to undergo abortions to maintain the one-child policy. More recently, anthropologist Susan Greenhalgh, a Chinese population policy expert, reported that one out of every eight Chinese women married in the 1970s had suffered the trauma of a second or third-term abortion (Evans, 2000). There were many reports of full-term abortions, involuntary sterilization, forcible insertion of IUDs, the abandonment of female children, and female infanticide.

In response to some of these conflicts, the Chinese government relaxed the one-child policy in 1989. Rural families could have two children, but urban families were still restricted to one. This policy, known colloquially as "the one son or two child policy," placed a burden on second children who were females. Second-born daughters were subject to being placed in orphanages so that a family might have a son. China's orphanages are struggling to keep up with the number of female children. Additionally, the various minority groups have no restrictions on the number of children they can have. The minorities argued that through the one-child policy, the majority would quickly become the dominant group in their regions. They viewed the policy as an attempt to reduce their population and pressured the government to relax restrictions on their population growth. Recently, in April 2000, the Chinese government ruled that all the children of "only children" can have two children. But the government still offers higher rewards to those couples that have only one child. The Chinese government believes that the key to the success of its population-control efforts is the system of rewards offered to compliant families. Whether the people are willing to transform their fundamental cultural traditions to conform to government regulations is a question to be answered in the future.

TECHNOLOGICAL CHANGE

Ever since the Industrial Revolution, the scale of technological change has become global rather than local. Industrial technology—computers, electronics, and advances in global communications—has spread from the core nations to the developing countries. For example, as previously discussed, the Green Revolution has altered the nature of food production. Technical information on agricultural production is spread through television and satellites to villages in countries such as India and Pakistan.

Energy-Consumption Patterns

High energy consumption is not only creating environmental hazards; it has also led to increased depletion of resources. High-energy, industrialized societies such as the United States consume a major portion of the world's nonrenewable energy and resources. For example, in 1987, the United States used over 2 billion tons of energy (the equivalent of coal), and the former Soviet Union used 1.8 billion. In contrast, Mexico used 140 million; Egypt, 33 million; Bangladesh, 6.8 million; and the Sudan, 1.5 million (*Information Please Almanac,* 1991). In 1997 the United States, Russia, and China were the leading producers and consumers of energy. These three countries produced 39 percent and consumed 41 percent of world energy. In that same year, the United States representing 5 percent of the world's population, consumed 18.6 million barrels of petroleum per day—almost 26 percent of world consumption (*Time Almanac,* 2000). The U.S. Geological Survey estimates that there are about three trillion barrels of proven reserves of oil worldwide. The entire world should reach its peak levels of oil production in 2037, after which output is expected to fall precipitously. The 23 percent of the world's population residing in industrialized countries is consuming about 58 percent of the energy reserves that the planet is capable of producing.

Were semiperipheral and peripheral countries, with 77 percent of the world's population, to adopt the same consumption patterns as the core nations, nonrenewable energy supplies and resources might not be sufficient to support global economic development (Schusky, 1990). For example, as peripheral countries adopted mechanized farming, they increased their consumption of fossil fuels, leading to a worldwide jump in energy use. Between 1950 and 1985, the energy used to produce a ton of grain increased from 0.44 barrels of oil per ton to 1.14 barrels. By 1985, fossil-fuel energy used in farming totaled 1.7 billion barrels, about one-twelfth of the world oil output of 21 billion barrels per year (Brown, 1988).

Loss of Biodiversity

One of the major concerns regarding the consequences of globalization on the planet is the loss of biodiversity. **Biodiversity** is the genetic and biological variation within and among different species of plants and animals. Biologists are not exactly certain of how many species of plants and animals exist; new species are discovered every day. Some biologists think that there may be as many as 30 to 100 million species, or even more. Approximately 250,000 flowering plant species, 800,000 lower-plant species, and 1.5 million animal species have been identified (Raven, Berg, & Johnson, 1993). About 50 percent of these species live in tropical rain forests. As humans, we are dependent on these living organisms for survival; in both preindustrial and industrial societies people rely on plant and animal species for basic foodstuffs and medicinal applications.

Many plant and animal species are threatened with extinction, causing a loss of biodiversity. Biologists estimate that at least one species becomes extinct each day. And as globalization continues, it is estimated that perhaps as many as a dozen species will be lost per day. Biologist E. O. Wilson writes in *In Search of Nature* (1996) that each year an area of rain forest half the size of Florida is cut down. If that continues, by 2020 the world will have lost forever 20 percent of its existing plant species. That is a loss of 30,000 species per year, 74 per day, 3 per hour. He goes on to say that we know almost nothing about the majority of plants and animals that the rain forest comprises. We haven't even named 90 percent of them, much less studied their properties or tapped their potential value. Wilson suggests that it is likely that a substantial portion of the planet's biodiversity will be eliminated within the next few decades. With the increase of industrialism, mechanized agriculture, and deforestation, as many as one-fourth of the world's higher-plant families may become extinct by the end of the next century.

Wilson believes that we are entering the greatest period of mass extinction in the planet's history. We have very limited knowledge of the world's plant and animal species. For example, there are approximately 250,000 different flowering plant species, but 225,000 of them have never been evaluated with respect to their agricultural, medicinal, or industrial potential (Raven, Berg, & Johnson, 1993). One out of every four prescription drugs comes from flowering plants. Yet less than one percent has been studied for pharmacological potential. Many of these plants could be exploited as new food crops, pharmaceuticals, fibers, or petroleum substitutes. As long as biodiversity can be preserved, it represents a wealth of information and potential resources that can be extremely beneficial for humanity. In addition, with the new developments in genetic engineering, which depends on biodiversity (genetic variation), humanity may be able to find new resources that provide solutions for food and health problems.

PESSIMISTS VERSUS OPTIMISTS ON GLOBAL ISSUES

Two basic perspectives—one negative, one positive—have influenced the analyses of global trends affecting the environment, population, and technology.

The Doomsday Model

The negative perspective is sometimes referred to as the Doomsday Model, or the neo-Malthusian approach. This model predicts that if current population, environmental, and technological trends continue, they will produce a series of ecological disasters that will threaten human existence. In the 1970s, a group of scientists and academics known as the Club of Rome assessed these global trends and predicted worldwide scarcities and a global economic collapse. Using elaborate computer models developed at the Massachusetts Institute of Technology, these scientists concluded that current global trends in population growth, energy-consumption patterns, and environmental pollution will exhaust the world's natural resources within the next 100 years.

The Optimists: The Logic-of-Growth Model

The Doomsday Model has been challenged by optimists such as Julian Simon (1981), who foresee a more promising future for humankind. Simon noted that health improvements, including a decrease in infant mortality and an increase in life expectancy, are a global trend. Simon also argued that pollution has abated in most societies that have experienced economic growth. Simon believed that as development and economic improvements continue in different societies, people will spend money to solve pollution problems.

Sometimes this perspective is referred to as the logic-of-growth model. This **logic-of-growth model** assumes that natural resources are infinite and that economic growth can continue indefinitely without long-term harm to the environment. For example, this model notes that Malthus had not foreseen the biotechnological revolution in agriculture that made land much more productive than was true in eighteenth-century England. Economists such as Simon believe that food-production problems in regions such as Africa can be attributed to farm collectivization, government attempts to control the prices of agricultural commodities, and other institutional problems. Simon cites statistics indicating that on a worldwide level, food prices per person are decreasing, and food production per person is increasing.

The logic-of-growth theorists cite evidence showing that the costs of energy and other natural resources have actually fallen over time because humans have found creative technological solutions for producing and extracting these resources. For example, Simon argues that the increase in the price of oil in the 1970s was purely political. The cost of producing a barrel of oil is still about 15 to 25 cents. He notes how people in the past responded to shortages of firewood used for heating by turning to coal, and from coal shortages by using oil. Simon believed that this ongoing process of creative innovation will continue.

Simon and other logic-of-growth theorists further suggest that population growth is a stimulus for, rather than a deterrent to, economic progress. The title of Simon's major book is *The Ultimate Resource* (1981), which he considers to be the human mind. Productivity and solutions for economic and environmental problems come directly from the human mind. In the long run, therefore, population growth helps to raise the standard of living in society by utilizing creative ideas and technologies to extract solutions. Although Simon and other logic-of-growth theorists admit that, in the short term, population growth may inhibit economic development, they conclude that countries ought not restrict population growth forcibly and that eventually technological innovations and human creativity will solve our problems, just as they have in the past.

The Pessimists and the Optimists: An Assessment

Most likely, both the pessimistic and the optimistic predictions regarding global problems are exaggerated. Predicting the future is risky for any social scientist, and to project complex global trends regarding population growth, environmental destruction, and technological change over many decades is highly problematic. The optimists believe that, ever since the beginnings of civilization, humanity has benefited from technological progress. A comprehensive view of the past, however, challenges this assumption. For example, the emergence of intensive agriculture—one of the major developments in human history—produced benefits for small segments of the population but adversely affected the majority of people by contributing to higher disease rates, increased inequality, and other problems. Conversely, the pessimists tend to underestimate the human capacity to devise technological solutions to global problems.

Anthropological research may help assess these global issues in a more cautious and analytic manner. With its holistic approach, anthropology has always been concerned with precisely those aspects of human interaction with the environment that are now being recognized widely by scientists studying global environmental change. The U.S. Committee on Global Change (1988) called for the development of an interdisciplinary science for understanding global change. The discipline of anthropology represents a prototype or model for the interdisciplinary science that would be needed to understand these changes (Rayner, 1989). Anthropological data can help assess the causes of such phenomena as the greenhouse effect by examining land-use choices and the impacts of economic activities. Anthropology may assist in the development of policies on matters such as agriculture, biotechnology, pollution, and population growth by providing information on the links between local practices and global processes.

Ethnographic Research on the Green Revolution

An example of how ethnographic research can illuminate global problems involves studies of the Green Revolution in underdeveloped countries. Optimists such as Simon cite the Green Revolution as one of the advancements made through technology and human creativity. In their view, the Green Revolution contradicts the basic assumptions made by the neo-Malthusians that population will outgrow the finite resources (food) of a particular area of land. Use of hybrid species of high-yield wheat and rice and highly mechanized agricultural techniques has increased food production to a degree that could not have been anticipated by Malthusians of past ages.

However, many cultural anthropologists who have studied the adoption of mechanized agriculture in developing countries have found that these innovations have created unintended economic and social problems. In most cases, only wealthy farmers have the capital to invest in irrigation equipment, chemical fertilizers, and large tracts of land. To extend their landholdings, wealthy farmers buy out smaller farmers, creating a new class of landless peasants and a small group of wealthy farmers, which intensifies patterns of inequality and related economic and social problems (Schusky, 1990).

Vaccinating cattle before they are shipped to a feedlot. Industrial societies have changed the nature of agricultural production. Large corporate farming that depends on expensive energy and heavy capital investment has resulted in the decline of family farming.
Courtesy of Joe Munroe/Photo Researchers, Inc.

In addition, cultural anthropologists find that in areas such as Mexico, where the Green Revolution was adopted enthusiastically, the increased agricultural yields in grains are often used to feed animals raised for human consumption. Anthropologist Billie Dewalt (1984) discovered that more than 50 percent of the annual grain production in Mexico was used to feed animals such as pigs, chickens, and cattle. His research indicates that people who can afford meat have benefitted from the Green Revolution. By increasing inequalities, however, the Green Revolution has reduced the percentage of the population that can afford meat. Dewalt concluded that the commercialization and industrialization of agriculture has not only widened the gap between rich and poor in Mexico; it has led to the underutilization of food, energy, and labor, thus hindering rather than promoting agricultural development.

Case Study: The Green Revolution in Shahidpur

One ethnographic study has shown that when the Green Revolution is carried out under the right conditions, it can be successful. Cultural anthropologist Murray Leaf (1984) studied the effects of the Green Revolution in the Punjab region of northern India. Leaf conducted research in a Sikh village called Shahidpur from 1964 to 1966 and then returned in 1978. The years 1965 and 1978 mark the onset and complete adoption, respectively, of the Green Revolution in Shahidpur. Thus, Leaf was able to view the beginning and end of the process. During this period, the village switched from subsistence to mechanized agriculture.

The villagers adopted new strains of wheat, tractors, insecticides, and an irrigation technology on an experimental basis to determine whether this would increase their yields. Wealthy farmers adopted the technology readily, investing their capital in equipment and land. Poor peasants, however, also took the needed capital investment risks (with the support of government development agencies), and the risks paid off. Leaf's research demonstrates that, in contrast to modernization theory, poor peasants are not constrained by traditional cultural patterns that might inhibit rational strategies of investment and savings. When these peasants saw they would directly benefit from these investments, they were willing to accept the economic risks.

More important, the villagers were willing to acquire the knowledge and technical skills needed to manage and ensure the continuity of their agricultural production. Through a university extension center, new plant varieties and technologies were adopted on an experimental basis. The people could directly see the results of their agricultural experiments and respond appropriately to various conditions. The education was a low-cost investment with government-subsidized tuition even for the poorest families. Furthermore, the university center provided training in the maintenance and repair of farm equipment and in other nonagricultural employment fields.

Leaf suggested that a key to the success of the Green Revolution in this region (in contrast to many other rural areas) is that government officials were more interested in development than in control. Government advice was always linked to the actual reactions among the villagers. Channels of communication were always open between local and regional levels. Leaf's valuable ethnographic study has some suggestive insights for those interested in furthering the Green Revolution in the Third World. Much more ethnographic research needs to be done, however, to evaluate the successes and problems in implementing the Green Revolution.

Case Study: The Conservation of Wood in Haiti

Another area in which ethnographic research has increased our understanding of a global problem is the growing shortage of wood for fuel and construction in developing societies. This problem is most acute in regions where growing populations practice intensive agriculture. Peasant farmers spend several hours each day searching for firewood, the principal cooking fuel in poor households. This practice results in the cutting of forests, which take a long time to grow back. Deforestation has become a worldwide ecological challenge.

Anthropologist Gerald Murray (1989), who conducted research among the rural peasants in Haiti, helped design a plan to solve the problem. European powers such as the French had developed Haiti as a sugar-exporting colony. They found it profitable to cut forests to clear land for sugar cane, coffee, and indigo for European consumers. After Haiti became inde-

A Haitian farmer at work.
COURTESY OF PAUL A. SOUDERS/CORBIS.

pendent in the nineteenth century, foreign lumber companies continued to cut and export most of the nation's hardwoods. These activities, combined with population growth that created land scarcities, greatly reduced the amount of forest area. The Haitian government tried to develop a reforestation project but failed to secure the cooperation of most of the peasants. The government blamed traditional peasant attitudes and patterns of land use for the project's failure.

In contrast, Murray argued that neither traditional land-use patterns nor peasant attitudes were responsible for the failure of reforestation. He discovered that the peasants did not cooperate with the project because they did not see any immediate benefits. Most of the trees with which the peasants were familiar took many years to grow. Moreover, the peasants believed that planting trees on their small tracts of land would interfere with crop cultivation. They also feared that even if they reforested the land, the government would assume ownership of the trees and thereby deprive them of the use of the land.

Because of his study, Murray was invited to help design a reforestation plan. With assistance from other anthropologists and development specialists, he designed a program that introduced fast-growing hardwood trees as an additional cash crop for peasant farmers. The increasing demand for this type of wood for charcoal and construction made it an ideal commodity. Thousands of trees were planted all across Haiti. In addition, the plan called for the trees to be completely owned and managed by the peasantry rather than by the government. The peasants could harvest the trees whenever needed, and they knew that they would receive the direct benefits from the project. After several years, the peasants constructed their houses and sold charcoal from the new woods. Murray views this type of peasant-managed, cash-crop production as a feasible option for many Third World peasant communities.

A Global Solution for Global Problems

In June 1992 in Rio de Janiero, Brazil, representatives of 178 nations gathered at what was known as the Earth Summit. These representatives tried to set the stage for managing the Planet Earth through global cooperation. The issues were the environment, climate change induced by the greenhouse effect and global warming, population growth, deforestation, the loss of biodiversity, air and water pollution, and the threats of globalization throughout the world. Although the Earth Summit was successful because it received so much international attention and created worldwide awareness of global issues, the specifics of how soon problems were going to be solved, how much it would cost, and who was going to pay became extremely complicated.

A follow-up summit on climate change was held in Kyoto, Japan, in December 1997. The Kyoto Summit was organized by the Organization for Economic Co-operation and Development (OECD), which represents most industrialized countries of the world. The OECD is committed to helping its member countries move toward sustainable development for the planet's life-support system. The Kyoto Summit resulted in a protocol agreement endorsed by 110 countries to try to reduce greenhouse gases and stabilize atmospheric changes that would mitigate increasing global warming.

The Kyoto Protocol established targets and set the stage for international monitoring of greenhouse gas emissions from various countries. The Kyoto agreement set a target of overall reduction of 5.2 percent in greenhouse gases from 1990 levels by the year 2012. The European countries set a target of reducing their emissions by 8 percent; the United States by 7 percent; and Japan by 6 percent. The United Kingdom took it upon itself to set higher targets and committed itself to a 20 percent reduction of emissions by 2010. Part of the agreement encouraged the industrial countries to become partners with the developing countries to help curb greenhouse gas emissions throughout the world.

Not surprisingly, many leaders of developing countries blamed the industrialized countries for the problems. Leaders of developing countries view themselves as victims of industrialized countries. For example, the Rio Declaration was going to contain a statement of principles on deforestation that would legally prohibit developing countries from burning their tropical rain forests. The developing countries objected to this statement because it was unfairly focused on the tropical forests and included nothing regarding the deforestation of the old-growth forests in the United States, Canada, and Europe. When a compromise could not be reached, the legally binding statement was scrapped for a weaker statement with no legal implications.

In addition, the industrialized countries, including the United States, were very reluctant to participate in some issues. For example, with respect to global warming, Japan and the European community had established limits on carbon dioxide emissions. In 2001, with the election of George W. Bush as president, the U.S. administration dropped out of the Kyoto Summit agreement. The Bush administration claimed that the treaty was unacceptable because it would harm the U.S. economy. They contended that the cost of curbing greenhouse emissions from coal-burning power plants and automobiles was too great a burden on the U.S. economy and would result in the loss of jobs and profits. The U.S. administration argued that the Kyoto agreement made exceptions for countries such as China and India, who did not have to reduce their emissions although these countries were emitting substantial amounts of greenhouse gases. Thus, the Bush administration opted out of the agreement, stating that it was unfair because it did not hold developing countries to the same strict emissions standards as the developed countries.

Many of the developing countries at the Rio de Janeiro summit felt that their number-one priority was economic survival rather than saving the environment. Developing countries wanted to adopt industrialization as rapidly as possible to induce economic development. Although they agreed to some of the environmental mandates of industrialized countries, they did so only by requiring the industrialized countries to contribute large sums of money toward those efforts. This resulted in various conflicts between the have and have-not countries.

The Sustainability Model

Obviously, the problems resulting from globalization are extremely complex and are not going to be resolved without some sort of global unity. Anthropological research in countries throughout the world has resulted in a perspective sometimes known as the sustainability model. The **sustainability model** suggests that societies throughout the world need environments and technologies that provide sustenance, not only for the present generation, but also for future generations. This model encourages resource management that does not degrade the environment for future generations. The sustainability model is opposed to the logic-of-growth model, which assumes that economic and technological growth will inevitably bring progress. The sustainability model is more realistic in assessing environmental and technological change, and recommends policy changes to inhibit problems that are induced by globalization. Some countries are beginning to adopt this sustainability model of development by limiting their emissions, curbing population growth, and cleaning up pollution. However, these global problems cannot be solved by country-by-country solutions. The challenge for this generation is to provide a global, internationally based organizational context for the resolution of these problems. Neglecting these global problems is bound to result in massive difficulties for the future of humanity. Anthropological research can help in assessing these problems and thereby promote the model of sustainability.

Economic Trends

As indicated in earlier chapters, the contemporary global economy began with European expansion in the mercantilist and colonialist periods. Ever since World War II, this world economic system has been divided into core, semiperipheral, and peripheral countries, with the United States the leading core country. Trading and financial institutions in the capitalist countries controlled the international organizations such as the World Bank and the International Monetary Fund. The industrial-socialist countries of Eastern Europe and the former Soviet Union tried not to participate directly in the capitalist world economic system and also tried to create their own client states in areas such as Cuba, Angola, and Afghanistan. By the 1980s, however, new developments in the world economy were producing a radical restructuring of the world economic system.

Multinational Corporations

One of the major factors behind the emergence of the global economic network is the multinational corporation. In many ways, multinational corporations have opened the door for globalization by promoting the spread of technical and cultural knowledge to non-Western societies. In the modern era, multinational corporations have expanded to the point that some anthropologists consider them a new societal institution beyond the state. For example, anthropologist Alvin Wolfe (1977, 1986) discussed how multinational corporations have integrated the manufacturing processes at a supranational level. Multinational corporations have reorganized the electronics industry, garment manufacturing, and the automobile industry. Today, products might be manufactured in several different countries, and the financing and organization of labor carried out by the multinational corporation. Wolfe suggested that this process will continue. The multinational corporations will eventually assume the management of global affairs, and the nation-state will disappear.

Jobs and Growth: A Positive Assessment

Given their power and influence, multinational corporations have become highly controversial. With their tremendous capital assets, they can radically alter a society. Some theorists believe that multinational corporations can enhance global economic development, thereby reducing poverty and hunger. As these corporations expand into Latin America, Africa, the Middle East, and Asia, they bring capital and technology and provide employment. From this vantage point, they create jobs and spur both short- and long-term economic growth.

Neocolonialism: A Negative Assessment

Dependency theorists, however, suggest that multinational corporations have actually intensified the problems of developing countries. They contend that these corporations create benefits for a wealthy elite and a small, upwardly mobile middle class, while the vast majority of the population remains in desperate poverty. Because the multinational corporations tend to invest in capital-intensive commodities, the majority of the population does not participate in the modernization of the economy. Furthermore, the entire society becomes dependent on corporations that are based outside the region, which inhibits self-sufficiency and the development of a more diversified economy.

According to this view, multinational corporations are simply the forerunners of a new form of neocolonialism, aimed at supplying the industrial world with natural resources and cheap labor. Multinational corporations based in core societies encourage peripheral societies to incur loans to produce a limited number of export-oriented commodities, a process that creates a cycle of economic indebtedness and increased dependency. In contrast to the older forms of colonialism, the core countries do not incur the expenses of maintaining direct political control over these societies; rather, they keep the peripheral nations in a state of dependency and maintain indirect political control by making contributions and paying bribes to politicians. In certain cases, however, when core countries feel threatened by political developments in peripheral nations, they resort to direct military intervention.

McDonald's restaurants are one sign of globalization in non-Western countries.
COURTESY OF MARK RICHARDS/PHOTOEDIT.

Case Study: The Potlatch Corporation

As with other global developments, these issues can benefit from ethnographic research. In one example, anthropologist Paul Shankman (1975, 1978) researched the changes generated by a multinational corporation on the island of Western Samoa. The corporation studied by Shankman was a large wood-product firm called the Potlatch Corporation, based in the northwest coast region of the United States and named after the famed redistributional exchanges of Native Americans in that region. The Potlatch Corporation surveyed the tropical hardwood trees in a portion of Western Samoa and found a dozen species that could be used for furniture and veneers. To facilitate the leasing of large amounts of land in Western Samoa (bypassing traditional landholding arrangements), the Potlatch Corporation requested that the Samoan government set up an agency to act as a broker on behalf of the corporation. Potlatch eventually won a number of concessions from the Samoan parliament.

Although Potlatch claimed to be committed to the economic development of Western Samoa, Shankman found that the monetary rewards from leasing the land did not prove as great as the people had expected. For example, Potlatch leased 28,000 acres of land for $1.40 an acre. In one project in which it leased land from a group of seven villages, the average yearly income from leasing amounted to less than $11 per person. Royalties paid on cut timber were also low, amounting to 4 cents per cubic foot, part of which was to go back to the government for reforestation.

The Potlatch Corporation did provide jobs for three hundred people in Western Samoa, making it one of the island's largest employers. Shankman discovered, however, that most of these people were formerly employed in agriculture, civil service, and light industry. Through the Potlatch projects, labor was simply shifted from other sectors of the economy to forestry. Thus, Potlatch did not really create jobs; rather, it simply shifted them to new sectors.

Shankman believed that Potlatch's leasing policies would ultimately create a scarcity of land, and more peasants would be forced to produce on marginal land. Moreover, Shankman suggested that the inflated cost of living generated by the company, through higher wage notes, in addition to the negative consequences such as erosion of the rain forest caused by rapid lumbering, may result in long-term negative costs to the people of Samoa.

Shankman also noted that the risks assumed by the people of Western Samoa were much greater than those of the multinational corporation. If Potlatch were successful, it could recoup its initial investments very quickly. Were it to lose revenue, it could simply leave the area. In contrast, the peasants did not have any capital to fall back on were they to lose their land. Moreover, they had to live permanently with the economic, social, and ecological changes brought about by Potlatch's policies. Eventually, the Potlatch Corporation pulled out of the region. As Shankman (1990, 2000) concluded: "So much for the commitment to economic development of Western Samoa."

Other anthropologists are conducting research similar to Shankman's. The consensus at this point appears to confirm his charges that the expansion of multinational corporations has created new forms of economic dependency and neocolonialism. Thus, in the short run, the global changes wrought by multinational corporations appear to have had negative consequences for developing societies. Whether this will be true over the long run remains to be seen.

Emerging Economic Trends

Driven by new technological and scientific developments in areas such as biotechnology, telecommunications, microprocessor information systems, and other high-tech industrialization, the world economy continues to undergo rapid changes. The globalization of the world economy has produced a vast array of products and services in interlocking markets. World trade has accelerated over the last few decades, stimulating greater economic interdependency. These trends have resulted in a restructuring of the world economic system.

Changes in Socialist Countries

The globalization of the economy has had traumatic consequences for the industrial, socialist-based economies of the former Soviet Union, Eastern Europe, and other peripheral socialist economies such as China and Vietnam. These state-administered economies did not produce the extensive economic development that they had promised. Government officials in these countries promoted five-year plans for economic development, but these plans did not lead to the production of prized consumer goods or a higher standard of living.

Anthropologist Marvin Harris (1992) advocates a cultural-materialist approach in explaining the downfall of the former Soviet Union and Eastern European communism. Harris suggested that the infrastructure, which encompasses the technological, economic, demographic, and environmental activities directed at sustaining health and well-being, has a primary, determinant role in the functioning of a sociocultural system. The serious deficiencies and weaknesses in the infrastructure of the former Soviet Union and Eastern Europe undermined the entire fabric of society. For example, the basic energy supply based on coal and oil production became stagnant, and the generating plants for electricity were antiquated, leading to periodic blackouts and frequent breakdowns.

Harris described how the agricultural and marketing system for the production and distribution of food resulted in severe shortages, delays in delivery, hoarding, and rationing. In addition, increasing problems with, and costs incurred by, industrial pollution led to the deterioration of the socialist economies. According to Harris, the infrastructural deficiencies of these socialist systems had fundamental consequences for the basic health, safety, and ultimate survival of the people in these societies. These deficiencies eventually led to the societies' systemic breakdown.

The industrial-socialist societies faced major economic crises. Repeated failures in agriculture and industry led to frustration and unrest among the populace. Global communications with other societies, particularly those with much greater access to consumer goods, caused many people in socialist states to become frustrated with the inadequacy of their systems. These people began to question the aims and policies of their leaders.

The Soviet Union: Perestroika and Glasnost

In the former Soviet Union, Communist Party leader Mikhail Gorbachev responded to the people's criticisms and the economic crisis facing the country by instituting a series of reforms and economic restructuring known as *perestroika*. In effect, this policy involved the reintegration of the former Soviet Union into the world-capitalist system. New joint ventures with capitalist firms were undertaken; McDonald's and other multinational corporations from the West and Japan were invited to participate in the Soviet economy. Soviet industrial corporations were reorganized to emphasize competition and the maximization of private profits for individual firms. Wages and salaries in Soviet industries were no longer to be controlled by the government; rather, they would reflect market conditions and individual productivity.

To carry out *perestroika*, Gorbachev had to confront the bureaucratic elite that dominated the Soviet political economy. Because these reforms directly threatened the bureaucratic control of the political economy, he faced much resistance by government officials. Some of these bureaucrats were ideologically committed to the Marxist–Leninist model of communism and did not want the Soviet Union integrated into the world-capitalist economy. Others believed that tinkering with the economy with these reforms would induce more hardship for the Soviet people. For example, after the introduction of *perestroika* and the removal of government-controlled price restraints, the costs of food and other basic commodities skyrocketed.

As a means of implementing his economic reforms, Gorbachev also called for *glasnost*, usually translated as "openness," which involved the freedom to criticize government policies and officials. Newspapers and other media were allowed to express views that were in opposition to Communist Party dictates. *Glasnost* also permitted greater political freedom of expression as well as democratic elections and a multiparty political system. The policy of *glasnost* led to mass demonstrations against the former Soviet government and eventually to criticism and the downfall of Gorbachev himself.

As a result of the severe economic difficulties and subsequent political crises in the Soviet Union, many of the non-Russian republics began to declare sovereignty and independence. Regions such as Estonia, Lithuania, the Ukraine, Kazakhstan, Uzbekistan, Turkmenistan, and Azerbaijan cut their political ties with the Soviet Union. Although Gorbachev attempted to frustrate these developments, sometimes with a show of military force, the Soviet empire began to collapse. Eventually, all of the non-Russian regions formed their own independent republics. The independent republics not only cut political ties, leaving the Russian republic by itself; they also began to restrict the export of their domestic commodities into Russia. This exacerbated the difficult economic conditions within the Russian state itself.

The successor to Mikhail Gorbachev, Boris Yeltsin, attempted to further the *perestroika* and *glasnost* policies of his predecessor. Yeltsin's primary goal was to transform the remains of the state-managed centralized economy of Russia into an economy in which managerial and consumer decisions are based on market forces and the economy is in private hands. The Yeltsin government tried to radically restructure the political economy by ending price and wage controls, reducing or eliminating subsidies to factories and farms, slashing military expenditures, introducing new taxes, and balancing the national budget.

The United States and other European economic leaders supported these policies, which became known as *shock therapy*. This economic shock therapy had some positive consequences, but most economists agree that the peculiarities of the Soviet system were bound to prolong the process of economic reform. In the meantime, many Russians who were accustomed to subsidies and government benefits had to endure substantial hardships. A number of Russian bureaucrats began to use their positions to acquire economic assets through illegal maneuvers. *Ponzi schemes,* which used fake banks and financial institutions to gain large sums of capital from government organizations and the general population, were prevalent during this shock therapy period (Titma and Tuma, 2001). In addition, a lack of knowledge of how capitalism, free labor, and the market economy operate has resulted in major economic declines in agriculture and industry. In 2000, Vladimir Putin, Yeltsin's prime minister, was elected president of Russia, promising to continue the economic reforms and democratization of Russian society. The question for future developments in Russia is whether the people can be patient enough to endure these economic difficulties.

Eastern Europe

Stimulated by the policies of *perestroika* and *glasnost,* the Eastern European nations of East Germany, Poland, Czechoslovakia, Hungary, Romania, Bulgaria, and Yugoslavia began reforms of their socialist political economies. These countries had been restricted to trading primarily with the Soviet Union and among themselves. In the German Democratic Republic (East Germany), mass demonstrations and migrations of people to West Germany led to the fall of the communist government and the destruction of the Berlin Wall. Solidarity, a popular outlawed labor union led by Lech Walesa, toppled the government of Poland. Polish workers demanded economic reforms and a better standard of living than that offered by the socialist model. Democratic elections led to Walesa's becoming prime minister. Walesa subsequently visited the United States and other Western countries in search of foreign investment. Many of the Eastern European socialist-bloc societies actively sought reintegration into the world-capitalist economy as a means of stimulating both economic growth and democratic freedom.

In a book entitled *What Was Socialism and What Comes Next* (1996), anthropologist Katherine Verdery, who did most of her ethnographic work in the East European country of Romania, summarizes some of the problems and dilemmas facing this region. She writes about how a different sense of time prevailed during the socialist period in Eastern Europe, and the new forms of capitalism and its industrial work rhythms based on progress and linear models are disrupting these societies. Verdery notes that new resurgent patterns of gender inequality based on older patriarchal forms are reemerging in these postsocialist Eastern European countries. During the socialist period, gender relations were supposed to have been equalized. However, Verdery describes how the socialist government in Romania reconfigured gender roles, making women dependent on a patrilineal-paternalistic state. After the downfall of socialism, Romania, as well as Poland, Hungary, and other postsocialist countries, have been emphasizing a return to "traditional values" regarding gender, which positions the woman once again in the home and doing household chores. To some extent, this gender organization of postsocialist society defines housework as "nonwork." As these Eastern European economies become more capitalistic, women will probably be drawn into the work force, but in the meantime, these women are returning to the older patriarchal forms of family life.

In the final chapter of her book, Verdery comments on how the transformation of Eastern Europe and Russian societies may take a much different path toward capitalism than the Western European or U.S. societies have taken. The privatization of property is likely to involve very different processes than in Western societies. Former socialist leaders will undoubtedly use the legal and political process to develop economic opportunities for themselves, as they transfer the state enterprises into private hands. Verdery suggests that black markets, organized crime, and the manipulation of the legal and state apparatus by former socialist bureaucrats will all have consequences for these postsocialist societies. The future of these postsocialist societies cannot be predicted based on models of how Western capitalist states developed.

China

Since Mao Zedong's death, China, under leaders such as Deng Xiaoping, introduced many tenets of capitalism. Instead of relying on Communist Party cadre who wanted to instill egalitarian ideals, the new leadership sought to develop leaders with technical, agricultural, and scientific expertise. They encouraged students to obtain education in the United States and other Western nations. They abolished the commune system and reorganized agricultural and industrial production based on individual profits and wages for farmers and workers. The Chinese government called for modernization in agriculture, industry, science, and defense.

Although promoting economic change, the Chinese government has not endorsed political reform. Party bureaucrats remain entrenched in power and resist all pressure to relinquish their authority. The absence of political freedom resulted in mass demonstrations by students and others in Tiananmen Square in Beijing in 1989. The Chinese government crushed this freedom movement with military force and has continued to repress any form of political dissent that threatens its authority. Whether economic development and reintegration into the world economic system can work in China without corresponding political freedom is a question that remains to be answered.

Vietnam

Confronted with being one of the poorest countries in the world, the Vietnamese government in 1981 introduced a series of economic reforms called *doi moi* (Pike, 1990). Some of the younger politicians in Vietnam are calling for greater participation in the world economic system, the introduction of private enterprise, and individual material benefits in the form of wages and salaries. The Vietnamese reformers face the same problem as those in China and the Soviet Union. With their memories of their colonial experience and wars against the capitalist nations, conservative bureaucrats who are committed to Marxist–Leninist ideology oppose reintegration into the world economic system. Reformers, in contrast, actively seek support from capitalist countries and the international community to pursue their economic liberalization policies and democratization. Recently, it appears that reformers are having the stronger influence regarding state policies. For example, they were instrumental in the negotiations that resulted in the United States lifting its trade embargo against Vietnam in January 1994. This shift in U.S. policy will undoubtedly lead to increasing trade and capitalist economic activity in Vietnam.

Changes in the Core Societies: The United States and Japan

The globalization of the world economy has also had dramatic effects on the core industrial societies, such as the United States and Japan. The United States currently exports about one-fifth of its industrial production. This is double what it was exporting in the 1950s, and that proportion is rapidly increasing. About 70 percent of those exported goods compete directly with goods produced by other nations. Some U.S. states depend heavily on the international economy. For example, approximately one-half of the workers in Ohio work directly on exports such as tires and automobiles. Honda, the major automobile company in Japan, has a large plant in Marion, Ohio. Most American corporations now conduct business on a global level. Although the United States remains the world's largest economy, with a gross national product twice the size of that of its nearest competitor, it no longer dominates as it did in the past. In fact, at the beginning of the twenty-first century, the United States had one of the largest trade deficits and the largest foreign debt of any nation.

In contrast, Japan has maintained a trade surplus. During the past several decades, the United States and Japan have engaged in global economic competition. This competition needs to be considered in the context of the world economic system.

In the 1920s, in the early phases of Japanese industrialization, Japan's population began to expand. Lacking adequate natural resources such as fertile land, raw materials, and energy supplies, Japan became increasingly dependent on imported food and other raw materials. To secure a food supply to support its growing population, the Japanese began to act as an imperial power in Asia, colonizing Korea and Taiwan and expanding into China. Japanese imperialism in Asia was one of the direct causes of World War II.

During its occupation of Japan following World War II, the United States encouraged the development of corporate capitalism. The U.S. government viewed Japan as a capitalist

Japanese factories are moving to new areas of the world such as Indonesia.
Courtesy of Pierre Bessard/REA Agency/CORBIS SABA.

center that could be used to forestall the spread of communism in Asia. Some of Japan's *zaibatsu,* wealthy family conglomerates, were broken up into smaller concerns. Others, such as the Mitsui and Mitsubishi families, were encouraged to invest in new equipment and technologies to induce rapid capitalist growth. Large sums of U.S. capital were funneled into corporations such as Sony to stimulate corporate capitalism. These policies led to the "economic miracle" in Japan that occurred in the 1960s. By the end of that decade, Japan had become one of the world's leading exporters.

The Japanese government, however, realized that it was still dependent on energy and food from other regions of the world. The government constantly reminded its population that Japan must "develop exports or die." The government organized the Ministry of International Trade and Industry (M.I.T.I.) to mobilize industrial firms to export products such as automobiles and electronics to ensure a balance of funds to pay for its heavy imports of food and energy. The M.I.T.I. helps finance Japan's huge exporting corporations so that it can maintain a favorable balance of trade. By the late 1980s, Japan had a large trade surplus. However, it imported approximately 8 tons of fuel, food, wood, and other raw materials for every ton of goods it exported.

Both Japan and the United States, as well as other core capitalist countries, have become postindustrial societies, with a large component of their economy devoted to the service sector. At the same time, many of the basic manufacturing plants of these industrial economies are relocating into developing countries to exploit the cheaper labor supply. Japanese multinational corporations have relocated auto factories and other industries to developing Asian countries such as Indonesia and Thailand. Ford Motor Company has relocated an engine manufacturing plant in Mexico. As the core countries become increasingly internationalized, economic interdependency accelerates. Some theorists believe that this interdependency may become a key component in resolving conflict among nations in the global village.

The Semiperipheral NICs

Another result of the globalization of the economy is the rise of the newly industrializing countries (NICs) from a peripheral to a semiperipheral status in the world economic system. Included here are the nations of South Korea, Hong Kong, Singapore, and Taiwan. Popularly known as the "Little Dragons of Asia," they compete with the economic might of Japan. Both Taiwan and Korea were colonies of Japan, whereas Hong Kong and Singapore were colonies of Great Britain. As with other colonized nations, they became peripheral dependencies. These countries, however, are rapidly industrializing and have broken their bonds of dependency. In some industries, such as electronics, these nations have marketed products that compete with core countries like Japan.

The success of the NICs reflects the changing division of labor in the world economic system. As the multinationals relocated some of their labor-intensive industries to low-wage regions, the NICs were able to absorb some of these jobs. Like Japan, their success is partially due to U.S. economic support. In particular, during the 1950s and 1960s, the United States viewed South Korea and Taiwan as part of the capitalist bloc in Asia. The United States invested large sums of capital and foreign aid into these countries, thereby enabling them to develop as capitalist centers. In addition, as in Japan, the governments in these countries directed the modernization of the economy through massive investment into export industries.

The NICs have changed the context of the world economy through low-cost production methods and aggressive marketing. They have created a unique niche in the world economic system by exporting products that compete directly with those produced by the core countries. In many cases, they have expanded their overseas markets through joint ventures with multinational firms based in core countries. In other cases, they have created their own multinational corporations. For example, NIC multinational corporations have become global competitors as producers of semiconductors for electronic and computer equipment. The world's largest plastic firm is Formosa Plastics, based in Taiwan. The best-selling imported car in Canada is the Pony, made by Hyundai in South Korea.

Political Trends

As the world economy becomes more integrated, major political changes are taking place in the global network. During the 1950s, some modernization theorists predicted that the various nations would become very similar as they were brought closer together in the global economy. People everywhere would share the same goods and services and eventually the same cultural values. This similarity would set the stage for a unified world government. Certain current trends indicate that such a movement may be taking place; for example, in 1999, fifteen European countries agreed to accept the "Euro" as the form of currency exchange in order to facilitate trade and to help develop a unified European economy. The EU (European

Union) covers some 1.2 million square miles and contains 375 million people speaking 11 different languages. It is currently the largest market in the world, and its gross domestic product (GDP) rivals that of the United States.

In addition, a unified European parliament has been established, and Europeans no longer need passports to travel among the 15 different countries. Some Europeans are beginning to think of themselves as "Europeans" rather than Italians, Greeks, Germans, Irish, or British. The nation-state may be giving way to larger political organizations and processes. At the same time, however, other political tendencies seem to indicate movement in the opposite direction; in many areas the nation-state appears to be fragmenting along linguistic, ethnic, and religious lines.

In considering these global political trends, many anthropologists suggest that the nation-state is too small for the immense problems in the world political economy: capital flows, economic development, management of technology, environmental and demographic trends, production of commodities, and labor problems. Organizations such as the United Nations, International Monetary Fund, World Bank, World Trade Organization (WTO), NAFTA, the EU, and the multinational corporations appear to be in the process of displacing the nation-state in the management of the global economy. Although the United Nations has not been effective in producing an international consensus on global problems, it may become more important in the future.

At the same time, the nation-state may be too large to care for the different needs of people at the local level. Government officials representing the nation-state may not have enough contact with the populace in local areas to respond to their needs, which can range from housing and food to the opportunity to express their cultural values. One sign of the fragmentation of the nation-state into smaller components is the increase of ethnic and religious tensions at the local level.

Ethnic Trends

Ethnic unrest and tension are prevalent in today's world. Newspapers and television news are rife with stories about ethnic violence among the peoples of the former Soviet Union and Eastern Europe, Africa, Sri Lanka, India, Ireland, the Middle East, and the United States.

Anthropologists have been systematically examining ethnicity since the 1960s. An ethnic group is a collectivity of people who believe they share a common history and origins. Members of ethnic groups often share cultural traits such as language, religion, dress, and food. Today the countries of Latin America, Africa, the Caribbean, the Middle East, and Asia are plural societies that contain many ethnic groups.

As globalization occurs, with its rapid integration of nation-states, markets, and information technology, and as the management of economic and political development goes to the World Bank, the International Monetary Fund, the EU, the United Nations, and large multinational corporations, many peoples at the local level feel threatened by these global processes. Citizens of various countries lose faith in their government's abilities to represent their interests in these pluralistic societies. These globalization processes often exacerbate ethnic tensions and conflicts.

We looked at the development of ethnonationalist movements in Latin America, the Caribbean, Africa, the Middle East, and Asia. These ethnonationalist movements were, to some extent, a result of earlier colonial policies and new post–Cold War trends in globalization. Many ethnic groups have expressed a desire to return to a more simple way of life and traditional culture and behavior. They distrust the new global managers, and ethnonationalism is a reaction to these globalization tendencies. Restoring ethnic autonomy is sometimes seen as a strategy to rectify the globalization process.

The revival of local ethnic tendencies and identities is developing in the West as well as in non-Western countries. Anthropologists are studying the ethnic resurgence of the Scots and why they want more independence in the United Kingdom, and why Quebec wants to separate from the rest of Canada (Handler, 1988; Cohen, 1996). These local ethnic movements for autonomy and separatism are a response to the weakening of older nation-state loyalties, induced by globalization. As globalization is fraught with anxieties and produces uncertainties in structures and institutions, and as it develops in anarchic, haphazard fashion carried along by economic, technological, and cultural imperatives, the ethnic group becomes the refuge for people who feel as if they have no control over these new forces.

Religion and Secularization

Just as ethnic trends have created contradictory political trends, there are ongoing, contradictory religious trends in the context of globalization. Generally, traditional religious beliefs and rituals become separated from economic, social, and political institutions in industrial societies, and religion becomes a private affair for most people.

After the Enlightenment, social thinkers such as Auguste Comte and Karl Marx, as well as early anthropologists, predicted that as societies became increasingly industrialized and modernized, secularization would eradicate religious institutions and beliefs. Though secularization has occurred, however, religion has not disappeared in these societies. Even in places such as the former Soviet Union and Poland, where government authorities prohibited religious beliefs and institutions, religion remained a vital force.

To some extent, religious institutions have survived in industrial societies because religious leaders have emphasized many of the cultural values—for example, nationalism—espoused by other institutions. In addition, the persistence of religion may also be a product of the secularization process itself. Many recent religious revivals have occurred in those societies that have been most affected by modernization. As globalization introduces sweeping political, social, and ideological changes, many traditional beliefs and values are challenged. To cope with these destabilizing transformations, many people are reemphasizing traditional cultural values, including religion. For example, the fundamentalist movements in North America, whether Catholic, Jewish, or Protestant, can be partially understood as a reaction against secularization and modernization. The same can be said of Buddhist, Hindu, and Islamic fundamentalism in other parts of the world.

As people recognize that globalization is not incidental to their lives but rather a recognizable transformation in their everyday circumstances, they draw on religious substance as a means of restoring power over their lives. The reconstruction and reinvigoration of their

Vietnamese boat people.
Courtesy of AP/Wide World Photos.

religious identity gives some people a sense of greater control in what appears to be a runaway world. Fundamentalist religious movements articulate the uncertainties and distress brought about by expanding globalization and advocate alternative ways of organizing life on a more localized level.

The Role of Anthropology

Although the political, ethnic, and religious trends discussed in this chapter are essentially global, they also obviously affect people on the local level. Not surprisingly, therefore, cultural anthropologists are actively documenting the local responses to global political and religious trends of people in the agricultural regions of Latin America, Africa, the Middle East, Asia, and nonstate societies, as well as in industrialized societies. Cultural anthropologists have recorded the various dislocations of global political and religious processes in these societies and the ways in which people have attempted to cope with these global changes. The continuing agony of separatist, ethnic, and religious conflicts in Bosnia, Kosovo, Sri Lanka, and elsewhere threatens people throughout the world. Existing institutions such as the nation-state have not been

Jerry Falwell has been a leader of fundamentalist Christianity in the United States.
COURTESY OF JOHN TROHA/STOCKPHOTO.COM.

able to manage this local conflict. Perhaps by understanding the specific aspirations of these different peoples, national governments and the international community will be more responsive to their diverse needs and interests.

As anthropologists identify the cultural variations that hamper international coordination, they may help to contribute to the reduction of ethnic and religious tensions worldwide. Anthropologist John Bennett (1987) recommended that anthropologists synthesize their local studies (the micro level) with studies of global conditions (the macro level) to identify trends that militate against international cooperation. Anthropologists should make a concerted effort to understand the underlying historical and cultural motivations that contribute to ethnic and religious conflicts. In doing so, they may aid in humankind's understanding of its existence and the need for cooperation in the global village.

SUMMARY

Numerous global trends are altering the way of life in all societies. Environmental changes induced by globalization—the greenhouse effect, the depletion of the ozone layer, and atmospheric pollution—are creating new problems that may threaten the existence of our planet.

Population growth has declined in the core countries but has risen in many Third World societies because of a combination of reduced mortality rates and continued high birth rates. Technological changes resulting from industrialism have increased the consumption of energy and other raw materials.

Global environmental, demographic, and technological changes have led to two different perspectives: one pessimistic and the other optimistic. Pessimists predict that population growth and expanded industrialism will result in global economic collapse. Optimists tend to see human creativity and technological solutions as the salvation for humanity. Both the pessimistic and optimistic views are probably exaggerated. Anthropologists have examined specific cases regarding the adoption of mechanized agriculture and reforestation projects to understand better these worldwide problems.

Various global economic trends have developed in recent decades. Multinational corporations are creating more economic interdependency among nations. Ethnographic research, however, indicates that the changes introduced by multinational corporations may not always generate economic development in Third World societies. Other global economic trends include the reintegration of socialist societies into the world-capitalist system. Russia, Eastern Europe, China, and Vietnam are abandoning orthodox forms of socialism to join the world-market system.

The core countries such as the United States and Japan compete with one another in the global economy. This competition has resulted in the expansion of multinational corporations into various areas, leading to a new global division of labor. Countries such as South Korea and Taiwan have been moving from peripheral to semiperipheral status in the world-market system.

In contrast to global economic interdependency and modernization, political, ethnic, and religious trends often move in the opposite direction. Ethnic separatist movements often divide people, making the promotion of national goals difficult. Religious fundamentalist movements often result from the rapid modernization processes that erode traditional cultural beliefs. Anthropological studies of these trends improve our understanding of both local aspirations and global processes.

8. Refugees:

Worldwide Displacement and International Response

Stephen Lubkemann

Lubkemann, an applied anthropologist and demographer who works in West Africa, takes a broader, systemic view of the refugees, and the non-governmental organizations that so affect their lives. He outlines the basic terms that constrain and define the status of refugee. This article presents and analyzes case studies, unraveling the cultural, legal, economic and political factors that shape refugee dilemmas. Note the role of anthropologists working with and in NGOs in mitigating the plights of displaced persons.

Throughout history people have been forced to flee their homes in order to escape war, persecution, and natural disasters. The twentieth century has witnessed massive forced migrations. Political conflicts have been motivated by the widespread growth of ethno-nationalism, resistance to colonial rule, and the "Cold War" confrontation between capitalism and communism. Economic processes such as impoverishment due to development policies and global environmental degradation also have resulted in widespread population displacement.

Forced migration has been particularly affected by the emergence of "total warfare" in which non-combatants have increasingly borne the brunt of wartime violence. According to the Independent Commission on International Humanitarian Issues, 95% of the casualties suffered in World War I were combatants and only 5% were civilians, whereas in most current conflicts civilians often account for 90% or more of wartime casualties. Technology has also greatly increased the destructiveness of armed conflict thus causing greater displacement to occur.

REFUGEES AND INTERNALLY DISPLACED PERSONS

While attempts to assist uprooted people occurred throughout history, only in the twentieth century did international standards and institutions for protecting displaced people emerge. The 1951 United Nations Refugee Convention defines "refugees" as "individuals who are out-

113

side their own country and are unable to return as a result of a well-founded fear of persecution on grounds of race, religion, nationality, political opinion, or membership of a social group." Refugees are entitled to safe asylum, education, and medical care, and to not be repatriated against their will. The rights of refugees also include freedom of thought, of movement, and freedom from torture or degrading treatment. The convention defines the duties of states to uphold these rights as a matter of international law. It also requires refugees to uphold the laws of their host countries and to be noncombatants.

It is important to understand that displacement is a process that includes but is not limited to those who meet the legal criteria for "refugee" status (often called "Convention Refugees"). In fact, the vast majority of those who are forcibly uprooted from their homes do not fit the criteria that would allow them to be categorized as "Convention Refugees." Some are internally displaced persons within their own countries (known as "IDPs"). Others have been forced to move for reasons other than those specified in the convention, such as natural disasters, environmental degradation, or extreme economic duress. The number of those who are displaced worldwide is thus three or four times larger than the number of those who are officially designated as "Convention refugees." Those without "Convention refugee" status are not entitled to the legal protections that the Convention affords.

Moreover, those adversely affected by displacement often include people other than forced migrants themselves—such as the host populations in the impoverished third world nations where most uprooted people are re-settled. Thus the majority of those who suffer as a result of displacement do not benefit from the legal rights and entitlements afforded to "Convention Refugees" by international law.

COMPLEX CAUSES AND EFFECTS

Displacement is one of humanity's harshest and most traumatizing conditions and thus constitutes one of the international community's most pressing moral and ethical dilemmas for the 21st century. Armed conflict has persisted sometimes for decades in many places throughout the world such as Angola, Somalia, Sri Lanka, Kurdistan, Colombia, Rwanda, Afghanistan, Palestine, and Kashmir. In such contexts, displacement is not an exceptional interruption in the flow of "normal" life. Instead it has become an integral feature of social life that shapes all aspects of everyday routine. Anthropologists who strive to understand how social and cultural life are organized in these societies must examine how displacement affects many different dimensions of social life, including subsistence strategies, household formation, gender relations, and national identity.

In my own work with Mozambicans who fled their country's civil war, fifteen years of displacement resulted in radical changes in the way residence and marriage were organized. While leaving their wives and children in safe areas within Mozambique, many men migrated to South Africa to avoid being conscripted by the military. Because the war persisted for so long, many of these men eventually constituted second households by also marrying South African women. Although polygamy (men having multiple wives) was already a feature of these men's society, it had never before been "transnationalized" in this way. In this case long-term displacement created a new form of transnational community in which households, kinship networks, and economic strategies panned international borders. This form of social organization had not existed before the war but persisted after it.

Over the last three decades social scientists and policy-makers have begun to recognize refugees as more than simply the unfortunate by-products of conflict. They have started to study how displacement and forced migration affect broader processes of social change and international security. Some of the issues and phenomena that affect displacement and are, in turn, influenced by refugees are development, demographic change, immigration, ethno-nationalism, public health, the environment, and conflict resolution. In the social sciences anthropologists have played a leading role in investigating the causes, organization, and effects of displacement and have focused, in particular, on how displacement affects social relations, organizations, and identities.

CAUSES OF DISPLACEMENT

Typically those fleeing wars and political violence have been designated "involuntary migrants" as distinguished from "voluntary migrants," a term reserved for those who migrate primarily to improve their economic situation. Increasingly anthropologists have questioned the sharpness of the distinction between political and economic motives for migration by showing that political conflict and economic wellbeing are often closely related. Researchers have pointed out that people who migrate because their economies or subsistence environment have been devastated by war are also "involuntary migrants," even if they have not been directly targeted by military violence. In places like the Sudan or Ethiopia, governments have forbidden the distribution of food aid in insurgent areas in an effort to starve populations thought to be harboring enemy troops.

Wars also can produce forced migration by constricting the options that people have for coping with adverse environmental conditions. During times of famine in Mozambique, rural peasants traditionally coped with food shortages by temporarily moving to urban centers where they could find short-term work, enabling them to purchase food. However, during the Mozambican civil war, the fact that the government held most of the urban areas while the insurgency held rural areas made it virtually impossible to safely transit back and forth between the two. Intense drought conditions resulted in massive forced migration across international borders because the political conditions of the war impeded traditional mechanisms for coping with environmental hardship. Such examples demonstrate how economic, environmental, and political processes can be complexly interrelated in ways that make it difficult to reasonably distinguish "political" from "economic" motives, or migration as either "voluntary" or "involuntary."

Political processes such as nationalism and state-building can result in different forms of displacement. The Indonesian government has pursued a policy of forcibly relocating many of its citizens of the dominant ethnic group on the main island of Java to outlying islands in an attempt to influence the ethnic balance of power and cultural practices of ethnic minorities. This policy of "transmigration" is a deliberate attempt to build a unified national identity by "Javanizing" ethnic minorities. Unsurprisingly this policy has aggravated ethnic tensions and resulted in violent conflict that has produced displacement in its own right.

Development initiatives are another major cause of displacement. Colonial development projects often displaced tens or even hundreds of thousands of people to make room for settlers (as in South Africa, Zimbabwe, Mexico, and the United States) or to complete projects such as building massive dams. American anthropologist Elizabeth Colson has conducted one of the most important studies of the longterm social effects of development-induced displacement in her fifty years of research on the Gwembe Tonga in Zambia. The Tonga were displaced as the result of a dam project. The ongoing construction of the massive Three Gorges Dam on China's Yellow River provides a contemporary example of a major development project that will eventually displace up to 10 million people.

Economic and applied anthropologists also have shown how prevailing macro-economic policies such as "structural adjustment" can affect social and political environments in ways that produce forced relocation. Structural adjustment economic policies generally oblige governments to reduce their public expenditures, often resulting in the loss of jobs and public services. These policies also can produce cost-of-living increases as governments stop subsidizing the cost of food or other basic amenities. Anthropologist James Ferguson demonstrates the consequences of such policies in Zambia where people who have worked their entire lives in urban areas have been forced to relocate to less expensive rural areas and to pursue unfamiliar agricultural subsistence strategies.

More recently, environmental degradation also has been identified as a major cause of forced migration. Researchers working in Bangladesh and Africa coined the term "environmental refugees" to refer to those displaced because of environmental degradation or natural disasters such as earthquakes, floods, and volcanic eruptions. Although it is caused by natural events such as these, environmental displacement also is influenced by social, political, and economic factors. People who are economically and politically marginalized are more likely to have to live in areas vulnerable to catastrophic events and are thus more likely to become environmental refugees. Research is just beginning to consider the potential effects of worldwide environmental trends such as global warming on the potential future displacement of such marginal populations as those bordering the Sahel in Africa.

EFFECTS OF DISPLACEMENT

Displacement has a broad range of political, economic, social, and psychological effects, which anthropologists and other social scientists have begun to focus their research attention on. The experience of displacement, particularly when it is prolonged, often leads to the forging of socio-political consciousness and national political identity. Millions of Palestinians, Rwandese, and Afghanis have been living in camps or other forms of exile for decades. In such cases, multiple generations actually have been born and grown up in conditions of displacement. Contrary to prevalent media depictions of refugees as merely passive victims of larger circumstances, anthropologists working with these populations have demonstrated how the experience of prolonged displacement can motivate people to politically organize and react against the perceived causes of their displacement. Not surprisingly, refugee camps in Palestine and Afghanistan have proven to be fertile recruiting grounds for military groups fighting against Israel and in successive conflicts in Afghanistan. Both the Taliban and the earlier anti-Soviet mujaheddin movements, which the Taliban ousted, originated within Afghan refugee communities in Pakistan.

Anthropologists working with refugees in Kenya, the Democratic Republic of the Congo, Uganda, Macedonia, Turkey, Rwanda and Burundi also have examined how national political stability can be affected when massive population movements influence ethnic composition and balances of power within host countries. For example, during the international coalition's war against Iraq in 1990, Turkey feared that a massive influx of ethnic Kurds from Iraq would further strengthen the Kurdish resistance movement within its own borders. Turkey, therefore, refused entry to displaced Kurds attempting to flee the regime of Saddam Hussein.

The rapid arrival of large numbers of destitute and desperate refugees usually has significant, though often contradictory and socially differentiated economic impacts on host populations. Researchers in East Africa have demonstrated how the arrival of large numbers of refugees may drive down the price of labor in host areas. This may provide a boon, on the one hand, to more wealthy segments of the host population who are in a position to hire labor. However, it may also drive down wages and increase competition for jobs with other poorer locals who also subsist by providing labor. Similarly massive population influxes may increase pressure on scarce resources such as land or fuel. The influx of Mozambican refugees into Zimbabwe during the 1980s eventually produced a popular backlash because there was already stiff competition for land within Zimbabwe, and Mozambicans were occupying more and more of it. Such effects can increase socio-economic differentiation (i.e. increasing the gap between the rich and poor) within host populations, creating new forms of social tension and conflict. These socio-economic impacts are particularly pronounced in many third world countries that bear the brunt of the world's refugee burden, and in which poverty may already be widespread.

These impacts are likely to be further pronounced if displaced populations do not settle in visible refugee camps or receive official assistance but rather "self-settle" in the midst of host populations. Anthropologists working in Africa and Latin America have provided most of the few in-depth examinations of these so-called "self-settled" refugees. Throughout the 1970s and into the 1980s, there was evidence that many self-settled refugees were able to successfully integrate into local host communities in rural border areas, usually by drawing on extended kinship or ethnic ties that spanned these borders. Recent work by anthropologists point to the fact that an increasing number of the self-settled seem to be establishing themselves in major urban centers rather than in rural areas bordering their countries of origin. While it is clear that the self-settled comprise a majority of the displaced (some estimates range as high as 80% of all displaced), exact estimates are hard to come by. Since the majority of these individuals are technically illegal immigrants, they have a vested interest in concealing their national origins in order to avoid deportation.

Anthropologists have been particularly successful and pioneering in working with self-settled refugees because their fieldwork methods allow them better access to these populations. Through long-term interaction with their subjects, anthropologists are able to build stronger, more trusting relationships than are possible through other methods. This rapport also provides for a deeper and more holistic understanding of the complex social effects of displacement. Many anthropologists have consequently become strong advocates for the refugee populations with whom they work. The precarious legal status of many displaced people and their traumatic histories force anthropologists to grapple with difficult ethical dilemmas and with the challenge of how best to protect their research collaborators.

Anthropologists have increasingly examined how displacement is a highly gendered process that reorganizes social relations and identities. In many refugee situations women and children comprise over 80% of the refugee population. There is also evidence that wartime violence and displacement often have more negative economic and social effects on women than on men. For example, refugee women are usually more vulnerable to predatory sexual violence than refugee men. A great deal of policy research has attempted to identify the most "vulnerable groups" within displaced populations, such as women-headed households, children, the elderly, and those with disabilities, in order to identify ways to provide greater assistance and protection.

Anthropologists have shown that culturally specific social systems play an important role in constituting vulnerability. Vulnerability is not merely a function of biological factors such as age or sex. It is primarily related to the ways in which social roles bind people to certain obligations and entitle them to certain rights. Social roles vary widely across different cultures. In my own work in Mozambique, I was able to show organizations assisting refugees that their assumptions that elderly widows were more vulnerable than elderly widowers was incorrect because it did not account for the way the local kinship system worked. In this particular social context, elderly women almost always were supported not by their husbands but by their sons and his wife or wives. Elderly men, on the other hand, depended on their wives for support. The loss of a spouse was therefore much more consequential for elderly men than for elderly women.

Displacement also may have profound effects on the gendered distribution of labor, on the way gendered relationships like marriage or parentage are organized, and on how gendered and other social roles change in terms of the obligations and rights these imply. Thus, for example, in rural Mozambique, displacement had profoundly disempowering effects for women. It reconfigured gender relations and the social institution of marriage in very detrimental ways for many women. Displaced women who resettled in refugee camps were unable to engage in subsistence agriculture which was their primary economic activity and the basis of their social influence within their households. On the other hand, many men were able to continue their primary economic activity—labor migration. The fact that many of these migrant men took additional wives in their migration destinations also disempowered their Mozambican wives. These wives who remained behind in refugee camps found it difficult to claim their share of their husbands' earnings. Conversely, in other contexts, such as among Eritrean refugees settled in Canada, women have been able to assume new social roles previously unavailable to them, resulting in their relative empowerment vis-à-vis Eritrean men.

The experience of having to adapt to an unfamiliar social and cultural environment can make forced migration and resettlement particularly difficult experiences. It is important to realize that displaced people arrive in new societies with their own sets of values and aspirations. The maintenance of particular cultural differences may become crucial to refugee constructions of meaningful identities and life strategies in novel social environments. For example, several anthropologists who have worked with Hmong refugees from Cambodia in the U.S. have noted the critical role that religion has continued to play in organizing these refugee communities and in constituting a sense of social identity.

Differences between the cultural norms of refugees and those of host societies concerning appropriate codes of social behavior sometimes create tensions between refugees and the communities in which they have resettled. Exposure to new value systems and cultural norms can also generate conflict within refugee communities and households themselves. Men and women, or different generations, often have divergent views about which features of their own original culture should be maintained and which from the new host society should be adapted as their own. Anthropologists working with Afghani and Laotian refugees in the U.S. and with the Palestinians in Germany have taken particular note of intergenerational differences in how parental authority is regarded. For example, anthropologist Dima Abdulrahim has documented the disputes that arise within Palestinian refugee households in Germany over whether or not fathers should have the right to dictate whom their daughters should marry.

Those studying other groups such as the Sudanese or Ethiopians in the U.S., the Mozambicans in South Africa, or the Burundians in Tanzania have noted how internal tensions and arguments often emerge over changing norms in the way gender roles and relationships are defined. In my own work I found that Mozambican women who joined their husbands in South Africa often observed that there was a greater sharing of domestic tasks by men in South African households. They consequently began to question the gendered division of labor within their own households. Mozambican men resisted the erosion of their privileges. In many cases they eventually went out of their way to avoid having their Mozambican wives join them in South Africa in order to prevent them from exposure to new norms.

EFFECTS ON HEALTH

The psychological effects of exposure to violence and displacement are attracting increased attention from mental health experts, including medical and psychological anthropologists. The trauma of displacement can make adaptation to new and unfamiliar social and cultural environments particularly difficult. Anthropologists have demonstrated how different cultural beliefs play a central role in the way individuals interpret and cope with traumatic experiences such as displacement. The challenges of adaptation may be further intensified by the uncertainty and insecurity of temporary status or a sense of being highly constrained in a refugee camp environment. Prolonged dependence on aid in long-term refugee camp situations can lead to diminished self-esteem and a sense of dependency and disempowerment.

One of the most fruitful recent areas of collaboration between researchers and organizations assisting refugees has been in understanding and improving humanitarian reactions to the health problems faced in complex emergencies. The catastrophic mortality rates in the Rwandan refugee camps in eastern Zaire (now the Democratic Republic of the Congo) sounded a wake-up call within the humanitarian community that has since sparked greater collaboration with the CDC (Center for Disease Control), as well as research and training programs on refugee health at leading schools of public health such as Johns Hopkins and Columbia University.

In 1999 the National Research Council Committee on Population created a Roundtable on Forced Migration to assess and encourage research on the demographic effects of displacement. Research on refugee mortality and morbidity represents only the first step in a much needed examination of the broader demographic effects of forced migration. It is worth noting that Africa is the continent with the greatest number of IDPs (internally displaced persons), the world's highest fertility rates, fastest urban growth, and highest rates of HIV. Remarkably, however, the relationship of forced migration to these important demographic processes has scarcely been examined to date.

THE ANTHROPOLOGY OF HUMANITARIAN ACTION

Anthropologists working on refugees have focused largely on how displacement affects and is affected by social organization. Increasingly many of us see the necessity of also focusing on the larger political economic systems and organizations that intervene in the lives of the displaced. The humanitarian regime consists of those organizations that assist or interact with displaced populations, the systemic relationships among these organizations, and their institutionalized set of practices. The anthropology of humanitarian action focuses on the social, cultural, economic, and political factors that shape those practices and the relationships of power among those organizations.

The UNHCR (United Nations High Commissioner for Refugees), created in 1950 after World War II, following post war reconstruction in Europe, continues to play the leading role in international efforts to assist and protect refugees and displaced people worldwide. Throughout the last decade of the twentieth century, the number of "persons of concern" to the UNHCR rose from 14.92 million to 22.26 million.

Regional international bodies such as the OAU's (Organization of African Unity) and the OAS (Organization of American States) extended the definition of refugee to include individuals and groups forced to flee their countries because of conditions of generalized violence and insecurity rather than because of individual-specific persecution. At best these criteria only have been applied within these regions. Unfortunately countries throughout the world increasingly have followed the lead of Western European and North American governments in pursuing more restrictive asylum granting policies that limit the number of refugees allowed to settle within their borders.

Such policies are a reaction by the governments of industrialized nations to two decades of rapid growth in immigration. This flow has been caused by people fleeing deteriorating political and economic conditions in developing countries such as Haiti, Mexico, and Nigeria and in former communist bloc countries, such as Romania and Nicaragua. Such people come seeking greater opportunity in the West. The globalization of mass communication has increased awareness of the opportunities available in many industrialized nations. The development of international transportation systems has facilitated transcontinental travel. These aspects of globalization have played an important role in motivating international migration.

The UNHCR only can advise individual states on how to interpret the Refugee Convention's criteria when applying these to individuals seeking asylum within their own borders. Consequently governments always have been able to restrict whom they accept as refugees in ways that serve their political and economic interests. Fears of the negative economic effects of excessive immigration have led industrialized nations to interpret the convention's criteria in ever more restrictive terms. Thus, for example, in several cases in North America during the 1990s, courts recognized that asylum seekers fled their countries of origin because of a legitimate fear of violence but still denied them refugee status, because it was determined that they were being persecuted for "nonpolitical" reasons (such as sexual orientation or gender).

Governments also have developed ways to provide temporary relief for those fleeing insecurity without incurring the legal obligations implied in granting "convention refugee" status. Throughout Europe and North America, different forms of TPS (Temporary Protection Status) have emerged that provide an interim solution to populations fleeing generalized violence until it is safe for them to return. Initially put forth as a short-term measure, TPS does not usually provide the social benefits to which refugees are entitled, such as education and employment or the possibility of seeking asylum or permanent resettlement. However, the prolonged insecurity and challenging conditions in countries such as Liberia and Guatemala have led to annual renewals of TPS status in the U.S. for displaced populations from these countries for up to a decade.

My work with Liberian refugees in the U.S. has shown how the TPS status has had mixed effects. On the one hand, it has constrained people's economic mobility and social integration into American society. The constant uncertainty over whether TPS will be renewed serves as a disincentive for longer-term social investment in their host communities. On the other hand, the threat of TPS termination has mobilized Liberian community members around a common cause as they lobby for permanent residence status. This has allowed them to transcend longstanding ethnic and socio-economic divisions that played a significant role in causing the Liberian civil war in the first place.

In the most extreme cases, industrialized nations have resorted to more severe measures to prevent the influx of forced migrants. European Union states have refused entry to asylum seekers on the grounds that they already had passed through "safe countries" en route from their countries of origin. Heavy fines have been imposed on airlines that transport asylum seekers who do not already have visas. Even more draconian and legally dubious measures have involved intercepting refugees before they arrive on host country shores and turning them back without asylum hearings. This was the U.S. government's policy towards thousands of Haitian boat people who sought to land on American shores during the 1990s. This package of increasingly restrictive measures represent a policy of "containment," often described as an attempt to create "fortress" regions that make access to forced and other migrants more difficult.

Such policies have not stemmed the rising tide of forced migrants. Instead they have produced greater levels of clandestine immigration into industrialized nations. Moreover they have placed the economic burden of displacement on other less-industrialized countries, which are even more adversely affected by massive refugee influxes. Meanwhile the levels of financial assistance that industrialized nations provide to international organizations and developing nations to assist refugees also has diminished. Unsurprisingly, the willingness of governments everywhere to host refugees has eroded. In this environment refugees throughout the world have experienced rising levels of violence and hostility from host populations and governments. Even governments that have long proven to be generous hosts to large refugee populations such as Iran and Tanzania undertook large-scale forced repatriations during the late 1990s and closed off their borders against further refugee flows.

The restriction of asylum also increasingly reduces the options for the displaced in ways that subject them to greater risk of violence. One example is the creation of so-called 'safe zones' within conflict areas as an alternative to allowing refugees to cross international borders. European

Union countries already overwhelmed by massive population influxes that resulted from the fall of the Berlin Wall urged the creation of "safe zones" in Bosnia-Herzegovina because of their reluctance to receive refugees from the former Yugoslavia. However, insufficient military means for ensuring their safety led to notorious calamities in 1995 when the safe zones in Srebrenica and Zepa were overrun, and thousands of Bosnian civilians were massacred.

Restrictive immigration policies do not prevent forced migration because they fail to address the root causes of migration—namely the precarious political and economic conditions that compel people to move. The growing worldwide reluctance to accept refugee resettlement and the increasing trend towards civil (as opposed to interstate) warfare has resulted in a dramatic increase in the number of IDPs worldwide. The appointment in 1992 of the first UN Special Representative on Internally Displaced Persons represented a critical step in institutionalizing international concern for this issue.

The nature of post-Cold War conflicts presents considerable new challenges to organizations that want to assist the displaced. Many civil wars—such as those in the former Yugoslavia and Rwanda—have been driven by ethno-nationalist sentiments aiming to create ethnically homogeneous countries. In these conflicts military forces have directly targeted civilian populations in an effort to eliminate or forcibly uproot minorities—a process called "ethnic cleansing." In such cases humanitarian efforts to assist the displaced do not serve the interest of warring parties and are often hindered. Long-term solutions to the displacement produced by ethnically-driven violence may be particularly difficult to find. Repatriation attempts that bring ethnic groups back into contact often spark further violence, "revenge killings," and new displacement—as was most recently the case in Kosovo.

In other situations warring parties have developed an interest in the persistence of conflict. The "blood diamond trade" in Sierra Leone and narcotrafficking in Colombia are cases in which the targeting of populations and ongoing displacement help perpetuate the conditions of violence, instability, and insecurity upon which illegal profitable activities thrive. Finally, in places such as Somalia, humanitarian aid itself has been increasingly appropriated by combatants. In these cases, ironically, assistance is transformed into a means for supporting the conflict that is producing displacement in the first place!

The problems of IDPs and the fact that fortress policies do not successfully contain forced migrations has led the international community to consider how to prevent displacement in the first place, by addressing its root causes. In the 1990s the international community took unprecedented steps by intervening in the internal affairs of Iraq and Serbia (Kosovo) in order to protect displaced people but also to prevent forced migration flows across international borders.

Ultimately, however, there is still reluctance on the part of most states and international organizations to challenge the principle of national sovereignty by interfering in the internal affairs of other countries. In conflicts that have produced large numbers of IDPs such as in Sierra Leone, Iraq, Chechnya, Colombia, and Bosnia-Herzegovina, assisting displaced populations has presented new challenges to policy-makers. The UN is an organization premised on the sovereignty of its members. Moreover the UNHCR can only act at the request and with the permission of sovereign governments. These realities have made it difficult for the UNHCR to provide assistance in some of these cases. The international NGO (non-governmental organizations) community remains divided on this issue. Some organizations have taken positions in cases such as Sudan and Sierra Leone that clearly prioritize assistance at the expense of considerations of national sovereignty.

THE ROLE OF NGOs

Over the last three decades international NGOs, including CARE, OXFAM, the International Rescue Committee, Doctors Without Borders, Catholic Relief Services, and Save the Children, have come to play a pivotal role in organizing and providing assistance to displaced and war-affected people worldwide. Many of these organizations work with UNHCR, doing much of the operational work on the ground. Increasingly they have influenced policy-makers and national governments by bringing the plight of displaced people to the attention of the global media, as in the recent cases of Rwanda and Kosovo.

Policy makers and humanitarian organizations have increasingly moved beyond merely providing assistance to protecting those assisted and those assisting from violence. Some organizations in the international humanitarian community have started to place a greater emphasis on promoting the human rights of the displaced. Thus the NGO, Doctors Without Borders—recipient of the 2000 Nobel Peace Prize—publicly denounces human rights violations, even if this insults a government and thereby prevents them from carrying out assistance activities. In some situations in which assistance has been diverted to serve the interests of combatants (such as in the Rwandan refugee camps in Eastern Zaire), or where human rights violations have been particularly grave (such as the Taliban's mistreatment of women in Afghanistan), some NGOs have ceased their assistance activity altogether. Other organizations such as the International Red Cross have chosen not to comment on human rights violations and remain politically neutral in order to continue providing assistance, even if it is diverted or has unintended and undesired consequences.

HUMANITARIAN ACTION

Anthropologists have increasingly examined the activities of the organizations that provide assistance to refugees. Barbara Harrell-Bond's landmark study, *Imposing Aid* (1986), confronted humanitarian organizations with research demonstrating that their activities were often more responsive to external pressures such as funding and inter-organizational rivalry than to the needs of the refugees themselves. My own work with the Humanitarianism and War Project showed how NGOs in Mozambique are primarily accountable to the interests of the government agencies that fund them rather than to the people who receive their services. As a result, decisions are often made that do not create sustainable solutions to the problems that are most important to locals. Instead assistance often serves to promote the international visibility or political agendas of donors.

Anthropologists also have shown that humanitarian assistance that does not create sustainable solutions or use local capacities causes considerable harm rather than helping refugee or other war-affected populations. In Mozambique my work demonstrated that the unwillingness of modern medical doctors to work with traditional medical practitioners created local suspicion and hostility that proved detrimental to public health. Locals tended to visit traditional medical practitioners first because they were less expensive. Since these practitioners had been alienated by the hospital doctors, they rarely referred sick patients to hospitals but instead would refer them only to other traditional medical practitioners. Consequently, patients often would arrive at hospitals only after a disease had progressed to a degree at which the costs for curing it were exceedingly high.

There have been important, recent collaborative attempts to improve humanitarian action and advocacy. The establishment in the mid-1990s of INTERACTION—a coalition of over 165 associations involved in humanitarian work—and the SPHERE initiative, to establish a voluntary charter with standards and ethical principles for humanitarian action, represent important developments in this direction.

Refugees and displacement are increasingly recognized as only one aspect of a set of interrelated political, economic, and military problems constituting what have come to be called "complex emergencies." Humanitarian assistance is only one component necessary for the solution of these challenges and by itself cannot solve the problems that displaced people face. International humanitarian assistance continues to gradually expand in scope to provide assistance to all populations affected by displacement (including IDPs, hosts, and even those left behind by forced migrants in devastated war zones—the "displaced in place"). However, it has become increasingly evident that humanitarian action only can be effective if the more fundamental political and economic roots of displacement and conflict are addressed. Anthropologists will continue to play an important role in studying the experiences of the displaced and the effects of displacement. However, they also have an important role to play in understanding the international political systems within which displacement occurs and in identifying the social factors that constrain and shape responses to displacement.

FURTHER READING

Ahearn, Frederick L. ed. 2000. *Psychosocial Wellness of Refugees: Issues in Qualitative and Quantitative Research.* Berghahn Books.

Bascom, Jonathan. 1998. *Losing Place: Refugees and Rural Transformations in East Africa.* Berghahn.

Black, Richard. 1998. *Refugees, Environment, and Development.* Longman.

Black, Richard, and Koser, Khalid, eds. 1999. *The End of the Refugee Cycle? Refugee Repatriation and Reconstruction.* Berghahn.

Cernea, Michael, and Christopher McDowell. 2000. *Risks and Reconstruction: Experiences of Resettlers and Refugees.* World Bank.

Cohen, Roberta, and Francis Deng. 1998. *Masses In Flight: The Global Crisis of Internal Displacement.* The Brookings Institute.

Colson, Elizabeth. 1971. *The Social Consequences of Resettlement.* Manchester University Press.

Daniel, E.V., and J. Knudsen, eds. *Mistrusting Refugees.* 1995. University of California Press.

Giles, Wenona, Helene Moussa and Van Esterlik, eds. 1996. *Development and Diaspora: Gender and the Refugee Experience.* Artemis Press.

Godziak, Elzbieta M., and Dianne J. Shandy, eds. 2000. *Rethinking Refuge and Displacement: Selected Papers on Refugees and Immigrants Volume VIII.* American Anthropological Association.

Hanes, David W., ed. 1996. *Refugees in America in the 1990s: A Reference Handbook.* Greenwood Press.

Harrell-Bond, Barbara. 1986. *Imposing Aid: Emergency Assistance to Refugees.* Oxford University Press.

Indra, Doreen, ed. 1999. *Engendering Forced Migration: Theory and Practice.* Berghahn.

Krufeld, Ruth M., and Jeffrey L. MacDonald. 1998. *Power, Ethics, and Human Rights: Anthropological Studies of Refugee Research and Action.* Rowman and Littlefield Publishers.

Kushner, Tony, and Katharine Knox. 1999. *Refugees in an Age of Genocide: Global, National, and Local Perspectives During the Twentieth Century.* Frank Cass.

Loescher, Gil. 1993. *Beyond Charity.* Oxford University Press.

Lubkemann, Stephen C. 2002. "Refugees." In *World at Risk: A Global Issues Sourcebook,* pp. 522-544. CQ Press. [This article, "Refugees," formed the basis for the much shorter AnthroNotes essay.]

Malkki, Lisa H. 1995. *Purity and Exile: Violence, Memory, and National Cosmology Among Hutu Refugees in Tanzania.* University of Chicago Press.

Minear, Larry. 2002. *The Humanitarian Enterprise.* Kumarian Press.

UNHCR. 1997. *The State of the World's Refugees: A Humanitarian Agenda.* Oxford University Press.

Van Hear, Nicholas. 1998. *New Diasporas: The Mass Exodus, Dispersal and Regrouping of Migrant Communities.* University College London Press.

REFUGEE PERIODICALS AND SERIALS

Disasters: The Journal of Disaster Studies, Policy and Management, published quarterly by the Overseas Development Institute and Blackwell Publishers, Oxford UK.

Forced Migration Review, published quarterly by the Refugee Studies Center, Oxford University, Oxford UK.

Humanitarianism and War Project Occasional Paper Series, published by Tufts University, Boston, MA.

International Journal of Refugee Law, published quarterly by Oxford University Press, Oxford, UK.

International Migration Review, published quarterly by the Center for Migration Studies, NY

Journal of Refugee Studies, published quarterly by Oxford University Press, Oxford, UK

New Issues in Refugee Research, occasional paper series published by the UNHCR Policy Studies Group, Geneva, Switzerland.

Refugee, published six times per year by the Centre for Refugee Studies, York University, Toronto, Canada.

Refugee Survey Quarterly, published quarterly by Oxford University Press.

Refugees, published quarterly by UNHCR, Geneva, Switzerland.

Selected Studies on Refugees and Immigrants, published annually by the Committee for Refugees and Immigrants (CORI), American Anthropological Association, Washington, DC.

State of the World's Refugees, published bi-annually by the UNHCR, Geneva, Switzerland.

World Refugee Survey, published annually by the US Committee for Refugees, Washington DC.

Stephen C. Lubkemann is assistant professor of anthropology at George Washington University and adjunct assistant professor of research at the Watson Institute for International Studies at Brown University.

9. Transnationalism, Localization, and Fast Foods in East Asia

James Watson

This article demonstrates to the readers how local consumers in Asia take the apparently homogenous processes of transnational capital and readjust McDonald's practices. The author is using the case of one fast food chain to show that the Western capitalism is changed as it

enters the markets, and the cultures of consumption, of the non-western world. This article is central in understanding how the emerging global culture and economy unfolds. Anthropological investigation uncovers quite a complex picture as global corporations must adapt to local cultures. This article shows the interactive development of capitalism and the articulation of consumption and identity.

On November 22, 1994, the *Wall Street Journal* announced that the world's busiest McDonald's restaurant, located in the heart of Beijing, would have to move to make room for a new commercial development. Within hours the story was picked up by wire services and splashed across the pages of newspapers and magazines around the world. McDonald's managers had situated their first Beijing outlet within a stone's throw of Tiananmen Square, one of China's primary tourist spots and a public arena for the celebration and contestation of Chinese national identity. News of the move came as a shock to company officials who were operating on the assumption that they had a 20-year lease on the premises. The message of the surprise relocation far outweighed its immediate commercial impact: If this could happen to McDonald's, potential investors reasoned, no one was safe.

Under ordinary circumstances, news of a restaurant relocation is unlikely to attract much attention. But this, of course, was no ordinary restaurant: it was McDonald's. The very name, its "Mc" prefix, and the ubiquitous Golden Arches are recognized and imitated throughout the world. McDonald's has become a saturated symbol, so laden with contradictory associations and meanings that the company stands for something greater than the sum of its corporate parts.

McDonald's sells more than food. In Beijing, for instance, a new class of yuppies has embraced the company as a means of connecting to the world outside China. Many of the people Yunxiang Yan interviewed said they did not like the food, but assumed that something more profound was at issue when eating at McDonald's. In Korea, by contrast, hamburgers and similar meat products have long been a feature of the national diet, so the actual taste of McDonald's standard fare is not considered new. But many Koreans equate eating a Big Mac with cultural and economic treason. Similarly in Taiwan, eating has become a political act and one's choice of restaurant—mainlander-owned or Taiwanese—may be taken as a reflection of attitudes toward independence or reunification with China. McDonald's and other fast food chains have boomed on this precarious terrain, assisted perhaps by the common perception that "foreign" foods are politically neutral. Meanwhile, in Japan McDonald's has made the transition from exotic to ordinary and the restaurants have blended into the local scene. Much the same can be said of Hong Kong. Since the early 1970s, an entire generation of Japanese and Hong Kong children has grown up with McDonald's; to these people the Big Mac, fries, and Coke do not represent something foreign. McDonald's is, quite simply, "local" cuisine.

McDonald's and the Cultural Imperialism Debate

Today over 30 million customers will be served at approximately 20,000 McDonald's restaurants in over 100 countries (See Table 1). In 1995 the system-wide sales of McDonald's Corporation totaled US$30 billion, $14 billion of which derived from restaurants outside the United States. A new McDonald's opens somewhere in the world every three hours.

Table 1: McDonald's Restaurants by Country, 1990–1995		
	1990	**1995**
Systemwide	11,803	18,380
United States	8,576	11,368
Japan	*776*	*1,482*
Canada	626	902
Germany	349	649
England	356	577
Australia	269	530
France	150	429
Brazil	63	243
Mexico	21	132
Taiwan	*43*	*111*
Sweden	49	106
Hong Kong	*51*	*98*
New Zealand	46	98
Philippines	32	83
Singapore	34	78
China	*1[a]*	*62*
Malaysia	22	58
South Korea	*4*	*48*
Thailand	6	39
Indonesia	0	38

SOURCE: 1995 Annual Report, McDonald's Corp., McD36-3030, p. ii.
[a]Shenzhen Special Economic Zone.

What do these statistics mean? The answer, of course, depends upon one's point of view. Some readers no doubt welcome McDonald's ascendancy as evidence that free market values prevail everywhere, irrespective of geography or cultural differences ("All the World's a McStage"). This viewpoint is reflected in the news media that track McDonald's and report on its every triumph ("Big Mac Goes to Mecca"). In preparing for this project I read thousands of newspaper, magazine, and trade journal articles about the worldwide fast food industry. There can be little doubt that McDonald's enjoys a special, perhaps even privileged, relationship with U.S. media—a tribute to the company's virtuosity in public relations. Positive articles far outweigh negative or neutral ones. The reverse appears to be true in Britain, owing largely to McDonald's disastrous decision to sue local environmentalists ("Big Mac Makes a Meal of It As Libel Trial Drags On"). With the possible exception of Korea, media reports in East Asia tend to be positive. The Chinese media could barely restrain their enthusiasm for McDonald's during the restaurants' first three years of operation in the People's Republic; the company was celebrated as a model of modernization, sanitation, and responsible management.

More recently, however, Chinese political leaders have expressed alarm at the growing influence of McDonald's, Kentucky Fried Chicken (KFC), Pizza Hut, and other foreign food firms. As Chinese state policy has begun to encourage an indigenous fast food industry, local media coverage has shifted accordingly. Chinese leaders appear to be aligning themselves with

European and American intellectuals who have long equated McDonald's and its rivals in the fast food industry as agents of *cultural imperialism*—a new form of exploitation that results from the export of popular culture from the United States, Japan, and Europe to other parts of the world. "Culture" in this context is defined as popular music, television, film, video, pulp fiction, comics, advertising, fashion, home design, and mass-produced food. Corporations that are capable of manipulating personal "tastes" will thrive as state authorities lose control over the distribution and consumption of goods and services. Popular culture, in this view, generates a vision, a fantasy, of the good life, and if the Big Mac, Coke, and Disney cartoons are perceived as an integral part of that life, American companies cannot lose.

Theorists who write about cultural imperialism argue that it is the domination of popular culture—rather than outright military or political control—that matters most in the postmodern, postsocialist, postindustrial world." One of the clearest expressions of this view appeared recently on the Op-Ed page of the *New York Times*. The voice is Ronald Steel's: "It was never the Soviet Union, but the United States itself that is the true revolutionary power. . . . We purvey a culture based on mass entertainment and mass gratification. . . . The cultural message we transmit through Hollywood and McDonald's goes out across the world to capture, and also to undermine, other societies. . . . Unlike more traditional conquerors, we are not content merely to subdue others: We insist that they be like us.

McDonald's as a Corrosive Force?

Does the spread of fast food undermine the integrity of indigenous cuisines? Are food chains helping to create a homogenous, global culture better suited to the needs of a capitalist world order?

This book is specifically designed to address such questions. The authors of the following case studies have different perspectives on the cultural imperialism debate, reflecting circumstances in the societies studied. We do not celebrate McDonald's as a paragon of capitalist virtue, nor do we condemn the corporation as an evil empire. Our goal is to produce ethnographic accounts of McDonald's social, political, and economic impact on five local cultures. These are not small-scale cultures under imminent threat of extinction; we are dealing with economically resilient, technologically advanced societies noted for their haute cuisines. If McDonald's can make inroads in these societies, one might be tempted to conclude, it may indeed be an irresistible force for world culinary change. But isn't another scenario possible? Have people in East Asia conspired to change McDonald's, modifying this seemingly monolithic institution to fit local conditions?

The essays in this book demonstrate that the interaction process works both ways. McDonald's *has* effected small but influential changes in East Asian dietary patterns. Until the introduction of McDonald's, for example, Japanese consumers rarely, if ever, ate with their hands; this is now an acceptable mode of dining. In Hong Kong, McDonald's has replaced traditional teahouses and street stalls as the most popular breakfast venue. And among Taiwanese youth, french fries have become a dietary staple, owing almost entirely to the influence of McDonald's.

At the same time, however, East Asian consumers have quietly, and in some cases stubbornly, transformed their neighborhood McDonald's into local institutions. In the United States fast food may indeed imply fast consumption, but this is certainly not the case everywhere. In Beijing, Seoul, and Taipei, for instance, McDonald's restaurants are treated as leisure centers, where people can retreat from the stresses of urban life. In Hong Kong, middle school students often sit in McDonald's for hours—studying, gossiping, and picking over snacks; for them, the restaurants are the equivalent of youth clubs. More will be said about the localization process in the following chapters. Suffice it to note here that McDonald's does not always call the shots.

Globalism and Local Cultures

Those who have followed academic and business trends in recent years are aware that two new "isms" are much in vogue—globalism and transnationalism. Many writers use these terms interchangeably. In my view the two -isms represent different social processes and should not be conflated. Globalism describes an essentially impossible condition that is said to prevail when people the world over share a homogenous, mutually intelligible culture. Proponents of globalism assume that electronic communications and mass media (especially television) will create a "global village." This global system is sustained, the argument proceeds, by technologically sophisticated elites who speak the same language (American English), maintain a common lifestyle, and share similar aspirations. To quote one observer of globalism, Benjamin Barber, the "future [is] a busy portrait of onrushing economic, technological, and economic forces that demand integration and uniformity and that mesmerize peoples everywhere with fast music, fast computers, and fast food—MTV, Macintosh, and McDonald's—pressing nations into one homogeneous global theme park, one McWorld tied together by communications, information, entertainment, and commerce."

In its most recent guise, globalism has resurfaced as a logical projection of the digital revolution. According to various digirati, notably those associated with *Wired* magazine, Internet enthusiasts have already begun to create a global culture that will negate—or at least undermine—the traditional state. Web visionaries also predict that ideologies based on class, religion, and ethnicity will recede as the global system becomes a reality. This new utopian literature is reminiscent of early Marxist visions of a stateless, classless world devoid of ethnic and religious divisions. Underlying globalist theories is the idea that people the world over will share a common culture, but few of these modern visionaries bother to clarify what they mean by "culture"—it is simply taken for granted.

From the very beginning of anthropology as an academic discipline, debates about the meaning of culture have united and divided anthropologists. Of late, the tone of this debate has become especially strident, separating the good from the bad, the enlightened from the ignorant. In its earlier usage culture was defined by most anthropologists as a shared set of beliefs, customs, and ideas that held people together in coherent groups. In recent decades, however, the notion of coherence has come under attack by ethnosemanticists, who have discovered that people in supposedly close-knit groups (bands of hunters, factory workers. bureaucrats) do not share a single system of knowledge. Culture, therefore, is not something that people inherit as an undifferentiated bloc of knowledge from their ancestors. Culture is a set of ideas, reactions, and expectations that is constantly changing as people and groups themselves change.

In this book the operative term is "local culture," shorthand for the experience of everyday life as lived by ordinary people in specific localities. In using it, we attempt to capture the feelings of appropriateness, comfort, and correctness that govern the construction of personal preferences, or "tastes." Dietary patterns, attitudes toward food, and notions of what constitutes a proper meal (a concept discussed by all contributors) are central to the experience of everyday life and hence are integral to the maintenance of local cultures.

As noted above, there are serious questions attending the use of the term "culture," and the word "local" is similarly problematic. Both notions imply an inherent sameness within a given population, irrespective of class, gender, or status differences. When this style of analysis is carried to its logical extreme the result is essentialism, which leads one to assume that "the Chinese" (for example) share an essential, irreducible core of beliefs and attributes that separates them from other categories of people, such as "the Koreans." It is obvious that all Chinese do not share the same mental framework, nor do they always agree on what constitutes appropriate or correct behavior.

Readers will note that the authors of this book have made efforts to highlight class, gender, and status differences, especially in relation to consumption practices. One surprise was the discovery that many McDonald's restaurants in East Asia have become sanctuaries for women who wish to avoid male-dominated settings. In Beijing and Seoul, new categories of yuppies treat McDonald's as an arena for conspicuous consumption. Anthropologists who work in such settings must pay close attention to rapid changes in consumer preferences. Twenty years ago McDonald's catered to the children of Hong Kong's wealthy elite; the current generation of Hong Kong hyperconsumers has long since abandoned the Golden Arches and moved upmarket to more expensive watering holes (e.g., Planet Hollywood). Meanwhile, McDonald's has become a mainstay for working-class people, who are attracted by its low cost, convenience, and predictability.

One of our conclusions in this book is that societies in East Asia are changing as fast as cuisines—there is nothing immutable or primordial about cultural systems. In Hong Kong, for instance, it would be impossible to isolate what is specifically "local" about the cuisine, given the propensity of Hong Kong people to adopt new foods. Hong Kong's cuisine, and with it, Hong Kong's local culture, is a moving target. Hong Kong is the quintessential postmodern environment, where the boundaries of status, style, and taste dissolve almost as fast as they are formed. What is "in" today is "out" tomorrow.

Transnationalism and the Multilocal Corporation

It has become an academic cliché to argue that people are constantly reinventing themselves. Nevertheless, the speed of that reinvention process in places like Hong Kong, Taipei, and Seoul is so rapid that it defies description. In the realm of popular culture, it is no longer possible to distinguish between what is "local" and what is "foreign." Who is to say that Mickey Mouse is not Japanese, or that Ronald McDonald is not Chinese? To millions of children who watch Chinese television, "Uncle McDonald" (alias Ronald) is probably more familiar than the mythical characters of Chinese folklore.

We have entered here the realm of the transnational, a new field of study that focuses on the "deterritorialization" of popular culture. As Arjun Appadurai notes, the world economy can no longer be understood by assuming that the original producers of a commodity necessarily control its consumption. A good example is the spread of "Asian" martial arts to North and South America, fostered by Hollywood and the Hong Kong film industry. Transnationalism describes a condition by which people, commodities, and ideas literally cross—transgress—national boundaries and are not identified with a single place of origin. One of the leading theorists of this new field argues that transnational phenomena are best perceived as the building blocks of "third cultures," which are "oriented beyond national boundaries."

Transnational corporations are popularly regarded as the clearest expressions of this new adaptation, given that business operations, manufacturing, and marketing are often spread around the globe, to dozens of societies. The Nike Corporation, a US-based firm that began operation in Japan, is an excellent case in point. One of the company's most popular products is the Air Max Penny, inspired by an American basketball player whose nickname is Penny. The shoe contains 52 separate components produced in five countries (Japan, South Korea, Taiwan, Indonesia, and the United States). By the time it is finished, the Penny has passed through at least 120 pairs of hands. The final product is assembled by Chinese workers in a Taiwanese-owned factory just north of Hong Kong; design work is done by American technicians at a research center in Tennessee. Nike itself does not own any factories. Instead, the company relies on an international team of specialists who negotiate with manufacturers, monitor production, and arrange shipment.

The classic model of the transnational corporation assumes a non-national, or even anti-national, mode of production controlled from a headquarters complex located somewhere in the First World. Dispersed production and centralized control would certainly appear to be the norm in the transnational food and beverage industry: Coca-Cola's far-flung empire is based in Atlanta; KFC in Louisville; Heinz in Pittsburgh; Kellogg's in Battle Creek, Michigan; Carr's, the biscuit maker, in Carlisle, England. The list could easily fill this page and the next.

At first glance, McDonald's would appear to be the quintessential transnational: It operates in more than 100 countries and maintains a sprawling headquarters complex in Oak Brook, Illinois—the home of Hamburger University. On closer inspection, however, the company does not conform to expectations; it resembles a federation of semiautonomous enterprises. James Cantalupo, President of McDonald's International, claims that the goal of McDonald's is to "become as much a part of the local culture as possible." He objects when "[p]eople call us a multinational. I like to call us *multilocal,*" meaning that McDonald's goes to great lengths to find local suppliers and local partners whenever new branches are opened. To support his claims, Cantalupo notes that, in 1991, there were fewer than 20 American expatriate managers working in overseas operations. Yunxiang Yan discovered that only one American—a Chinese-speaker—worked in the Beijing headquarters of McDonald's; all of the managers encountered by Sangmee Bak in Seoul were Korean nationals; and in Japan, decisions have been in local hands since the company's opening in 1971. In fact, it was McDonald's early experience in Japan that set the tone for future overseas operations. As John Love notes, the Japanese case "proved that the key to success in the international market was the same as it was [in the United States]: local control by local owner-operators."

Research in this book reveals that McDonald's International retains at least a 50 percent stake in its East Asian enterprises; the other half is owned by local operators. Soon after McDonald's opened in Korea, a major political debate erupted over the disposition of local profits. Was the goal of the company to enrich American stockholders or to help build the Korean economy? Korean managers confronted their critics by arguing that local franchisees owned half the business and that a high percentage of profits was plowed back into its Korea-based operations. Sangmee Bak notes that local managers insisted that the Korean business environment was so complicated that foreigners could not hope to survive on their own. They took great pride in their accomplishments and told Bak that theirs was a Korean business. In Korea—as in China, Taiwan, and Japan—McDonald's goes out of its way to find local suppliers for its operations. Hong Kong is the lone exception; owing to its special geographic circumstances, raw materials are no longer produced there, and nearly everything McDonald's uses has to be imported. (Since its repatriation on July 1, 1997, however, one could argue that Hong Kong no longer relies on "imports," given that most of its supplies come from mainland China.)

McDonald's localization strategy has been so successful that two of its East Asian managers have become international celebrities: Den Fujita, Managing Director, Japan, and Daniel Ng, Managing Director, Hong Kong. These men are credited with turning what appeared to be impossible tasks ("Selling hamburgers in Tokyo or Hong Kong? You must be joking!") into dramatic success stories. Fujita and Ng are media stars in their respective countries; like Ray Kroc, founder of McDonald's in the United States, they have become entrepreneurial legends who extol the virtues of hard work, personal discipline, and the free market. (Another such living legend is, of course, George Cohon, President of McDonald's Canada and the impresario of McDonald's Moscow; in 1991 *Pravda* proved it had a sense of humor by designating Cohon a "Hero of Capitalist Labor.")

Behind each of these success stories lies the ability to discern, and respond to, consumer needs. Daniel Ng, for instance, established his own research unit and ran focus groups to monitor the changing attitudes of ordinary customers; he is also a keen observer of the popular culture scene in Hong Kong. The independent natures of these local managers (not to mention their sheer chutzpah) underline the obvious: McDonald's transnational success is due in large part to its multilocal mode of operation. There is, however, another critical factor in the equation—good timing.

The Family Revolution in East Asia: Children as Consumers

It is certainly no coincidence that the startup dates for McDonald's (see Table 2) correspond to the emergence of new classes of affluent consumers in the various East Asian countries. Rising incomes have produced dramatic changes in lifestyles, especially among young people who live and work in metropolitan areas. Decisions regarding employment and consumption no longer require consultations with an extended network of parents, grandparents, adult siblings, and other kin. Married women are working outside the home in increasing numbers, which in turn has affected gender relations, child-rearing practices, and residence patterns. A majority of newlyweds are opting for neolocality (forming a new household separate from those of their parents) or creating new arrangements that defy convention. In Taiwan, for instance, professional women often insist on living near their own parents, rather than follow the more "traditional" pattern of patrilocality (living with or near the husband's parents). The crucial factor here is the household labor—childminding, cooking, shopping—provided by the working woman's mother, whose assistance makes her daughter's professional life possible.

Table 2: Startup Dates for McDonald's in Various Countries			
1955	Franchising begins in U.S.A.	1984	Taiwan
1967	Canada	1985	Thailand
1971	Japan	1985	Mexico
1971	Australia	1986	Turkey
1971	Germany	1988	South Korea
1972	France	1990	China (Shenzhen Special Economic Zone)
1973	Sweden	1990	Russia
1974	England	1991	Indonesia
1975	Hong Kong	1992	China (Beijing)
1976	New Zealand	1992	Poland
1979	Brazil	1993	Israel
1979	Singapore	1994	Saudi Arabia
1981	Philippines	1995	South Africa
1982	Malaysia	1996	Croatia

SOURCES: *1994 Student Information Packet,* McDonald's Corporation, McD1-1274, p. 38; *New York Times,* Nov. 12, 1995, and Feb. 5, 1996.

In response to these changes a new family structure has emerged, one that focuses on the needs and aspirations of the conjugal unit, the married *couple.* Conjugality brings with it an entire set of attitudes and practices that undermine older assumptions regarding the meaning of life. Should married couples strive, regardless of personal cost, to promote the welfare of the larger kin group and support aging parents? Or should they concentrate on building a more comfortable life for themselves and their immediate offspring? Increasingly, the balance is shifting toward conjugality and away from the family norms that guided earlier generations.

The shift also coincides with a dramatic decline in the birthrate and a rise in the amount of money and attention lavished on children. China's single-child-family policy has helped produce a generation of Little Emperors and Empresses, each commanding the affection and economic support of two parents and in many cases four grandparents. McDonald's has capitalized on the Little Emperor/ress phenomenon, treating children as independent decision makers who command substantial resources. Similar patterns of indulgence are common in Taiwan and in Japan, where children command impressive amounts of spending money. In 1995, Hong Kong parents gave junior high school students an average of US$107 per month to spend on snacks and entertainment.

McDonald's restaurants first appeared in East Asian cities during the early phases of this family revolution. When one looks closely at the historical sequence summarized below, it is obvious that entrepreneurial flair alone cannot explain the corporation's phenomenal success rate.

Tokyo, 1971

An affluent middle class has matured by the early 1970s, and a new generation of consumers can afford to eat out on a regular basis. McDonald's takeoff corresponds to the emergence of the "teens," a hitherto unrecognized stage in the Japanese life course. For the first time in Japanese history, all young people are expected to stay in school until age 18. These leisured youths become avid consumers of American-style fast foods and popular culture.

Hong Kong, 1975

McDonald's opening date marks the beginning of a long economic boom in Hong Kong as the British colony becomes an international services center and a transshipment port for the China trade. A white-collar middle class rapidly replaces Hong Kong's postwar working class. By the mid-1970s the majority of residents are living in neolocal, conjugal units and are preoccupied with their own offspring rather than a wider network of kin. Children and young adults emerge as full-fledged consumers in the late 1970s and early 1980s. McDonald's becomes the "in" place to eat.

Taipei, 1984

McDonald's is the first foreign food company allowed to operate in Taiwan's previously closed market. The start-up corresponds to the beginning of a new political era, one in which local interests challenge the authoritarian rule of the Nationalist Party. The Golden Arches arrive just as Taiwan reaches takeoff as a major player in the global electronics and computer markets. Taiwan's emerging middle class begins to have time and money to spend on leisure activities. Family patterns change rapidly to accommodate urban life and the regular employment of married women. Older forms of childhood socialization, emphasizing filiality and obedience, are gradually de-emphasized to accommodate practices that encourage consumerism. Taipei's youth embrace McDonald's as a symbol of their new lifestyle.

Seoul, 1988

McDonald's is the first foreign food chain permitted to operate in Korea. An indigenous middle class has emerged after decades of personal sacrifice and deferred gratification by the previous generation of workers. Salaried employees (mostly male) have little spare time for family activities, but their dependents begin to enjoy a lifestyle defined by consumerism. Korean children rapidly become knowledgeable consumers, eager to eat hamburgers, pizza, and American-style chicken. The persuasive power of this new generation is impressive: Many parents who object to foreign imports find themselves arranging birthday parties for their children at McDonald's.

Beijing, 1992

Family patterns in urban China have been changing rapidly since the introduction of economic reforms in the late 1970s and early 1980s. McDonald's enters the Chinese scene during a critical period of class formation; for the first time since the communist victory of 1949, independent entrepreneurs and business people are allowed to operate openly. Affluent families begin to distinguish themselves by engaging in conspicuous consumption and McDonald's becomes a powerful symbol of the new lifestyle. By the mid-1990s a booming market in children's entertainment (theme parks, video parlors, computer games) has emerged. McDonald's is expanding rapidly in China to capitalize on these cultural developments; plans call for up to 600 outlets by the year 2003.

One conclusion is obvious: McDonald's could not have succeeded in East Asia without appealing to younger generations of consumers, children and teenagers. The corporation makes a point of cultivating this market and invests heavily in television advertising aimed specifically at children. Birthday parties have become a key element in this strategy: Prior to McDonald's entry into the local scene, festivities to mark the specific birthdates of youngsters were unknown in most parts of East Asia. In Hong Kong, for instance, calendrical dates of birth were recorded for use later in life (in matching the horoscopes of prospective marriage partners, for instance), but until the late 1970s most people paid little attention to the annual event—if indeed they remembered it at all.

McDonald's and its rivals in the fast food industry have promoted the birthday party—complete with cake and candles—in their advertising and, as the case studies in this book make clear, the celebrations have become the rage among upwardly mobile youngsters throughout East Asia. McDonald's also introduced other, localized innovations that appeal directly to their youngest customers. In Beijing, the company's ubiquitous male mascot, Ronald, has been paired with a female companion known as Aunt McDonald, whose job it is to entertain children and attend parties. In Taipei and Hong Kong, McDonald's offers parents a special party package that includes gifts and toys for each participant, plus the services of a hostess who leads the children in songs and games. Parties of this type have become an integral feature of the local culture.

More than any other factor, therefore, McDonald's success is attributable to the revolution in family values that has transformed East Asia. Furthermore, as demonstrated repeatedly in this book, the localization process depends heavily upon children: In Japan and Hong Kong, McDonald's did not make the transition from foreign import to "local" institution until the first generation of childhood consumers began to have children of their own. Generational succession is not yet complete in Taiwan. Children are driving the localization process. It is too early to call the outcome in Korea and China, but children everywhere are powerful agents of social change.

Standardization and Taste: The McDonald's System

One characteristic of this book distinguishing it from previous studies of the fast food industry is our focus on *consumption*: we place primary emphasis on the role of consumers. As noted in the Preface, we have chosen not to concentrate exclusively on *production*. Before we proceed, however, something needs to be said about McDonald's efforts to standardize its product, given that consistency and predictability are important keys to the company's worldwide appeal. What follows is a brief summary of the fast food industry, its history and productive processes. Readers who are interested in specific aspects of production (including management, labor relations, food sourcing, and mechanization) might wish to pursue the references cited in the endnotes.

McDonald's, of course, did not invent fast food, although the corporation is largely responsible for the standardization and automation we now take for granted in the industry. Nearly every country has a candidate for the original "fast" cuisine: fish and chips in Britain, noodles in China, station box lunches (*ekibentō*) in Japan, street kebabs in Turkey, sausage and bread in Germany (which later metamorphosed into the ubiquitous American hot dog). One key to McDonald's success is the constant push to speed up production without sacrificing consistency. Corporate goals announced in late 1995 include the filling of walk-in orders within 90 seconds and a guarantee that customers will never have to wait more than three-and-a-half minutes at drive-through windows. Company representatives monitor performance by making surprise visits to McDonald's outlets every quarter.

McDonald's has created a *system* that depends upon standardized procedures in everything from sandwich assembly to advanced management training at Hamburger University. An excellent summary of McDonald's operating procedures can be found in *Fast Food, Fast Talk*, a study of the standardization of work in the United States; the author, Robin Leidner, characterizes McDonald's as "an exemplar of extreme standardization." A 600-page *Operations and Training Manual* guides production. Nothing is left to chance; photo layouts show where the sauces should be placed on the bun, and the exact thickness of sliced pickles is specified. All equipment at McDonald's restaurants must be purchased from approved suppliers, and the architectural design of both interior and exterior is carefully controlled. McDonald's does not condone "absentee" owners, nor will it work with partnerships (i.e., multiple owners); franchise holders must be involved in the day-to-day management of the restaurant. In 1991 over 20,000 people contacted the company to inquire about new franchises; only 2,000 reached the interview stage and fewer than 200 were accepted.

As Robert Kwan, Managing Director of McDonald's in Singapore, puts it: "McDonald's sells . . . a system, not products." The aim is to create a standardized set of items that taste the same in Singapore, Spain, and South Africa. Many travelers have told me (with a tone of triumph in their voices) that they can indeed perceive slight differences in the taste of Big Macs they have sampled in Beijing or Paris. Such claims are, however, difficult to verify. Thomas Friedman of the *New York Times* reports that he has eaten Big Macs at McDonald's in 14 countries (all, no doubt, in the line of journalistic duty) and maintains that "they all *really do* taste the same." Based on personal visits to McDonald's in the five sites surveyed in this book—plus England, Germany, the Netherlands, and the United States—I side with Mr. Friedman on the question of taste.

McDonald's may not be able to control the taste responses of individual consumers, but it *can* make the experience of eating relatively predictable. The corporation pays close attention to restaurant design, down to the exact measurements of service counters, placement of overhead backlit menus (an innovation that is now widely imitated throughout the world), arrangement of seats and booths, color of walls and style of decorations, and the location of (standardized) disposal bins. Who has not had the uncanny sensation of déjà vu when entering a McDonald's restaurant in a foreign country? "It's just like home."

The familiarity factor is central to McDonald's success, especially in societies like the United States, where job mobility is a regular feature of family life. To many disoriented, lonely children, the Golden Arches symbolize more than just food; McDonald's stands for home, familiarity, and friendship. One finding of this book is that American children are not alone in this response. A surprisingly high percentage of young people in Tokyo, Taipei, and Hong Kong have grown up with McDonald's as their favorite venue for entertaining family and friends. It was not the power of corporate sponsorship alone that made McDonald's the "official food service partner" during the 1996 Olympic Games in Atlanta. Athletes from around the world were familiar enough with McDonald's fare to accept it without question, thereby avoiding potentially disastrous encounters with strange foods. Americans abroad report similar reactions. On his way home from China after an exhausting business trip, the CEO of Microsoft, Bill Gates, found himself in Hong Kong with a colleague, looking for a place to eat after midnight: "We were really happy to discover that they have 24-hour McDonald's in Hong Kong," said Gates, as he "wolfed down hamburgers."

Modified Menus and Local Sensitivities: McDonald's Adapts

The key to McDonald's worldwide success is that people everywhere know what to expect when they pass through the Golden Arches. This does not mean, however, that the corporation has resisted change or refused to adapt when local customs require flexibility. In Israel, after initial protests, Big Macs are now served without cheese in several outlets, thereby permitting the separation of meat and dairy products required of kosher restaurants. McDonald's restaurants in India serve Vegetable McNuggets and a mutton-based Maharaja Mac, innovations that are necessary in a country where Hindus do not eat beef, Muslims do not eat pork, and Jains (among others) do not eat meat of any type. In Malaysia and Singapore, McDonald's underwent rigorous inspections by Muslim clerics to ensure ritual cleanliness; the chain was rewarded with a *halal* ("clean," "acceptable") certificate, indicating the total absence of pork products.

Variations on McDonald's original, American-style menu exist in many parts of the world: Chilled yogurt drinks (*ayran*) in Turkey, espresso and cold pasta in Italy, teriyaki burgers in Japan (also in Taiwan and Hong Kong), vegetarian burgers in the Netherlands, McSpagetti in the Philippines, McLaks (grilled salmon sandwich) in Norway, frankfurters and beer in Germany, McHuevo (poached egg hamburger) in Uruguay.

Not all McDonald's menu innovations have been embraced by consumers: Witness the famous McLean Deluxe fiasco in the United States and a less publicized disaster called McPloughman's in Britain (a cheese-and-pickle sandwich). The corporation has responded to constant criticism from nutritionists and natural food activists by introducing prepackaged salads, fresh celery and carrot sticks, fat-free bran muffins, and low-fat milk shakes. These efforts may satisfy critics but they are unlikely to change McDonald's public image among consumers, few of whom stop at the Golden Arches for health food.

Irrespective of local variations (espresso, McLaks) and recent additions (carrot sticks), the structure of the McDonald's menu remains essentially uniform the world over: main course burger/sandwich, fries, and a drink—overwhelmingly Coca-Cola. The keystone of this winning combination is *not*, as most observers might assume, the Big Mac or even the generic hamburger. It is the fries. The main course may vary widely (fish sandwiches in Hong Kong, vegetable burgers in Amsterdam), but the signature innovation of McDonald's—thin, elongated fries cut from russet potatoes—is ever-present and consumed with great gusto by Muslims, Jews, Christians, Buddhists, Hindus, vegetarians (now that vegetable oil is used), communists, Tories, marathoners, and armchair athletes. It is understandable, therefore, why McDonald's has made such a fetish of its deep-fried potatoes and continues to work on improving the delivery of this industry winner. The Chairman of Burger King acknowledges that his company's fries are second-best in comparison to those of its archrival: "Our fries just don't hold up." A research program, code-named "stealth fries," is specifically designed to upgrade Burger King's offerings.

10. Across Space and Through Time:

Tomatl Meets the Corporate Tomato

Deborah Barndt

This article discusses how the economy of one area in Mexico has depended on the capital and consumption patterns in Canada and the U.S. It graphically portrays how tomato has transformed from a subsistence crop to a cash crop. The tomato story in this article is a good microcosm to tell us about how subsistence crop became an automobile-like commodity. North American corporations have even patented the seeds of certain strains of tomato. Ironically, Mexican tomato growers, whose predecessors domesticated the plant now have to pay for the seeds. Some local peasants have become wage workers for big tomato agribusinesses operated by corporations to the north. This article gives us a vivid description of production processes and the commodity chains.

The history of the tomato can reveal the unfolding global food system and the shifting role of women workers within it. In this chapter, we begin to excavate tangled *roots* and to follow the tangled *routes* of the tomato through the intertwining stories of Tomatl and the corporate tomato.

A group of popular educators from Mexico, the United States, and Canada created a skit at a 1994 conference dramatizing these two stories. "Tomasita Tells All: The True Story of the Abused Tomato" offers us a brief historical review of the shift from subsistence agriculture (Tomatl) to industrialized and globalized food production (the corporate tomato). A Mexican artist turned the drama into a cartoon story, excerpted on p. 142.

While the cartoons presented here simplify a long and complex history, they nonetheless reflect two distinct approaches to growing food that can be seen in contention not only across time but also in the present context. While the monocultural production depicted in the large fields of look-alike tomatoes predominates in the NAFTA era, subsistence agricultural traditions and sustainable farming practices persist not only among many Mexican campesinos

but also in the north where community-based rural and urban agricultural initiatives are reclaiming more ecologically sustainable production practices. Tomasita's story is definitely tangled, like roots and routes, across both time and space.

There are, in fact, competing strategies, in dynamic interaction through the production, distribution, and consumption of the tomato. In this chapter, we trace Tomasita's journey through history and across the continent, weaving two separate but interrelated stories. Two main characters introduce the contrasting approaches to growing food: Tomatl is the home-grown tomato, named with the Indigenous name it was given in Aztec times; the corporate tomato is the fruit in its more familiar commodified form, produced in large quantities through multiple technological interventions. While the focus will be on the journey of the corporate tomato, we will periodically refer to the contrasting and shorter journey of Tomatl, from pre-colonial to postcolonial times.

In tracing the trail from Mexican field to Canadian fast-food restaurant, we move through the three NAFTA countries, from south to north, on a journey that is clearly not a straight line. To simplify the story, I am dividing the process into three major stages following the trip north:

- the production of tomatoes in Mexico;
- their transport, trade, and distribution into the United States and Canada; and
- their commercialization and consumption in Canada.

Each stage will be graphically summarized, providing the traveler with a kind of road map. While the linear south-north trajectory suggested here reflects a predominant dynamic of the south producing for the north, all three phases—production, distribution, and consumption of tomatoes—take place in each of these three countries, as well as in others around the planet. This journey could, in fact, have many other starting and ending points, the processes described here playing out differently in other contexts.

I am building on the tradition of global commodity chain (GCC) analysis, an approach developed by Gary Gereffi and others to understand the current forms of capitalism in which production and consumption not only have crossed national boundaries but have been reorganized under a "structure of dense networked firms or enterprises." While my framing of the tomato story does not follow a classic commodity chain analysis, it does try to link the particular and general, the local and global aspects of tomato production and consumption.

Gereffi distinguishes between producer-driven commodity chains, in which transnational corporations control production networks, and buyer-driven commodity chains, in which large retailers and brand-named merchandisers shape and coordinate decentralized production networks while controlling design and marketing themselves. Because the corporate tomato moves from globalizing Mexican agribusiness and processing plants to Canadian supermarkets and restaurants that are also globalized, we will see both types of chains in their overlapping complexity.

This chapter foregrounds the story of the tomato, leaving the workers who move the tomato along this chain in the background for now. As the stories of women workers unfold in subsequent chapters, we will also see what commodity chain analysis suggests are the two primary factors in the restructuring of the global economy: the search for low-wage labor and the pursuit of organizational flexibility. What I bring to the commodity chain approach is an ecological perspective and a gendered analysis, integrating as well race, age, and regional differences.

In a popular education workshop with immigrant women in Toronto, Neema, a Trinidadian woman, described the global food system like this: "It seems like one big puzzle and we don't have all the pieces. So we've got to see if we can fit all the pieces together and get a clearer picture of what's going on." This is no easy task. In my particular telling of the tomato tale, the overall impression is of a long and twisty trail, a many-staged journey that no one under-

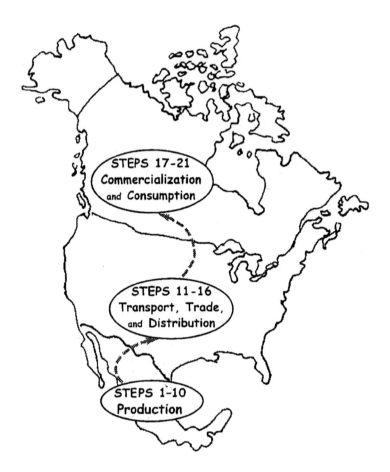

stands in its entirety. We were most struck by this fact as we interviewed campesino and company vice president, cashier and chief buyer alike: no one person has the whole picture; each actor in this complex chain perhaps has some sense of the steps that come just before and after his or hers, but sometimes not even that much.

Of course, each stage is perceived differently by each person engaged in it; these multiple subjectivities, in fact, make the story not only contradictory but also more human. It is a daunting task to piece together the puzzle. I have confronted roadblocks and detours, discovered diversions and surprising openings. In this telling, I have chosen to follow certain tangential paths and not others. This is a constantly changing process that I personally can't hope to unveil fully.

I am arbitrarily dividing the journey into twenty-one steps (for the corporate tomato's journey) and five stages (for Tomatl and alternative practices); each step or stage introduces a key issue to be explored later through the case studies of Mexican agribusiness and Canadian food retail and service industries. This brief review thus opens the windows to places and processes to be examined in more depth throughout the book. The tangled journeys make us realize we

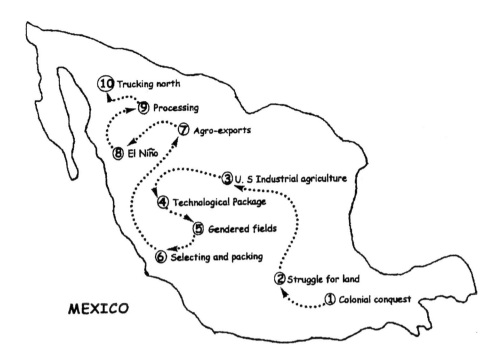

cannot separate our survival in the north from the survival of people in the south, nor the fate of human beings from the fate of the earth. The corporate journey is described in steps (numbers 1, 2, 3), while we can follow Tomatl's story (designated as stages and marked by Roman numerals—I, II, III) from the margins: the survival of more sustainable locally controlled growing practices.

TOMATL'S STORY FROM THE MARGINS

Stage I: Tomato's Beginnings in Pre-Hispanic America

The tomato originated as a wild plant in the Andean region (what is now northwest Peru), its seeds then probably carried north by birds to what is now Mexico, centuries before the time of Christ. First domesticated by the Mayans and the Aztecs, the fruit was named *tomatl*, which in Nahuatl, the language of the Aztecs, means "something round and plump." For centuries the tomato was a native crop grown by Indigenous peoples in Mexico to feed their families. Using traditional agricultural practices, they grew tomatoes in great variety, interplanted them with other crops, and rotated crops from year to year, in the context of complex local ecosystems. Wild tomato species, for example, supplied other varieties of tomatoes with resistance to nineteen major plant diseases.

COURTESY OF GETTY IMAGES, INC.

THE JOURNEY OF THE CORPORATE TOMATO

Step 1: Colonial Conquest of the "Love Apple"

In the sixteenth century, the Spanish conquistadores received tomatoes as part of tributes from Indigenous peoples in the Americas and eventually took the plant back to Europe along with other natural riches they had "discovered." There it was initially feared as poisonous and primarily considered decorative as a "love apple," until Italians began to embrace it in their cuisine. French settlers carried tomatoes to Quebec and Louisiana in the eighteenth century, and it was soon proclaimed medicinal and promoted by agricultural innovators such as Thomas Jefferson. Since then the tomato has been central to diets in the Americas and considered rich in vitamins (A and C) and minerals (calcium and potassium), especially when ripe. It has been bred into hundreds of hybrid forms; the most common big round red version, *Solanum lycopersicon* in Latin, is known in Mexico as *jitomate*. The tomato is now the most widely grown fruit in the Americas as well as the most heavily traded.

Step 2: The Struggle for Land (Campo)

In recent decades, many Mexican *campesinos* (which means literally "of the land, or *campo*") have lost access to lands for cultivating the plant, either individually or collectively in peasant communities. Indigenous peoples have struggled for land for centuries, especially after the Spaniards arrived and sent them to work as peons in the mines and plantations. Mestizo and Indigenous campesinos gained greater access to land through the Mexican Revolution (whose battle cry was "Land and liberty!") and through agrarian reforms under President Lázaro Cardenas in the 1930s. In the 1980s, Mexican neoliberal policies privatized *ejidos* (communal lands) and encouraged foreign investment, and in the 1990s, NAFTA increased agroexports. Since then, more and more campesinos from the southern states of Mexico have migrated to richer northern states to work as salaried labor for large agribusinesses. If they still own plots in their home regions, much of the land has been degraded through endless cycles of fertilizer and pesticide use.

Land, or the *campo*, is thus central to the story of the corporate tomato, particularly as it has become viewed as a natural resource and as private property by Western science and industrial capitalist interests, both national and international. The origins of the commodification of land are explored later in this chapter.

Step 3: Monocultures Led by U.S. Industrial Agriculture

Tomatoes were the first fruit produced for export in Mexico, beginning in the late 1880s, but their production intensified with the development of capitalist production in Sinaloa in the 1920s. Often financed by U.S. capital and inputs, Mexican companies adopted American industrial practices such as Taylorization, the assembly line production and standardization developed after World War I. The work was divided into small manageable units, and technology was introduced that didn't depend on physical force, opening up jobs for women. In the late 1920s, U.S. surplus and protectionist policies forced Mexican producers to standardize packing tomatoes in wooden crates to compete with U.S. producers. In the 1950s, two technologies revolutionized tomato cultivation: the use of plastic covering that kept the plants from direct contact with the earth and the growth of seedlings in greenhouses. By 1994, tomatoes accounted for 22.6 percent of the fruit and vegetable production in Mexico, even though they took up only 3.5 percent of the arable land.

Monocultural and cash crop production is a central feature of the global food system today. It has, however, eliminated many types of tomatoes; 80 percent of the varieties have been lost in this century alone. Now Indigenous and mestizo campesinos tend tomatoes as salaried workers in agribusinesses built on a Western scientific logic and rationalism. Each worker is relegated to a specific routinized task, in large monocrop fields or more recently in greenhouses (called "factories in the fields"), where the goal is to harvest thousands of tomatoes at the same time and in identical form.

This process is unveiled in rich detail through the stories of women workers. The industrialization of agriculture has, in fact, been accompanied by a feminization of agricultural labor, particularly in greenhouses and packing plants.

COURTESY OF KEVIN FLEMING/CORBIS.

STAGE II: COMBINING SALARIED WORK WITH SUBSISTENCE AGRICULTURE

While large monocultural agribusinesses dominate tomato production in Mexico, the campesinos who work seasonally for them cannot survive without also cultivating their own staple crops. As the case study of Empaque Santa Rosa, the Mexican agribusiness, shows, the low wages of industrial agriculture are based on the assumption that workers will combine salaried work with subsistence agriculture. For the poorer Indigenous migrant farmworkers, this is becoming less possible as they must migrate to more and more harvests to survive and as they lose access to arable land in their home states. But many peasants such as Tomasa and Pablo, featured in chapter 6, maintain their subsistence knowledge and more environmentally sustainable practices by growing basic foods in plots on hillsides outside their village, working in their *milpa* (cornfield) after returning from picking tomatoes in large plantations. This double day not only assures their survival but keeps traditional knowledges alive alongside more industrialized practices. The interplanting of corn, squash, and beans (called the "three sisters" by North American Aboriginal people) uses the advantages of each crop to improve the growth of the others while maintaining the fertility of the soil.

Step 4: Multinationals Control the Technological Package

Even though many tomato seeds originated in Mexico, they have now become the "intellectual property" of multinational companies, which claim patents on genetically modified forms of the seeds (see "The Genetic Moment and Neoliberalism," later in this chapter). They have been recreated in thousands of varieties, hybridized and more recently genetically engineered by multinational agribusinesses such as the U.S.-based Calgene and Monsanto and their counterparts such as Western Seed of Mexico. In 1996, Western Seed created, for example, a seed that is immune to the whitefly that destroyed thousands of tons of tomato production in Autlán, Jalisco, in the early 1990s. These seeds, selling for $20,000 a kilogram and geared entirely to the export market, have also been altered with genes that make the tomatoes last much longer before ripening ("long shelf life" tomatoes), so they can make the journey from Mexico to Canada without rotting en route.

For many Indigenous peoples and campesinos, this has meant not only a loss of ownership and control of the seeds but also a loss of their own knowledge about how to grow tomatoes in endless varieties. Ironically, Mexican producers such as Empaque Santa Rosa must now buy tomato seeds from foreign companies in the United States, Israel, and France; they also hire French and Israeli engineers who bring a whole technological package that must be used with the seeds, as well as an entire production process adopting European and North American management and work practices.

Agrochemicals are central components of the "technological package," and their origins in the Green Revolution are examined later in this chapter. Long before tomato seedlings are planted in the ground, for example, the soil has been treated with fertilizers to enrich the soil for growth. As the tomatoes grow, there is a constant barrage of a variety of agrochemicals—pesticides, herbicides, and fungicides—aimed at killing pests, bacteria, and fungi. Under the mantra of efficiency and productivity, they are heralded as making the plants grow faster, stronger, more uniform, and in greater quantity; they are also critical to the production of the blemish-free tomatoes demanded by the export market. The agrochemicals themselves are primarily imported from U.S. multinationals: Bayer, Dupont, Monsanto, Cargill. There is neither training in their use, however, nor protective gear provided for workers in fields where pesticides are sprayed by hand, combine, or small plane. Every year an estimated three million people are poisoned by pesticides.

STAGE III: ZAPATISTAS, NAFTA, AND FOOD

It is no coincidence that the poorest field-workers are Indigenous families from the south, forced away from their land for the myriad of reasons named earlier. Nor was it an accident that the Zapatistas chose 1 January 1994, the inaugural day of the North American Free Trade Agreement, as the moment for an uprising of Indigenous communities who have lost their land and livelihoods through colonial practices and neoliberal policies. The Zapatista struggle, for bread and dignity, has been transformed into an international movement that is reclaiming Indigenous rights and knowledges as critical not only for the survival of poor campesino communities but also for the survival of the planet. Food is a political centerpiece of this initiative, reflecting the continuing struggle for the land (campo) as well as for cultural identity of campesinos and Indigenous peoples.

Step 5: Centered Fields: Women Workers Plant and Pick

Primarily young women plant the seeds in Empaque Santa Rosa's large greenhouses in Sinaloa and nurture them into seedlings, ready to be distributed to production sites in other parts of the country. Once shipped to Sirena, they are transplanted in the surrounding fields by the few full-time workers hired by Santa Rosa from neighboring villages. The young plants are watched carefully over the first few weeks, pruned by campesino women who pluck off the shoots so the stems will grow thicker, faster, and straighter. If tomatoes grow from a main stalk, they take up less space, are less vulnerable to pests on the ground, and are easier to pick. When the plants reach a certain height, women workers tie the vines to strings that hold them up, so they can grow without being crushed on the ground.

As one of the most labor-intensive crops, tomato picking requires many more person hours and careful work than does picking bananas, for example. While most agribusinesses in the United States now have mechanical harvesters that pick tomatoes very fast and in massive amounts, in most Mexican monocultural plantations, tomatoes are still handpicked by campesinos. Hired by the companies, many of them are Indigenous families who have been brought on a one- to two-day journey from the poorer southern states for the harvest season, and they live precariously in migrant labor camps near the fields.

At Empaque Santa Rosa, the tomato workers usually start picking tomatoes at 7:30 A.M., stop for a lunch at 10:30, and are finished by 2:30 P.M., by which time the sun has become unbearably hot. They pluck them fast, too, so that they can fill the quota of forty pails a day to earn their twenty-eight pesos (approximately U.S. $5 in 1997). Both men and women (as well as children) pick tomatoes, but women pickers are considered more gentle, so there is less damage to the crop. Men, on the other hand, are the ones who stack crates on flatbed trailers that they pull by tractor from the field to the packing plant. This gender dynamic needs to be understood in the context of a *machista* culture perpetuated by an international sexual division of labor.

Step 6: Selecting and Packing the Perfect Tomato

Men unload the tomatoes in crates from the trucks and dump them into chutes that send them sailing into an agitated sea of 90 percent chlorinated water, a bath to remove the dirt, bacteria, and pesticide residue from their oversprayed skins. They are dried by blasts of warm air, then moved along on conveyor belts through another chute that coats them with wax. It keeps the moisture in and the bacteria out, protecting the tomatoes from further breakdown during the long journey, but it also gives them a special shine that makes them more attractive to wholesalers and shoppers in the north.

Not all tomatoes will make the longer trip north, as only the "best" are selected for export. To be chosen, they must be large, well-shaped, firm, and free of any cracks, scars, or blemishes. The "nimble fingers" that decide which tomato goes where belong to young women, many of them brought by Santa Rosa from its larger production site in Sinaloa to handle this

COURTESY OF INDEX STOCK IMAGERY/TOM VANO.

delicate task. They sort the fruit according to grades and destinations but also by size (determined by how many fit into a box—e.g., 5 × 5s or 6 × 7s) and by color (from shades of green to red), because this is how the importers order them. In Santa Rosa's packing plants, tomatoes are sorted by hand, while in the greenhouses, they are sorted partially by a computerized system that weighs and scans them by laser, then sends them down specific chutes for packing by size and color.

As the tomatoes move along the conveyor belt, primarily women sorters determine their destiny. If they are perfect by international standards, they are deemed "export quality" and divided into second and first grades. If they are regular sized, they go to belts for national consumption and are again categorized as second and first grade. The domestic tomatoes are sent to the big food terminals in Guadalajara and Mexico City, where they may be sold at one-third the price that they will draw internationally.

Women packers have even more responsibility with the tomatoes. They pick them up from depositories that have divided them by color but often have to re-sort them, checking on the sorters' work. Then they put them gently but quickly into boxes. It's a contradictory tension for these women because they are paid by the box and not by the day (as the sorters are); so they try to put several tomatoes into boxes at the same time, while also being careful not to damage the fruit. The contents are inspected before being closed. In the past few years, as Empaque Santa Rosa has more fully entered the global export market, little round stickers are pasted on the skin of the tomatoes before they are packed up and sent off. Also delicately applied by women, these stickers indicate the particular variety of tomato, according to an international numbering system (e.g., Roma tomatoes are #4064, while cherry tomatoes are #4796).

Step 7: Tomatoes, Trade, and Agroexports

It is easy to tell the difference between those destined for local or export markets: if they're going north, they're packed in cardboard boxes with "Mexican tomatoes" written in English on the outside, often with Styrofoam or plastic dividers that hold each tomato in place; those chosen for domestic consumption are packed, without separators, in wooden crates marked with the company's Mexican label, Empaque Santa Rosa. The real rejects are dropped unceremoniously through a big chute into a truck outside the packing plant arid sold to local farmers as animal feed.

Once packed and stickered, the boxes that will carry the tomatoes north are scaled, stacked, wrapped, and moved by men working in the packing plant. They are stacked into skids of 108 boxes and wrapped with a plastic netting that keeps them intact en route. Bar codes are also stuck on the skids by ticketers (usually men); when scanned, the lines on the bar code identify the company, tomato variety, the field they were grown in, the day they were packed, and so forth, allowing inventory to be recorded and problems to be traced. An additional sticker bears a number identifying the worker who packed and inspected the boxes at the point of origin. Men driving motorized forklifts deposit most skids directly onto big trailer trucks, while leaving others in temporary storage.

Structural adjustment programs and neoliberal policies in Mexico in the 1980s encouraged agroexports, and NAFTA in the 1990s opened the doors for competition with northern producers. Tomatoes are one of the few Mexican crops to really "win" with NAFTA, because Mexico maintains the comparative advantage with more intense and consistent sun, easier access to land, and cheaper labor than the United States and Canada. Empaque Santa Rosa, for example, used to produce tomatoes as much for domestic production as for export, but it now sends 85 percent of its harvest north across the border; an ever-increasing number of greenhouse operations produce cherry tomatoes entirely for export. Mexico ships seven hundred thousand tons of tomatoes annually to the United States and Canada. Prices are better in the north, and with the asymmetry of currencies and wages, companies like Santa Rosa can make much more money in the export market.

Tomatoes are ordered by international brokers who request them not only in specific sizes, but also in different shades, from green to red (1 = green, 6 = red). Their journey north may be delayed while the company owners wait for the prices in the United States to rise so they can be sold for more profit. Thus, they might be stored away in refrigerated rooms at the packing plants or near the food terminals, at a temperature that keeps them from ripening too fast, remaining there for a few days up to a week, until the market is more favorable. When the producers decide to fill an order, then, depending on the color requested as well as the destination, the tomatoes may be gassed with ethylene, the same substance that naturally causes ripening, so that the ripening process, temporarily slowed down, is now speeded up. The doors of the storage rooms are closed for twenty-four hours, while the tomatoes are gassed, as the ethylene is dangerous for humans to inhale.

Step 8: Erratic Weathers: El Niño or Global Warming?

Besides being sprayed incessantly with chemicals, tomatoes have been subjected recently to intense rains and even freak snowstorms. If a premature freeze occurs in the fields, the juice and pulp of the tomato freeze like ice, as though they had been put in a refrigerator. The journey for some tomatoes dead-ends here, causing the company economic losses and ending the work season prematurely for thousands of poor campesinos.

These erratic weather conditions are often blamed on El Niño, which originated in Peru and is caused by the clashing of hot and cold currents off the Pacific coast. But many contend that human intervention is also affecting global weather patterns, and crops have suffered from their erratic nature in recent years. Global warming is particularly accelerated by the emission of greenhouse gases into the atmosphere, slowly depleting the ozone layer. Among the greatest culprits of this process are the large trucks that transport food long distances, the focus of step 10.

Step 9: Detour to Del Monte Processing Adds "Value"

Second-rate tomatoes are sent in wooden crates to the major food terminals (in Guadalajara, Mexico City, and Monterrey), to local markets, and sometimes to food-processing plants. Santa Rosa, for example, supplies Del Monte, with tomatoes for processing into canned tomatoes, ketchup, or salsa at its plant in Irapuato, Guanajuato. Tomatoes received at Del Monte are dumped into an assembly line production that moves them along to be weighed and washed, sorted and mashed, then processed through cooking tanks, evaporating tanks, and pasteurizing tanks. Again, primarily women workers fill the bottles through tubes, and the bottles are capped, cooled, labeled, and packed into boxes.

While one might think Del Monte would prefer overripe tomatoes for processing, they actually prefer firmer varieties, so that the tomatoes won't get caught in the automated conveyor systems and mess up the technology for transporting them into the plant. More and more, however, ketchup producers like Del Monte are buying tomato paste rather than whole tomatoes, because the paste-making business draws on cheap labor and facilitates the process for the manufacturer. In bottled form, tomatoes join many other processed and frozen foods that are increasingly replacing fresh food in North America; they are sometimes called "value-added" products, although the real added value is reflected mainly in the price.

Step 10: Trucking: A Nonstop Dash North with Perishable Goods

Empaque Santa Rosa owns a few of its own trailer trucks to transport tomatoes to both domestic and northern markets; they guzzle fossil fuel and also contribute to the depletion of the ozone layer. More often, however, Santa Rosa contracts independent truckers to deliver tomatoes to the Mexican–U.S. border at Nogales. It often hires UTTSA, for example, a trucking company whose refrigerated units can carry fifty thousand–pound shipments of fresh produce. The tomatoes are sometimes precooled in a hydrocooling machine that brings their core temperature from 75 degrees down to 34 degrees, because if the temperature drops from 75 to 34 during the two-day journey north, the fruit might deteriorate.

Trucking is a male job. Truckers often work in pairs, so that one can sleep in the back of the cab, while the other takes over the driving. The trip to Nogales from Sirena may take thirty to forty hours, depending how many drivers there are; time is of the essence, because tomatoes are highly perishable and preferred at a certain ripeness, but not overripe. Their average life span, in fact, is 4.7 days, so the faster the drive, the quicker they arrive, and the more market days remain for the critical activity of selling them.

We now enter the second phase of the journey of the corporate tomato from Mexico to Canada, highlighting issues of trade and transport, inspection and distribution. While it involves processes in all three NAFTA countries, this phase is clearly controlled by U.S. regulatory agencies, political interests, and multinational corporate needs. Contending political, economic, and legal interests converge in activities around the borders, especially the highly charged U.S.–Mexican line.

Step 11: Controlling the Gates: Dumping, Drugs, and Deportees

To better control and facilitate the border inspection process, the U.S. Department of Agriculture (USDA) has installed its own inspectors within many Mexican agroexport plants to check the tomatoes before they're even loaded into the trailer trucks. Mexican environmental laws are not as strict as those in the United States and Canada, though NAFTA has provided some pressure to "harmonize." U.S.-based companies, however, sometimes "dump" pesticides in Mexico after they have been banned in their own country. The problem comes back to haunt them when tomatoes are exported back to the United States, carrying higher concentrations of agrochemicals and threatening the health of U.S. consumers.

The USDA hopes to eventually complete all inspections at the point of origin, in the Mexican plants where the tomatoes are packed. Nonetheless, loads of tomatoes are inspected again and again along the route to the border, and the trucks carrying them are stopped regularly by inspectors at four checkpoints. Usually it is not the tomatoes that interest them as much as other possible cargo that could be smuggled within the trucks, such as narcotics or Mexicans seeking illegal entry into the United States. Narcotraffic is actually a much more lucrative (and volatile) enterprise than tomato production, and a lot of the border activity centers on attempts to control or eradicate it.

The border patrol complex is located in a sandy ravine with desert brush competing with large-armed spotlights and police cruisers on the hillside, a veritable militarized zone. U.S. Customs officials, guns bulging at their hips, check for truck fraud and narcotics; the work of sniffing dogs has recently been complemented by high-tech X-ray equipment which can scan entire truckloads for suspicious objects. The increasing drug trade is just one more sign of deepening despair and uncontrollable violence in both countries, but particularly Mexico. The U.S. government and Mexican government have joined forces to address this matter.

Second to drugs is concern for the growing number of desperate Mexicans who try to escape poverty and unemployment, by illegally crossing the border, seeking work in the United States where they earn in one hour what they would make in a day at home. Horror stories abound about the ways they try to smuggle themselves in, under truck cabs, amid produce, or across rivers at night, and about how they are often captured, mistreated, and sent back to Mexico. It's ironic that tomatoes, as well as capital, are so welcome in the north, while Mexican

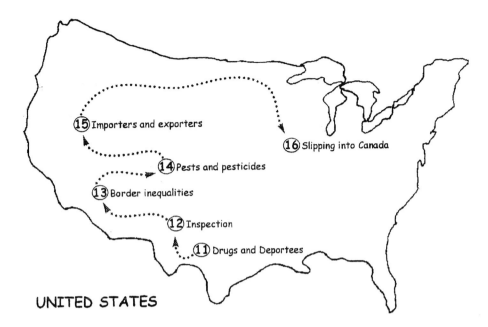

workers are not, except when they are wanted for menial tasks, at specific times, and under limited conditions.

Tomatoes account for 56 percent of the cargo of the nine hundred to thirteen hundred big trailer trucks that cross the Nogales border daily. Truck traffic has been increasing at such a dramatic pace since NAFTA (in peak season in 1998, over twenty-seven thousand trucks crossed here in one month) that new lanes are being added to the highway to ease the congestion.

Step 12: Checking for Quality: Appearance Matters

Most food inspection actually takes place on the Mexican side of the border.

At the complex of the Confederation of Agricultural Associations (CAADES), in Nogales, Sonora, six kilometers south of the U.S. border, tomatoes are run through a series of checks by the USDA officials. First they weigh the trucks, to be sure they don't surpass the total limit of eighty-eight thousand pounds; if the loaded trucks are overweight, they must unload and reload the tomatoes in smaller trucks. Then a USDA inspector goes through a truckload and randomly stamps boxes of tomatoes at the top, middle, and bottom of a skid. Ten boxes are opened and inspected at a time. An inspector also measures a few sample tomatoes with a metal frame to confirm their proclaimed size: from 4×4 to 7×7, referring to how many will fit into one layer of a standard box.

Some tomatoes get their temperature taken to be sure that the refrigeration of the truck has not failed; if they were packed pink and register higher than 50 degrees, they may be deteriorating too fast and are turned back. Of the long list of potential "quality defects" and "condition defects" used to check the tomatoes, most (such as "smoothness" and "color") relate primarily to the appearance of the fruit. To be deemed suitable as a U.S. No. 1 grade, no more than 10 percent of a load can have either quality defects or condition defects.

Step 13: The Line Is Drawn: Border of Inequalities

There is a stark contrast at the border between the huts dotting the hillsides on the Mexican side and the more elegant homes on the U.S. side; just as the price of tomatoes rises the minute they cross the line, the wages and standard of living also rise. The way business is organized on both sides of the border area also reflects this asymmetry between nations. A growing number of maquiladora plants, set up since the 1960s in the northern Mexican border by multinational companies, employ thousands of young women in assembling electronics, in piecing together garments, and, in lesser quantity, in food processing. On the U.S. side, on the other hand, an immense infrastructure of administrative offices and warehouses has been established to facilitate the speedy movement of tomatoes beyond the border to northern consumers. The border thus also separates the workers in the south (Mexico) from the managers in the north (the United States).

Step 14: Keeping Pests and Pesticides at Bay

Truckers that have passed the inspection in Nogales, Sonora, on the Mexican side, and are transporting tomatoes from a reputable agribusiness, can pass through the rapid transit lane, merely handing in the paperwork and moving quickly north. Others, however, may be directed into the U.S. Customs complex on the Arizona side of the border, for further inspections by the FDA and USDA. The Food and Drug Administration officials randomly select a box from a truck and cut a chunk out of a sample tomato to send to an FDA lab in Phoenix, Arizona. About 1 percent of the produce are tested for pesticide residues. This is one way officials can check to see whether Mexican tomato producers are following the standards regarding the acceptable levels of pesticide residue permitted in the United States. The lab testing may take a few weeks, by which time the chemically suspect tomatoes may have already been unwittingly digested by U.S. or Canadian consumers. Growers whose produce is proven to have certain chemicals above the legal limit are warned that enforcement action might be taken if the problem continues.

What can be detected more immediately, however, are the pests or plant life that may be carried inadvertently in the trucks or boxes in which the tomatoes are packed. USDA botanists don rubber gloves and check the fruit for microbes or markings (a hard scar may be evidence of a pest). If found defective, they may be sent back to Mexico for domestic consumption, sent on to Canada "in bond" (quarantined and wrapped with unbreakable metal straps), or sprayed by a Nogales fumigation company, with USDA officials monitoring the process. If, on the other hand, all goes well in the inspection, the border-crossing process will be complete within three to four hours, and the tomatoes are given official entry into the United States.

Step 15: Exporting/Importing: Brokers and Wholesalers

When a Mexican trucker is not certified to cross the border, he will pay an American trucker $20 to drive the truck through customs and to a warehouse a few miles north of the border. The warehouses are owned by exporters as well as brokers; Empaque Santa Rosa, for example, has its own office on the U.S. side to manage international sales and distribution within the United States and into Canada. The skids are unloaded in thirty to sixty minutes and stored temporarily in the warehouse. Throughout the day, brokers arrange sales by phone, fax, and increasingly by E-mail. This is clearly a man's world, and tomatoes are constantly repacked and reloaded on the trucks of brokers or distributors for U.S. and Canadian wholesalers and retailers.

The Blue Book lists hundreds of wholesalers and retailers in the United States and Canada who purchase tomatoes, especially during peak season. Loblaws supermarkets in Ontario, for example, brings up three truckloads of tomatoes daily from the Nogales border. Like other wholesalers and retailers in Canada, they deal with brokers or shippers in Nogales who receive their orders and seek out the best deal from warehouses in the area.

It takes about three days in refrigerated trucks (kept at 48 degrees Fahrenheit) for the tomatoes to reach Ontario from the Mexican border; if coming from Florida it's only two days, while from California it may be four. Three National Grocers trucks leave Nogales daily filled with three key varieties of tomatoes: the extra large Romas, vine ripes, and Gas Greens. Loblaws has its own warehouse, National Grocers, near the Toronto airport, open seven days a week, twenty-four hours a day, and employing one thousand people (mainly men). Supplying Loblaws, Zehrs, Value-Mart, No Frills, and some Atlantic chains, National Grocers also brings tomatoes in by air daily from around the world (France, Morocco, the Canary Islands, and Israel), especially between December and February when local hothouse production is closed down because of cold weather.

STAGE IV: CHALLENGING GLOBALIZED PRODUCTION: ECOLOGICAL FOOTPRINT

Activists and academics concerned about the often hidden ecological costs of production and distribution in a global food system that depends on moving tomatoes long distances have developed tools for measuring the impact of such practices. Neither transportation, which is heavily subsidized by government, nor environmental degradation (exacerbated both by the burning of fossil fuels and by the hydroflurocarbons in refrigerated units of trucks) appears either in the balance sheet of the companies or in the price we pay as consumers. One such tool, the ecological footprint, developed by William Rees, calculates both primary energy consumption and carbon dioxide emissions.

The footprints below represent the contrasting energy costs of producing tomatoes in Mexico and in Ontario greenhouses for Canadian consumption. Of the tomatoes imported annually into Ontario, 74 percent were from the United States, 22 percent were from Mexico, and 4 percent were from other countries. In 1997, Ontario's forty thousand tons of tomato imports (from North America) traveled over ninety-one million kilometers (i.e., 2,320 kilometers/ton). A recent study estimates that most tomatoes enter Toronto by truck but that

North American imports emit 221 tons of carbon dioxide into the atmosphere while the transportation of Ontario greenhouse tomatoes only emitted 67 tons. Air transport is even more damaging to the environment; according to a 1994 SAFE Alliance study, tomatoes arriving by air contributed 1,206 grams/ton • kilometer, compared to 207 for road travel, 30 for water, and 41 for rail.

Step 16: A More Permeable Border: Slipping into Canada

It's difficult to know how many Mexican tomatoes actually make it into Canada. One-quarter of the tomatoes sold in Ontario come directly from Mexico, but this doesn't include those that are shipped from Mexico to border states, then repacked under new U.S. trademarks and sent on to Canada. While the journey from Nogales to Sarnia may take as long as the Sirena–Nogales trip within Mexico, tomatoes have a much easier time at the Canadian border. Fortunately, the elongated inspection at the Mexican–U.S. border is not repeated, because the standards in the United States and Canada are pretty much the same. If the tomatoes pass as U.S. No. 1 grade tomatoes in Nogales, they're considered certified and won't be inspected again at the Canadian border.

Truckers who, since the deregulation of transportation in the late 1980s and NAFTA in the early 1990s, cross the border more regularly merely present a "confirmation of sale," which has often been previously faxed or sent electronically to both Canadian Customs and the

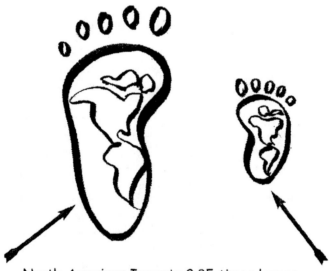

THE ECOLOGICAL FOOTPRINT

North American Imports 2.85 times larger than Ontario Greenhouse tomatoes

Canadian Food Inspection Agency (CFIA). A small number (about 4 percent) of the shipments are inspected by customs officials (and dogs), usually initiated as a search for contraband (drugs, weapons, liquor, tobacco), and secondarily a check on the quality of the tomatoes. If the fresh produce smells or appears spoiled, a CFIA inspector will be called in.

Tomatoes are the subject of intense communications between the brokers (shippers) at the U.S.–Mexican border, and U.S. and Canadian buyers (wholesalers), and then again between the brokers at the Canadian border and the buyers awaiting the arrival of fresh tomatoes. Ontario Produce, one of the key wholesalers at the Ontario Food Terminal, for example, has its own brokers negotiating the crossing of tomato shipments at Sarnia, Ontario. Ontario Produce faxes its record of the load, and its broker helps shepherd it across the Sarnia border. Customs officials check the shipper's manifest and the buyer's manifest, and if there are no problems, the tomatoes are allowed to enter Canada.

Finally, we move on to the third phase of the corporate tomato journey north, as it is received, inspected, and distributed in Canada, to terminals and then to supermarkets and fast-food restaurants.

Step 17: The Morning Zoo: Food Terminals Work While We Sleep

Tomatoes are delivered (by truck via Sarnia) to the Ontario Food Terminal, often in the middle of the night, to be ready for sale when wholesalers and retailers arrive from 4 A.M. on. Ontario Produce, one of largest of the twenty companies in the terminal, has eight buyers who order tomatoes from all over the world (Belgium, Spain, Italy, Mexico); while most are beefsteak tomatoes from Florida, they also buy tear drops, cherry, hothouse, and Roma (demanded by the ethnic market), and sell eleven truckloads a day. Ontario Produce sends its own three trucks out to pick up orders as well as to receive deliveries. If they arrive too early, the trucks may have to wait for hours before unloading, while wholesalers close down for a couple of hours to clean up and prepare displays of the best samples for the following day.

Once unloaded at the terminal, the tomatoes may be returned to refrigerated storage units, similar to the ones in Sirena, but with computerized temperature control, where they're kept at a temperature of 36 to 40 degrees. These units are equipped with catalytic generators to produce ethylene, a liquid that when released creates vapor that accelerates the ripening of the fruit. Signs around the heavily locked door warn of its highly flammable nature, indicating that smoking around it could cause an explosion. Whether or not the tomatoes are gassed depends on demand and price.

Wholesalers (or jobbers) like Joyce Foods arrive in the early morning to buy for fast-food restaurants, the primary customers for tomatoes. They prefer the firmer Florida tomatoes (without any markings) because they are more sliceable (e.g., for McDonald's Arch Deluxe or for pizzas). While importers and wholesalers have noted an increase in Mexican tomatoes since NAFTA, they are often too watery for fast-food use. Tomatoes that have been traveling several days from Mexico ripen at different times and, to different degrees, suffer from stem puncture, or deteriorate. Importers can claim for damages, but this involves lengthy court procedures, so they may just send them to be repacked. Women workers at Bell City packers near Toronto, for example, eliminate the decayed tomatoes, wash them again, and re-sort them

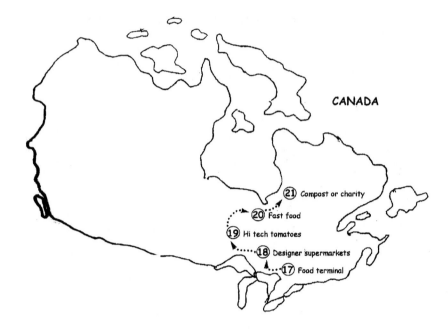

into six different colors through a computerized laser system and a mechanized assembly line similar to the one in the Santa Rosa greenhouse in Mexico.

STAGE V: LOCAL TOMATOES PICKED BY MEXICAN HANDS

In the summertime, fewer tomatoes are imported from Mexico, since Canadians can get them fresh from local farmers. Even the sales manager at Ontario Produce recognizes the difference: "Anything that is grown locally has a better taste than the imported merchandise. If you compare it with the local stuff, it is totally different, just like night and day."

There is also a growing greenhouse production of hothouse tomatoes in Ontario year-round. The climate can be carefully controlled in these sophisticated glass greenhouses, and the production is more predictable. Many people also prefer them, because they can ripen on the vine and thus are tastier than tomatoes picked green and sent on the long journey north from Mexico. With a growing demand for organic tomatoes, biological methods of pest control are being used in greenhouses as well.

National Grocers buys tomatoes for Loblaws from Mennonite farmers in western and southern Ontario. Ironically, many of the locally produced tomatoes are harvested by Mexican migrant farmworkers, men and women, who come north every summer as part of a government program called FARMS. Irena Gonzalez, for example, has been coming for thirteen years from July to October. While she is still only paid at minimum wage, she makes in an hour in Canada what she would make in a day in Mexico picking tomatoes.

Step 18: Designer Supermarkets and Multicultural Labels

A mixture of corporate tomatoes and (in season) locally grown tomatoes is delivered to Loblaws supermarkets, where they become part of a simulated village market within megastores, which now combine selling groceries with gourmet takeout, dry cleaning, pharmacy, photo processing, plant nurseries, art galleries, and even banking. The produce section has been moved to the front of stores to create the illusion of being closer to the source of food. The walls surrounding the tomatoes are brightly colored and well lit. With their waxed shiny surfaces, they are arranged artfully on carts, under umbrellas and a sign that says "Fresh from the Fields."

As part of a global retail market, Loblaws now proclaims that "Food Means the World to Us." Having come from Mexico, tomatoes are part of its global reach, either in fresh form or processed into one of Loblaws' corporate brand President's Choice sauces, Italian style plum tomatoes, or salsas and tacos being promoted in colorful Latino-style aisles, introducing Canadians and its multicultural population not only to new tastes but to new ways of being. The seduction of consumers into lifestyle foods and an illusion of diversity is a key theme.

Step 19: High-Tech Tomatoes and Computerized Cashiers

Corporate tomatoes can be purchased in fresh or processed form, and they are either punched in or scanned at the supermarket checkout lane. Fresh tomatoes are given PLU (product lookup) codes either on tickets or on stickers. Because they are of variable weight, they must first be weighed and their PLU numbers punched in to calculate their price. If a cashier is not sure of the type of tomato (nine different varieties are sold by Loblaws), she may check the visual inventory on her computer screen. Canned tomatoes or bottled salsa, on the other hand, can be quickly swiped through the scanner; their bar codes are read by a laser beam, and the type and price appear immediately on a printed receipt.

Global food production has become highly technologized in recent decades, and work practices have been transformed by the information revolution. The high-tech corporate tomato mediates a complex relationship between the worker and the technology; the electronic devices that control pricing and inventory, for example, can also monitor the productivity of cashiers such as Marissa, featured in chapter 4.

Step 20: Fast Food: Homogenized Tomatoes and Toys

McDonald's, which traditionally has targeted a young market, doesn't include tomatoes in the Big Mac, since many children don't like them. In 1996, however, when the fast-food giant's domestic sales were slipping, it created the Arch Deluxe for grown-ups, adding tomatoes; in 1999, it was replaced by the Big Xtra. McDonald's prefers to buy Florida beefsteak tomatoes that are pulpier, firmer, and easier to slice for a hamburger bun, while the tastier Mexican produce are juicier and more likely to fall apart. It is clearly a question of appearance and not of taste. The draw of McDonald's is often more the lifestyle, reflected in the glossy ads, billboards, TV commercials, toys, and videos that promote dominant popular culture. At the final destination of the corporate tomato, it becomes clear that tomatoes and hamburgers are not just food, nor even mere commodities, but symbols of a way of life.

Perfectly sliced tomatoes on a cookie cutter hamburger and bun are part of a global trend toward homogenized diets. In fact, the term *McDonaldization* is now equated with this rationalizing and homogenizing process, which is built on principles of efficiency, calculability, predictability, and control; other businesses and social institutions are increasingly modeled on practices similar to the fast-food restaurant. The resulting loss of both biodiversity and cultural diversity are key themes explored in the case studies.

The standardization of meals also fits a frantic lifestyle that devalues the preparation or savoring of food such as tomatoes, and the experience of commensality, or enjoying sharing a meal as an intimate social act. Homogenized consumption patterns in Canada parallel the monocultural production of tomatoes in the Mexican fields, both representing dominant practices at either end of the current global food system.

Step 21: Waste or Surplus: Compost or Charity?

There is a "paradox of hunger" reflected by a deepening poverty in the context of a relatively affluent Canada. Food retail giants such as Loblaws are by far the largest donors to a burgeoning network of food banks. Besides getting a tax write-off for its contribution, Loblaws also invites customers to buy goods, such as canned tomatoes, and add them to a donation box in the store. There are critics of this practice, and food bank organizers complain that the kind of items donated aren't always the most needed. Organic produce such as tomatoes, however, are disposed of in a different way; in collaboration with Organic Resources, Loblaws uses a system of underground holding tanks where wasted tomatoes are stored until they can be recycled as compost on experimental farms outside of Toronto. McDonald's takes a "total life cycle" approach to solid waste, where possible trying to recycle and/or compost solid waste, such as corrugated paper.

STAGE VI: FULL CIRCLE: SEEDS IN THE MULTICULTURAL CITY

Tomatl is well and alive and living in Toronto. One sunny May day, I made my way to Field to Table, the warehouse where FoodShare Metro Toronto is promoting a variety of food alternatives for low-income communities. Lauren Baker, who helped me trace the corporate tomato journey for two years, today sells me heritage tomato seedlings that she has grown on the first certified organic rooftop garden in Canada. There she has transformed organic waste into rich composting soil, which is then recycled in diverse urban agricultural projects.

Part of a growing food security movement, FoodShare recently launched a new project, entitled "Seeds of Our City." It draws on the rich knowledges of ethnic communities that are now part of Toronto's multicultural population and that have brought their own growing practices and food traditions to community gardens sprouting all over the city. They are vibrant examples of the survival and recovery of more ecologically sustainable growing traditions built on a closer relationship between production and consumption.

After taking my new seeds and native plants home to my backyard garden, I attended an afternoon cultural event at the Native Canadian Centre, also in downtown Toronto. As part of the Mayworks Festival of Working People and the Arts, a concert releasing a CD, *Food for*

Chiapas, offered music, drumming, poetry, and comedy by Latin American and native artists of diverse origins but all now living in Toronto. The benefit was also an educational event, reminding us of the struggles of Indigenous campesinos in Chiapas, whose access to land and to traditional practices has been threatened over centuries by the production of the corporate tomato. Since the implementation of NAFTA in January 1994, the Zapatista movement has strengthened the resistance of these people fighting for food, for land, and for dignity and has drawn international solidarity from many sectors of civil society. Their vision is also to reclaim a more just and sustainable relationship to the earth, one that recovers the practices of Tomatl in the twenty-first century.

11. Civilization and Its Discontents

Katharine Milton

Anthropologists are concerned about how local culture, heath, and economy are affected by the introduction of goods on the global market. Milton discusses how Amazonian Indians' subsistence patterns were affected by the Western material culture. The introduction of more effective tools, including rifles, resulted in the fast decimation of resources, especially game animals. Milton demonstrates how easily the delicate balance between humans and the environment could be disrupted by the use of new technologies. Disease, too, is an unintended consequence of the introduction of new cultural practices and a changing relationship with the environment. These Brazilian people are losing local knowledge they critically need for their survival. On every level, materially, ecologically and cognitively, their lives are changed.

For more than a decade now, I have led a double life. I spend part of my time in the United States, living in an apartment in Berkeley and teaching anthropology classes at the University of California. The rest of my time is spent in the Amazon Basin, where I live in the company of recently contacted Indian groups, studying their traditional ecology and features of their tropical forest environment. On returning to the United States after one of these extended stays in the jungle, I always experience culture shock as I strive to regain control of my possessions, which I have totally forgotten about.

Usually my first act is to retrieve my dust-covered car, which has languished for some six to eighteen months in a garage. The battery must be charged, and then I must wash and vacuum the car, fill it with gas, and check out its many parts. Once I am mobile, I rush to a large supermarket to stock up on cleaning supplies and food. My first few days are completely taken up with chores; there never seems to be a moment when I am not contemplating some type of home repair or new purchase.

And then there is my body. What a job it is to live up to what is expected of the average American. I must visit the dentist—often more than one kind of dentist—to be sure my teeth are performing at top level. The doctor must be seen for a checkup; my eyes must be examined, glasses and contact lenses adjusted, and so on. I begin to wonder how my friends in Berkeley manage to have any free time at all, since I have fewer possessions than they do— I own no television set, no stereo or compact disk player, no video machine, home computer, food chopper, or any number of other items my friends seem to dote on. I don't even own my apartment.

Plunged back into life in Berkeley, I see myself as a slave of material possessions, and I notice that I deeply resent the time and energy required to maintain them. Nothing could be more different from the life I have been leading with hunter-gatherers deep in the rain forests of Brazil, where people have almost no possessions, and those that they do have are made from local forest materials and are entirely biodegradable.

The groups I have visited live far from any cities, towns, or commercial enterprises. They include the Mayoruna and Maku from Amazonas State; the Arara, Parakana, and Arawete from Pará State; and the Guaja from Maranhão State—peoples so remote and little known that few outside their immediate geographic area have heard of them. Often I am one of the first non-indigenous females many members of the group have ever seen. With my pale skin and hair I am a truly terrifying apparition to younger children, who sometimes scream with fear when they first see me.

All these peoples have been recently contacted: only a few months or, at most, years have passed since the Brazilian Indian Bureau (FUNAI) managed to establish a formal relationship with them. Previously, these groups avoided or were strongly hostile to outsiders, but with contact, they have permitted a few Indian Bureau employees to live with them, to assist them, and at times, protect them in dealings with other Indian groups or members of the wider Brazilian society. Living with these people has given me the chance to see how even modest changes in their traditional lifeways—the introduction of something as innocent in appearance as a metal cooking pot or ax, a box of matches or some salt—can be the thin edge of a wedge that will gradually alter the behavior and ecological practices of an entire society.

These people typically live in small villages of fewer than a hundred inhabitants, in some cases in groups of only fifteen or twenty. Most practice slash-and-burn agriculture on a small scale, complementing crop foods with wild game and fish, forest fruits and nuts, and occasionally, wild honey. For some months life may revolve around the village, but sooner or later every group I have worked with leaves, generally in small parties, and spends weeks or even months traveling through the forest and living on forest products.

Throughout the forest there are paths that the Indians know and have used for generations. They travel mainly when wild forest fruits and nuts are most abundant and game animals are fat, but families or small groups may go on expeditions at other times of year as well. They trek a few miles, make a temporary camp, and then hunt, gather, and eat several meals in the area before moving on to a new site. At certain times of year, many groups relocate to the borders of large rivers, where they obtain turtle eggs or other seasonal river foods.

The accumulation of possessions would be an impediment to this seminomadic life style. Whenever individuals go on a trek, they carry everything they need. Leaving possessions behind in a thatch-and-pole hut, to be retrieved later, is not an option, since the humid climate and voracious insects would quickly destroy them. Great numbers of insects often live inside Indian dwellings, principally jungle cockroaches that hide in the roof thatch by day but come out by the thousands at night. Indians seem oblivious to them, letting them run about on their bodies and even crawl on the food so long as they are not perched on the next bite.

Granted, these are generally soft-bodied, small jungle cockroaches and not the tough, large roaches of our urban areas, but even so, I found it difficult to adjust to them. My frantic efforts to remove cockroaches from my body and clothes were regarded as strange by my Indian hosts. At one site, I resorted to storing my clothing each night in a heavy plastic bag, which I sealed shut and suspended from a piece of plastic fish line tied to a roof pole. Otherwise, at night, the roaches covered my shirt and pants so thoroughly that often the fabric could not be seen. Although the roaches would be gone the next morning, they would leave a musty smell; further, just the idea of wearing garments that I had seen coated with cockroaches gave me a squirmy, unclean feeling.

On the forest treks, the women are invariably the most burdened, something Western observers often find difficult to understand or accept. A woman will walk for hours carrying a toddler, a large palm basket containing fifty or more pounds of animal or plant foods, hammocks, a cooking utensil or two, a machete, and the family pets, such as parrots, monkeys, and young puppies. In all the groups I have observed, the women's legs and feet are deformed by the pigeon-toed walk they adopt to give them added traction and stability on the slippery, narrow forest trails. The feet of adult men turn in only slightly, because men usually carry nothing heavier than a bow and arrows (ostensibly to be free to take advantage of any hunting opportunities).

The most important possession the Indians carry with them, however, is knowledge. There is nothing coded in the genome of an Indian concerning how to make a living in a tropical forest—each individual must become a walking bank of information on the forest landscape, its plants and animals, and their habits and uses. This information must be taught anew to the members of each generation, without the benefit of books, manuals, or educational television. Indians have no stores in which to purchase the things they need for survival. Instead, each individual must learn to collect, manufacture, or produce all the things required for his or her entire lifetime.

Because people differ in their talents, the pool of community information and abilities is far greater than its component parts. Individual men and women have their own areas of expertise, as well as their share of general knowledge. Members of the group know whom to consult for special information on hunting practices, the habits of particular game animals, rituals, tool manufacture, crop varieties, and the like.

Tropical-forest Indians talk incessantly, a characteristic I believe reflects the importance of oral transmission of culture. When I lived with the Maku, I slept in a hammock inside a small communal palm shelter. If a Maku awoke in the middle of the night, he usually began to talk or sing in a very loud voice—apparently without any thought that anyone might object to this behavior. It was considered normal, what you do when you wake up in the middle of the night and aren't sleepy. Others learn, as I did, to sleep through it or, if they aren't sleepy, to listen to it. Vocal expression apparently is expected and tolerated in Maku culture, no matter what the hour, an indication to me of how much it is valued.

Unlike our economic system, in which each person typically tries to secure and control as large a share of the available resources as possible, the hunter-gatherer economic system rests on a set of highly formalized expectations regarding cooperating and sharing. This does not mean hunter-gatherers do not compete with one another for prestige, sexual partners, and the like. But individuals do not amass a surplus. For instance, no hunter fortunate enough to kill a large game animal assumes that all this food is his or belongs only to his immediate family.

Quite the reverse is true: among some forest peoples, the hunter cannot eat game he has killed or is restricted to eating only one specific portion of his kill. Game is cut up and distributed according to defined patterns particular to each group and based in large part on kinship and marriage obligations. A hunter may have amazing luck one day, moderate luck on another, and no luck at all on a third. But he can usually expect to eat meat every day because someone bound to him in this system of reciprocity may well make a kill and share the meat.

Despite the way their culture traditionally eschews possessions, forest-living peoples embrace manufactured goods with amazing enthusiasm. They seem to appreciate instantly the efficacy of a steel machete, ax, or cooking pot. It is love at first sight, and the desire to possess such objects is absolute. There are accounts of Indian groups or individuals who have turned their backs on manufactured trade goods, but such people are the exception.

When Cândido Rondon, the founder of the Indian Protection Service in Brazil, began his pacification efforts in the early 1900s, he used trade goods as bait to attract uncontacted Indians. Pots, machetes, axes, and steel knives were hung from trees or laid along trails that Indians frequented. This practice proved so successful that it is still employed (*see* "Overtures to the Nambiquara," by David Price, *Natural History,* October 1984).

Whether they have been formally contacted or not, forest-living groups in the Amazon Basin are probably well aware of steel tools and metal cooking pots. After all, such goods have been in circulation along trade routes in these regions for centuries, and an Indian does not have to have seen a non-Indian in order to acquire them. However, such manufactured goods are likely to be extremely scarce among uncontacted groups. When the Arara Indians were first approached in 1975, they fled their village to escape the pacification party. Examination of their hastily abandoned dwellings showed that stone tools were still being used, but a few steel fragments were also found.

Since they already appreciate the potential utility of manufactured goods, uncontacted Indians are strongly drawn to the new and abundant items offered to lure them from isolation. Once a group has been drawn into the pacification area, all its members are presented with various trade goods—standard gifts include metal cooking pots, salt, matches, machetes, knives, axes, cloth hammocks, T-shirts, and shorts. Not all members of the group get all of these items, but most get at least two or three of them, and in a family, the cumulative mass of new goods can be considerable.

The Indians initially are overwhelmed with delight—this is the honeymoon period when suddenly, from a position in which one or two old metal implements were shared by the entire group, a new situation prevails in which almost every adult individual has some of these wonderful new items. The honeymoon is short-lived, however. Once the Indians have grown accustomed to these new items, the next step is to teach them that these gifts will not be repeated. The Indians are now told that they must work to earn money or must manufacture goods for trade so that they can purchase new items.

Unable to contemplate returning to life without steel axes, the Indians begin to produce extra arrows or blowguns or hunt additional game or weave baskets beyond what they normally need so that this new surplus can be traded. Time that might, in the past, have been used for other tasks—subsistence activities, ceremonial events, or whatever—is now devoted to production of barter goods. In addition, actual settlement patterns may be altered so that the indigenous group is in closer, more immediate contact with sources of manufactured items. Neither of these things, in itself, is necessarily good or bad, but each does alter traditional behavior.

Thus, the newly contacted forest people are rapidly drawn into the wider economic sphere (even into the international economy: for example, the preferred glass beads for personal adornment come from Czechoslovakia). The intrusion of every item—mirrors, cloth, scissors, rice, machetes, axes, pots, bowls, needles, blankets, even bicycles and radios—not only adds to the pressure on individuals to produce trade goods but also disrupts some facet of traditional production.

Anthropologist Paul Henley, who worked with the Panare, a forest-based people in Venezuela, points out that with the introduction of steel tools, particularly axes, indigenous groups suffer a breakdown in the web of cooperative interdependence. In the past, when stone axes were used, various individuals came together and worked communally to fell trees for a new garden. With the introduction of the steel ax, however, one man can clear a garden by himself. As Henley notes, collaboration is no longer mandatory nor particularly frequent.

Indians often begin to cultivate new crops, such as coffee, that they feel can be traded or sold easily. Another is rice, which the Indian Bureau encourages forest peoples to plant because, of course, all "real" Brazilians eat rice every day. Rice is an introduced crop both to Brazil and to forest Indians. Traditional crop foods, the successful cultivation of which has been worked out over generations in the forest environment and which are well suited to the soil conditions in particular regions, may become scarce, with the result that the Indian diet becomes unbalanced.

Indians who traditionally plant manioc as a staple crop may be encouraged to increase the size of their fields and plant more manioc, which can then be transformed into *farinha,* a type of cereal that can be sold in the markets. Larger fields mean more intensive agricultural work and less time to hunt—which also affects the diet. The purchase of a shotgun may temporarily improve hunting returns, but it also tends to eliminate game in the area. In addition, shotgun shells are very expensive in Brazil, costing more than $1 U.S. apiece. Dependence on the shotgun undermines a hunter's skill with traditional hunting weapons, such as blowguns and bows and arrows, as well as the ability required to manufacture them.

Clearing larger areas for fields can also lead to increased risk from diseases such as malaria and leishmanaisis, because cleared areas with standing water of low acidity permit proliferation of disease-bearing mosquitoes and flies. New diseases also appear. Anthropologist-epidemiologist Carlos Coimbra, Jr., for example, has shown that Chagas disease, which is transmitted to humans by trypanosome-carrying assassin bugs, apparently does not yet affect Indian populations in lowland areas of the Amazon Basin. Only when Indians cease their semi-nomadic way of life and begin to live for prolonged periods in the same dwellings can Chagas-carrying bugs adjust their feeding behavior and begin to depend on human hosts rather than small rodents for their blood meals.

The moment manufactured foods begin to intrude on the indigenous diet, health takes a downward turn. The liberal use of table salt (sodium chloride), one of the first things that

Indians are given, is probably no more healthful for them than it is for Westerners. Most Indians do not have table salt; they manufacture small quantities of potassium salts by burning certain types of leaves and collecting the ash. Anthropologist Darrell Posey reports that the Kayapo Indians of Brazil make salt ash from various palm species and use each type for specific foods.

Sweets and other foods containing refined sugar (sucrose) are also given to Indians, whose wild fruits, according to research by botanists Irene and Herbert Baker, contain primarily other sugars, such as fructose. Indians find that foods containing sucrose taste exceptionally sweet, and they tend to crave them once sampled. While a strong, sugary taste in the natural environment might signal a rare, rich energy source, the indiscriminate consumption of canned foods, candies, and gums containing large amounts of refined sugar contributes to tooth decay and can lead to obesity and even health problems such as diabetes.

Results of dietary change are often difficult to anticipate. Anthropologist Dennis Werner found that the Mekranoti of central Brazil, who did not make pottery, traditionally roasted most of their food. But the introduction of metal cooking pots allowed them to switch to boiled foods. This, in turn, allowed nursing mothers to provide supplemental foods to their infants at an earlier age. Werner found that the average nursing period in the Mekranoti had dropped steadily from 19.7 months prior to 1955 to 16 months in recent years, which corresponded to the period of steady increase in the use of metal cooking pots in the village.

One of the first things the Indian Bureau doctors generally do after contact is try to protect the Indians from the Western diseases that may be communicated to them during their first prolonged interaction with outsiders. The doctors give them immunizations and may also hand out drugs to prevent or eradicate dangerous malarias. Pregnant women, infants, and preadolescents often receive massive doses of antibiotics. Antibiotics and antimalarial drugs, although helpful in some respects, may also have detrimental effects. For example, individuals exposed to antibiotics in utero or when young generally have teeth that are abnormally dark and discolored. Some drugs are reputed to interfere with fertility among women in recently contacted groups. If this lack of fertility combines with a drop in population size due to deaths from new diseases, a population can fall to a precarious low.

Perhaps the most critical disruption suffered by these groups, however, concerns how detailed information on features of the forest environment is diluted and forgotten. This is the pool of shared knowledge that traditionally has been the bedrock, the economic currency, the patrimony of each of these nontechnological forest societies. Manuel Lizarralde, a doctoral student at the University of California, Berkeley, who has done ethnobotanical work with the Bari of Venezuela, reports that in just a single generation there was a staggering loss of information about the identity of forest trees and their uses.

Despite this tale of disruption, disease, and destruction, many of the indigenous forest cultures are proving to be far more resilient than might be expected. The indigenous peoples remaining today in the Amazon Basin are true survivors who have successfully resisted the diseases, explorers, missionaries, soldiers, slave traders, rubber tappers, loggers, gold miners, fur traders, and colonists who have persistently encroached on them during the past five centuries.

Anthropologist Bill Balée, for example, has found that the Ka'apor Indians of Maranhão State, in peaceful contact with outsiders since 1928, still maintain many features of their traditional economy, social organization, and ritual life. He attributes this to the continued integrity of the nuclear family and the persistence of specific ritual duties between husband and wife that prohibit certain foods at different seasons or life stages. Such ritual practices have not only spared red-legged tortoises and other wild resources from being overharvested but have also diffused hunting pressures over a large area, thereby contributing to the persistence of the traditional economy.

Unfortunately, cultural persistence will do indigenous peoples no good if their tropical forest habitat is destroyed. Deforestation is primarily the result of outside influences, such as lumbering, cattle ranching, and colonization, that are permitted by government policies. Some estimates suggest that all remaining tropical forests will be destroyed by the year 2045.

Once the technological roller coaster gets moving, it's hard to jump off or even pause to consider the situation. Some say, so what? We can't all go back to the jungle, we can't all become forest-living Indians. No, we can't. But as I stand in my apartment in Berkeley, listening to my telephone's insistent ring and contemplating my unanswered mail, dusty curtains, dripping faucets, and stacks of newspapers for recycling, I'm not sure we wouldn't be far happier if we could.

Katharine Milton first traveled to Brazil in 1979 to expand her studies of howler monkeys, which she began five years earlier in Panama. [She is] a professor of anthropology at the University of California, Berkeley.

12. The Global Village:

Television, Tourism and Travel

George and Sharon Bohn Gmelch

Anthropologists are interested in how culture contact and post-colonial relationships influence people. Once a "sugar" colony of Britain, citizens of Barbados now travel to Britain and the United States, bringing new ideas and practices back to this Caribbean island. George and Sharon Gmelch also discuss how socialization in Barbados has changed since the introduction of American popular culture of Barbados, an island in the Caribbean. This article carefully explores how tourism, replacing the ebbing sugar industry, shapes the minds of Bajans. New patterns of behavior such as the "romance trade" and new commercialized festivals place locals in a moral quandary as traditional cultural values conflict with the economic realities of tourism.

Most people in St. Lucy are aware that Barbados is continually changed by its contact with the outside world. They know that events and political decisions made thousands of miles away in North America and Europe can have a profound effect on the island's economy—setting the price of sugar, determining the demand for hotel rooms, and, more recently, dictating structural readjustments that resulted in major civil service layoffs. In addition to the nearly half-million foreign tourists who stay on the island each year, many Bajans leave the country to work or study abroad or to visit relatives in North America and Europe. Both population movements introduce new ideas. On a daily basis television brings world news and North American popular culture directly into people's homes. "We're no longer an island," opined journalist Charmaine Gill. "Through telecommunications we belong to the world. We're part of the global village."

Philosopher Marshall McLuhan coined the term *global village* in the 1950s to refer to the single homogeneous world culture he believed the electronic media was creating. In many respects his prophecy seems to have come true, although it is due to more than just the spread of electronic media. Multinational corporations place legal and operational demands on small nations that they have little power to resist. At the local level, however, when people talk about the outside influences that most affect their lives, they identify three: television, tourism, and travel. In this chapter we examine the impact of these forces on people's lives. How much exposure do people in rural St. Lucy have to these phenomena? What changes do they think have taken place as a result? Although it is nearly impossible to separate the role played by television from that of tourism or foreign travel, there can be no doubt that, collectively, they have a profound impact on both the island and parish.

Television

Television arrived in Barbados in the 1960s; most people in St. Lucy acquired it a decade later. Today virtually every parish household has TV, and many people also own VCRs. Foreign lifestyles that were once the subject of speculation based on information gleaned from emigrants' letters home and returnees' tales are now displayed through talk shows, sitcoms, and films. World news is a part of everyday life. People in St. Lucy watched Nelson Mandela become president of South Africa and O. J. Simpson on trial. All homes receive the Caribbean Broadcasting Corporation (CBC) channel, which carries both North American and local programming. Since the late 1980s a subscription television service (STV) has been available, making U.S. networks such as the Cable News Network (CNN), the Entertainment and Sports Programming Network (ESPN), and Turner Network Television (TNT) available for a fee. At least 75 percent of Bajan households subscribe, although far fewer in St. Lucy than elsewhere in the island. In 1996 a new digital satellite system was being introduced, promising its subscribers hundreds of additional channels.

Most villagers are avid television and video watchers. In many homes the television set is constantly on, the sound seldom turned down. And, while it is still common to see neighbors talking together outside in the early evening, many more people are inside watching TV. Many families eat while watching TV. During our fieldwork so many people watched the nightly broadcast of "Days" ("Days of Our Lives"), an American soap opera, that telephoning someone between 6 and 7 P.M. was virtually taboo. An elderly woman we know was so absorbed in the drama that she yelled at the program's villains, fretted about the safety of her favorite character—"She just got to be careful 'cause I don't trust he. I don't trust he at'all, at'all, at'all"— and commiserated with a friend over the telephone immediately following each episode. Once darkness falls many villages seem eerily deserted; disembodied dialogue drifts through open windows into the street, and houses radiate a flickering blue glow.

North American shows dominate the television programming that Bajans watch and prefer. All of the channels available through subscription television originate in North America, as does most of the programming on Barbados' CBC. The most frequently watched and popular television programs are American soap operas, action series, and situation comedies, many of the latter with African-American stars. Many Barbadians worry about North American cultural penetration. "Man, we're the fifty-first state!" exclaimed one return migrant from the States.

> I came back home because I wanted my children to grow up in an unspoiled environment, but now Barbados is the same as the States. My kids want to wear

American clothes, eat American food, do American things, play American games. They're even watching American football and baseball on TV.

In the opinion of Sandra May Shorey of the Barbados National Trust, television programming should be controlled:

> Television should be tempered with more Barbadian and Caribbean-influenced programs. It's obviously easier to get "Days of Our Lives" and "Dallas" than something from Trinidad or Jamaica. Those countries produce very little, and what they have produced might not yet be of a standard high enough for the tastes of Barbadian viewers. But we don't really make an effort to get anything else. . . . We've never made an effort to develop programs, to explore our culture, because there's this ready-made culture, and we can just buy it.

Because commercial sponsors buy advertising time on programs they know are popular, the money to develop local programming remains limited. Nor can the government afford to support expensive program development. "We haven't got the money to do good programming—the gloss and the glitter. The government can't afford it," explained one man. "So how can we retain our culture? How can we compete with the rest of the world?"

Despite the enjoyment that television brings, villagers blame it for a variety of social ills. Communities and families, they say, are no longer as close. "People don't visit one another place like before—that gone," said an elderly neighbor of ours. "They visit more before TV." Television has made even children less sociable and less active. Instead of playing outside with their friends, many stay indoors to watch television alone or with their siblings. Research done by Monica Payne found that secondary school students watch an average of nineteen hours of television and videos each week. With time spent in school and travelling back and forth, there is little time left for socializing with friends. Villagers also hold television partially responsible for the growing alienation between the generations because children now spend less time talking to their parents and grandparents. The stories they once enjoyed are now considered "boring" in contrast to TV.

Bajans sometimes describe themselves as "quick to want and to acquire." Television fosters materialism and status striving. "It's impossible to see the equivalent of 'Dynasty' and 'Knots Landing' every night of the week, month after month, without assuming that you, the viewer, are also entitled to this standard of life," explained columnist and author John Wickham. Anxious to "improve" their lives, many people feel it is important to keep current with what is shown on TV. Some women watch television in order to track the latest North American fashions as well as to follow their favorite programs. Many young women in the parish flatly refuse to leave their homes to attend a party or concert unless they can dress in the latest style. Men are not immune. In the mid-1990s teenagers and young adults walked around the villages wearing Nike sweatbands and sport shoes, baggy name-brand jeans, and T-shirts emblazoned with American sports team logos. The son of a maid and a security guard we know begged his parents to buy him an expensive pair of Nike pump shoes—the equivalent of a week's combined wages—so he would feel comfortable at school. They gave in, reasoning that their modest income should not prevent him from being "happy." Advertising, of course, is based on creating dissatisfaction in viewers and linking happiness to a product.

Many villagers, like many Americans, believe that television and films contribute to violence and crime. The film *Colors,* which graphically portrayed the activities of a Los Angeles gang, is singled out as having spawned a number of mimic gangs in Barbados in the late 1980s. The parish's first reported gang made its appearance in 1989. Calling itself the "CBC gang," the youths reportedly broke bottles in the streets, stole coconuts, made noise, and hassled passersby. Expressing the shock of other residents, a resident of Broomefield said: "Well, we know that they have drugs all over Barbados. . . . But I never thought we would have lawless young people in St. Lucy walking about making other people miserable. You only hear about that kind of thing in Bridgetown." Gang names suggest media influence. In Bridgetown and neighboring areas the major gangs in the early 1990s were CNN, Vietnam, Beirut, and Q-8 (after Kuwait); in St. Lucy, CBC. Two are names of television networks, while three are countries or cities in which televised wars and violence had recently taken place.

Although the research findings are mixed, psychologists believe that television promotes aggression and violence in a number of ways. When violence is on TV, there is a greater tendency for children and adolescents to imitate it. The sheer frequency of violent acts and images on television normalizes violence and desensitizes children to real people's suffering. Both violent and high-action programs arouse their viewers, which can contribute to violent behavior in aggression-prone individuals. In a U.S. study, which followed children over a twenty-two-year period, from third grade through adulthood, Leonard Eron and Rowell Huesmann found that heavy television viewing was more predictive of later aggression than any other factor, including poverty, grades, single-parent homes, or exposure to real violence. When Barbadian police are interviewed about crime and youth gang activity, however, they emphasize the more direct influences of unemployment and drugs. Indeed, most crime and gang activity in Barbados is found not in rural St. Lucy but in Bridgetown and the more urban parishes of St. Michael, Christ Church, and St. James, where drugs and opportunities for crime are greatest, due to the large number of tourists.

Some people in the parish worry about the moral tone of much television programming and its long-term effect on the country. Many shows glorify material wealth, greed, corruption, casual sex, and power striving at any cost. "Adult programming," or pornography, available on satellite TV, is a particular concern to some. Although the number of parish households with satellite TV is currently small, those that have it receive fifteen adult channels from Canada. "It sickens me," said one father. "You wouldn't believe what you can see—I was talking to my friends about it this morning—it's gone past pornography. And who's to stop the children from seeing it? We're creating a sick society."

Television has a good side, of course, and this is the side that most villagers see. It provides inexpensive entertainment and can also play a positive educational role. Locally produced public service announcements, aired throughout the day, provide lessons on a variety of topics such as proper parenting, environmental awareness, and good citizenship. Documentaries and international news brought via CNN increase Bajans' awareness of social issues outside the country, although with an obvious American bias. "Before Anita Hill," claims one professional woman, "there was no concept of sexual harassment in Barbados. There was no name for it. I know I got no sympathy when I complained [five years earlier], so I dropped it." Bajans' current interest in diet and fitness is also attributed to the influence of North American TV.

Barbadians speak highly of once-popular programs like "The Fresh Prince of Bel Air" and "The Cosby Show" and of the positive images of family life they portrayed. Some people wish, however, that their positive social messages were emulated. "You see on "The Cosby Show" a lot of familial communication and families sitting down to eat [together], but this isn't adopted here," said one woman, "only the clothes."

Tourism

Tourism also ties Barbados to the outside world, bringing large numbers of foreigners to the island. In the early years tourists came to Barbados to recover their health in the island's warm air and salubrious sea breezes. Most stayed in small guest houses or in private homes. In 1751, for example, George Washington brought his older brother Lawrence, who was suffering from tuberculosis. They stayed for nearly seven weeks in country lodgings about a mile outside Bridgetown. Almost two centuries later tourist guidebooks still extolled the island's virtues as a "health resort," referring to Barbados as "the sanitorium of the West Indies."

By the early 1900s tourism had become a "notable feature" of Barbados' economy. No fewer than eleven steamships made regular calls. These early visitors tended to be wealthy, since transportation costs were high and the trip was long. They also stayed for substantial periods of time, weeks or even months. Although some large hotels had been built, most visitors stayed in guest houses or at small, exclusive "colony" or "club" resorts made up of individual bungalows, which fostered an intimate friendliness between visitors and local staff.

All this changed in the late 1950s and 1960s as the era of mass tourism got under way. With the jetliner travel was made faster and easier. Postwar affluence and the adoption of guaranteed holidays with pay for most North American and European workers gave people time off and money to travel. Sophisticated travel agencies and tour operators sprang up to package and promote Caribbean vacations. They popularized the idea of winter vacations in "exotic" tropical places and helped bring Caribbean holidays within the price range of many middle-income North Americans. Today nearly 400,000 tourists arrive in Barbados each year; an even greater number visit briefly aboard cruise ships.

Tourism now touches nearly everyone on the island. Many people in St. Lucy are employed in the industry as maids and security guards, waitresses and barmen, receptionists and gardeners. Others are self-employed food vendors, beach vendors, jet ski operators, and "beach boys." Still other people sell locally-grown produce to hotels and restaurants that cater primarily to the tourist market. The rest of the population experiences the indirect effects of tourism on Barbados' infrastructure, environment, and social climate.

Some of these effects are positive. By creating consumers for art and entertainment, tourism has encouraged the development of local music, dance, performance, visual arts, and crafts. The quantity and quality of live entertainment on Barbados is said to be high considering the island's small population. At the parish level this benefits primarily those young who can afford to visit hotels and nightclubs. Despite the availability of good local entertainment, however, many hotels and nightclubs persist in staging manufactured tourist shows such as limbo dancers and in playing North American Top 40 music rather than that of local artists. Tourism is responsible for the creation of a major cultural event that has been embraced by Bajans. "Crop Over" was originally a celebration held among plantation workers at the end of the sugarcane harvest. This "tradition" was introduced as a national celebration in 1974 to promote tourism during the slack summer season. Held at first in hotels with dancers dressed in colorful Trinidad-style carnival costumes, the new holiday was later reoriented to the local market and further developed by the National Cultural Foundation. It is now a popular national holiday that entices even Barbadians living abroad back home.

One negative consequence of tourism is its effect on the environment. Much of the south and west coasts of the island are covered with hotels and condominiums and tourist-oriented businesses such as restaurants, boutiques, and gift shops. While these provide local people with employment opportunities and offer some new services, they have created visual pollution. Along some stretches of coastline it is difficult for local people to catch a glimpse of the sea; most coastal property has been priced out of their reach. Only the steep cliffs, scarcity of beaches, heavy surf, and strong undertow along St. Lucy's coastline have saved it from similar development. Water pollution from hotel sewage and detergents are killing the reefs and eroding the beaches. Tourism also produces an enormous amount of garbage, which has overburdened the island's landfill, just as increased traffic overburdens the roads.

From the visitor's point of view, however, tourism is benign. It is simply a temporary trip away from home, for the purpose of rest or recreation, that brings money and employment to the island. Barbados promotes itself as a tropical paradise with a friendly population, the perfect place to get away from it all. The country's beauty lies "not only in its special location but in the relaxed hospitality of the Bajans—an intelligent, proud, and free people who cheerfully share their home with visitors from all over the world." In large measure Barbadians live up to their tourism industry image. Behind their rather reserved exteriors most people are friendly and surprisingly tolerant, often excusing tourist misbehavior with an indulgent "They're just here to have fun."

Yet tourism does place a social burden on the host population. While escaping their own obligations and commitments, tourists demand that local people fulfill theirs—serving food, cleaning rooms, entertaining, transporting, and providing a stress-free environment for sometimes boorish "guests." Tourists expect to be treated well no matter how they act, and they expect local people to be cheerful and courteous no matter how they feel. "I was startled to be spoken to in a gruff manner by a man behind the counter," groused a surprised Canadian tourist in a letter of complaint to a local newspaper, "telling me that I had no business coming in there [his shop] without a shirt."

The fact that most tourists are white and most Barbadians are black influences many tourist-local interactions. Racism—or expectations of it based on the country's colonial history and many Bajans' personal experiences as emigrants living in England, the United States, and Canada—can complicate interactions between tourists and locals. Some hotel employees, for example, render service to tourists indifferently. As one manager explained, "Too many of my people . . . equate service with servitude." A focus of training within the tourism industry has been teaching employees to be friendly and courteous. As Richard Haynes, then leader of the opposition, warned, "I urge . . . [Barbadians] to reflect on the damage which even a ten to fifteen percent decline in tourism expenditure will do to the Barbados economy and to further reflect on . . . the impact of such [racial] confrontation on tourism activity elsewhere in the Caribbean. . . . National pride, yes. Racism no."

The tourism industry in Barbados, however, has its own record of racism. "Until the 1960s," according to E. D. Archer, "black Barbadians were routinely refused service (or given the slowest service) in tourist hotels and restaurants." Hotel management still remains disproportionately white. Such discrimination made tourism a prime target of the short-lived student Black Power movement of the late 1960s. Many resorts continue to discourage locals from using their facilities. The nearest resort to St. Lucy, for example, recently adopted an all-inclusive plan in which tourists arrive having prepaid for everything, including food, drinks, and entertainment. Nonguests are no longer allowed onto the hotel's premises to eat in its restaurants, drink at its bars, or dance in its nightclubs, effectively banning all locals. The new plan also harms local businesses, since fewer tourists venture off hotel grounds. The presence of hotel security guards on the beaches discourages locals from using the public beach along the hotel's waterfront.

Race is sometimes overtly manipulated by both Bajans and tourists. Beach vendors occasionally use it as a sales strategy. A male vender of shell necklaces, for example, challenges tourists with the accusation, "You don't want to buy from me because I'm black." "Beach boys" (gigolos) who prey on female tourists similarly say: "Hi, I called to you earlier, but, when you didn't answer, I thought maybe it was because you don't like us black boys." Tourists, too, may introduce race into their interactions with local people. Some make overtly racist remarks to hotel staff. Martin Boyce, a former hotel entertainment director from St. Lucy, recalls the English tourist who criticized his speech: "I'm sure he was racist. . . . He wanted me to speak the way he was speaking. He wanted me to pronounce words the way he did. Like, I'm speaking bad. So I said, 'That's your English; this is my English. It's all English. I can understand you. If you can't understand me, I'm sorry!'" Other tourists simply make statements or ask questions that reveal how salient race is to them. One of us listened in surprise, for example, as an American tourist walked directly up to two hotel barmen and asked: "How do you guys feel about waiting on white people? Does it bother you?"

"Treat them well and they'll come back," advise public service announcements on television. The Caribbean Tourism Research Center (CTRC) holds workshops for teachers so that they can introduce tourism into Barbados' school curriculum. Heading the CTRC's list of recommendations is to teach students to be aware of their demeanor and of the need to change their deportment in order to match the expectations of visitors. The fact that people have to be told how to act indicates something of the unnatural strain tourism places on the local population. When tourists display their ignorance of Barbados, residents are annoyed and offended. Chupsing and raising his eyebrows, a hotel worker from St. Lucy said: "Tourists often tell me, 'I never heard of Barbados before I came here.' They don't have the slightest idea what Barbados is. They ask me about the size, what type of people live on the island, our language. Man, why they come?" According to a beach vender we know: "They think it [Barbados] somethin' like de wilderness of Africa. They expect to see de people runnin' round with a cloth about de waist." "People are surprised, when I speak," the owner of a small restaurant reported. "They say, 'My, but you speak well.'" "Their ignorance was sometimes profound," remembers a former hotel manager:

> They'd come and ask where they can get stamps. I'd tell them, "There's a little
> shop around the corner that sells stamps." They'd come back, "Well, they don't
> sell American stamps. We want to post a letter to the States." I'm telling you,

it's absolutely amazing. Any five-year-old in the Caribbean would know that, and they don't because to them the U.S.A. is the whole world. . . . Some of these people have saved up a long time to come to the Caribbean, and, when they get here, they figure everybody here has to be more ignorant than they are. They're just the tops, and aren't we glad they came!

Bajans who have prolonged contact with tourists sometimes benefit financially. Hotel workers and vendors who get to know a tourist well over a period of days or weeks may be given a substantial tip or gift at the end. In rare instances relationships between tourists and residents develop into friendships that are maintained over the years through letters and return visits, with the tourist sometimes helping finance a home improvement or business venture. One St. Lucy man we know was able to set himself up in the water ski business because of the financial help from a woman friend. Occasionally, Bajans travel with a tourist back to their home country to work or visit. A young St. Lucy woman who had looked after an American couple's children during their two-week vacation returned with them to the States to work as a live-in babysitter. Beach boys have traveled to Canada, the United States, and Europe to move in with their lovers. In *Colonial Madness* Lawrence Fisher discusses the role that relationships with tourists can play in creating jealousy and envy among villagers. He quotes a hotel maid:

> People come to visit me from the hotel at my house. They come to see me, or maybe they would bring me up [home] if the rain fall. If they have a party, they would come for me, an' I would work for them . . . [my neighbor] say "De white people think you are somebody, but they wouldn't know you aren't nobody."

The most intimate and visible tourist-local relationships are those between female tourists and "beach bums," or beach boys. These relationships are so well-known that many Bajans believe that any foreign woman who arrives on the island without a male companion has come with more than tourism's "three Ss"—sun, sand, and sea—in mind. While some women undoubtedly do have sex in mind, other women fall into romantic relationships with local men, which they believe are genuine and unique. "Romance tourism" as anthropologists Deborah Pruitt and Suzanne LaFont note in a study of beach boys in Jamaica, is not just a gender inversion of the "sex tourism" found in underdeveloped countries like Thailand or the Philippines, in which male tourists travel explicitly to avail themselves of the paid services of local prostitutes, most of whom have been forced into prostitution by poverty. Relationships between beach boys and female tourists, in contrast, even if paid, are voluntary and "constructed through a discourse of romance and long-term relationship." Unlike the local Filipina or Thai woman, the Barbadian beach boy in many respects has the upper hand. As sociologists Cecilia Karch and Graham Dann point out, he is the person who is on familiar ground, while the tourist is in a foreign land. He is knowledgeable about such relationships, while she may be unfamiliar with them. (Indeed, all she may know about local men is that the travel literature describes Bajans as "friendly.") Ironically, the beach boy may even act as a male protector, since foreign women often feel threatened by the hissing and explicit sexual comments many Bajan men direct at them. It is the female tourist who ultimately has control of the relationship, however, since she pays the bills, can break it off, and will leave the island to return home. She may be emotionally vulnerable, but it is the local beach boy who is financially dependent and who must show deference and appreciation in order to maintain the relationship.

Fantasy notions of "the Other" play a part in beach boy-tourist interactions. For the white tourist there is the idea of romance with a black man who she is likely to regard as "exotic," "natural," and more sexually endowed than a white man (according to the familiar saying "once you go Black, you never go back"). Most local beach boys are young and muscular and prowl the beaches in revealing swimsuits. Some wear dreadlocks, enhancing their exotic and natural appeal. Female tourists who at home might be considered plain, overweight, or too old for such a young man may be especially vulnerable to the beach boy's "sweet talk." "You married? You have a special friend?" he asks. "A beautiful girl like you should have a boyfriend," he responds, no matter how she has replied. "You need a Bajan boyfriend," he insists. "How you goin' to experience Barbados if you never sleep with a Bajan man?" Many beach boys now directly address the fear of AIDS, reassuring potential partners, "Don't worry, I practice safe sex." One jet ski operator and beach boy's motto is, "No accidents during the day, no AIDS at night!" For some women the offer presents an opportunity to experiment with their sensual sides while risking relatively little. Being a tourist is a liminal experience during which a person's behavior does not really count; she need never return to Barbados, and no one at home need ever know what she has done.

For the local beach boy, some of whom live in St. Lucy, relationships with tourists provide money, sex, intimacy with a foreigner, short-term comforts (e.g., dinner, drinks, a nice room), and enhanced status among their peers—as self-styled nicknames like "Dr. Love" suggest. Bajan masculinity is defined largely by sexual prowess, which includes the ability to satisfy women; what better evidence than the highly visible ability to attract foreign women. For many men such relationships mean money and even help with emigration. Most local people, however, regard beach boys as disreputables who are too lazy to find honest work. Yet they have a pragmatic attitude toward this special tourist-local relationship. "The people that are being approached are not innocent," claimed one villager. "They're both getting what they want [sex]. It's like trying a different type of food." According to a young woman we know: "The guys get a good time out of it. It's good for them. The only time it's a problem is when they [female tourists] mess with my guy." Being a beach boy is a young man's occupation, and most men move on to more respectable work by their thirties.

Other kinds of tourist-local encounters are undoubtedly more in keeping with the Tourism Board's assertion that "social interaction between people of diverse origins and cultural backgrounds" brings "positive benefits." We have both overheard many conversations in which tourists and local people shared information about their personal lives and their countries' customs, economy, and politics. A young hotel worker from St. Lucy, for example, struck up a conversation one afternoon with a Venezuelan couple who were swimming in a hotel pool. As they clung to the side, he practiced his Spanish with them, and they asked him to explain Bajan dialect. Together they talked about the need for people to learn other languages so they can better understand one another's cultures. The Mighty Gabby, Barbados' famous calypsonian, frequently talked to tourists during his early career as a singer on tour boats: "They'd talk about things I had no experience of—fascinating things, like countries, the size of them, the fastness of them, the kind of things that you could do there. . . . I was a young man having all this information fed to me. . . . I was fascinated, and I wanted to go see for myself."

What degree of contact do St. Lucy's residents have with tourists? Those who work in the industry, of course, have daily contact with tourists. But most people's exposure is limited to brief encounters and observations they make on the streets or in the stores of Bridgetown and Speightstown. One tourist behavior of which Bajans disapprove is their practice of wearing beach clothing in public. Locals interpret this as disrespect. "They walk around in these skimpy bathing suits. . . . Even in supermarkets you see men walking around without shirts and the ladies in only their swimwear," commented a woman with distaste. "A Bajan would be arrested if they were caught walking around with the lack of clothing that tourists walk around in." Local people are far from prudish; they just think that businesses and the streets of town are not the proper place. Some store owners have put up signs informing tourists: "No bare backs" and "No scantily dressed persons allowed in the store."

Few tourists stay in St. Lucy. To begin with there are no hotels. In the 1960s a large resort with an Olympic-size swimming pool was built at North Point, but management problems and its isolation from the centers of tourist activity led to its closing. Exposed to salt spray and strong winds for many years, it is now in bad condition. Tourists do visit the parish to enjoy its natural beauty. Most people go to the Animal Flower Cave, a wave-eroded underground cavern that opens beneath the cliffs onto the sea. Others come to see scenic Cove Bay with its view of Pico Teneriffe, a craggy rock spire just south of the bay.

Tourists who visit St. Lucy as part of an island-wide bus tour have minimal contact with villagers, speeding by on their way to the Animal Flower Cave or Cove Bay. They only leave the bus to see the sights and take pictures and are soon back on board. Those who travel in a hired taxi may see more and linger longer, but they too generally have limited contact with local people. Only tourists who rent "mokes" (open cars) and spend time exploring the island actually talk to villagers, typically while buying a cold drink at a rum shop or stopping to admire the view. It is not uncommon, however, to see even these more adventuresome tourists parked on the roadside bent over a map while glancing nervously in the direction of local people who could easily aid them. Some communities in the parish are never visited by even the most intrepid traveler, and thus the impact of tourism on many villagers remains indirect.

Tourism, like television, nevertheless transfers outside values and patterns of behavior to Barbadians through its "demonstration effects." Tourists become a reference group for the host society; they are living manifestations of the wealth St. Lucy's residents and other Barbadians so frequently see in film and on TV. Tourism thus contributes to a sense of relative deprivation. Even people who do not work in tourism have heard stories about how much hotel rooms cost. "Do you know at Sandy Lane that some people pay as much as two thousand dollars U.S. a day!" a member of Barbados' police force exclaimed during an interview about tourism and crime. Hotel workers watch as tourists purchase drinks and food at inflated prices, wasting much of it. Going to a restaurant for most villagers is an extravagance, done only to celebrate major family events such as a child's passing the Common Entrance Examination, graduating from college, or getting married. Tourists staying at the best hotels wear expensive clothing and jewelry. Others seem to flash their cameras, sports equipment, and money around. Many locals envy not only the tourists' ability to travel but also their possessions and apparent wealth. "The locals see what the tourists have and how they're living, and they want it," explained one hotel worker. "They don't see the fifty weeks of work behind it. They think it's easy."

One consequence of tourism that many people worry about is its effect on the work ethic of Bajan youth. Tourism is believed to raise expectations and the desire for material goods, at the same time giving some youths an opportunity to make "easy" money quick. The beach boy phenomenon is one example. Another is through drugs and crime, especially burglary and theft. According to one St. Lucy resident, the attitude of a growing number of youths is, 'Why should I work all week when I can make the same money in one drug deal or hustling the tourists?" "There's a feeling out there among the younger guys," elaborated a professor at the University of the West Indies,

> that there's a lot of money to be had and that "We want part of it, and we want it now." Serious steady work is not fast enough for them and doesn't pay well enough. So there's a tendency to hustle and perhaps cut corners for it [money]. There's a thin line between hustling and cutting corners and doing illegal things. . . . I think [tourism] has had that kind of impact, although it's hard to separate this from the impact of television, which has changed expectations— expectations that are unrealistic given the resource base of this country.

Because tourists have money and come to Barbados to have a good time, villagers reason, they provide a ready market for drugs. Selling to them has become a quick way for unemployed youths to make money. Indeed. the first four drug arrests in Barbados (for marijuana) occurred in 1971 just as mass tourism was getting under way; three of the four individuals arrested were tourists. By the 1980s cocaine and "rock" (crack) had also arrived on the island. Most drug dealing and crime occurs in areas with heavy concentrations of tourists, in the parishes of St. Michael, Christ Church, St. James, and, secondarily, in St. Joseph around the community of Bathseba. But St. Lucy is also affected. Barbados is one of many drug transshipment sites in the Caribbean, although a minor one compared to the Grenadines and Antigua, with couriers taking premium marijuana and crack to North America via airlines, yachts, and cruise and container ships. Drugs are often landed on isolated beaches—Maycock's, Duppies, Stroud Bay—along St. Lucy's coast.

Travel and Emigration

Foreign travel is also a major link to the outside world and a significant source of change at both the national and parish level. Emigration, prompted by poverty at home and opportunities abroad, has a long history on the island and was one of the earliest outside influences to affect the average Bajan. Today many people still travel abroad to work or study. Others go as tourists or to visit relatives overseas. Indeed, many people are members of "transnational families"—a term used by Rosina Wiltshire to describe Caribbean families who are spread across national boundaries, with relatives living on both sides of the Atlantic forming a network of linkages through which the normal family functions of economic support, decision making, and nurturing are shared. Approximately a quarter of St. Lucy's households currently have children living abroad. Most people regularly receive mail, telephone calls, and visits from family members living overseas. Many people visit relatives living in the United States, especially in Brooklyn, each year.

Most early emigration from Barbados was to other islands in the Caribbean and to South America. From the mid-1800s to early 1900s an estimated fifty thousand people left Barbados to work as seasonal agricultural laborers in British Guiana (Guyana) and Trinidad. Others emigrated to Suriname, St. Croix, and Cuba. During the construction of the Panama Canal an estimated forty-five thousand to sixty thousand people, including many from St. Lucy, left to work as "pick and shovel men" for ten cents an hour. Other Bajans emigrated to England, Canada, and the United States. They were fleeing the kind of poverty the Reverend F. Godson described in the parish in 1916:

> In Crab Hill and neighboring villages I came in contact with the worst pover-
> ty and destitution I ever saw up to then—except perhaps in one village in St.
> Kitts. It was a specially dry year, even for that area; there was little work on the
> plantations around and very little money; the people's own gardens were bare;
> and the price of imported foodstuffs, together with sugar, were soaring. So I
> met with hunger, rapes, dilapidated shacks, idling, and praedial larceny on an
> exceptional scale.

Emigration tides have waxed and waned over the years in response to conditions at home and the needs and policies of other nations. In 1924, for example, emigration to the United States virtually stopped as a result of legislation that placed national quotas on the number of immigrants allowed in. The entire British West Indies was limited to two hundred people; only five from Barbados. By the 1930s most emigration outlets in the Caribbean had also closed. One villager remembers those years: "There was nothing coming in terms of food. We ate sweet potatoes morning, noon, and night. It was a very hard time." Opportunities for emigration did not open up again until World War II, when Britain, Canada, and the United States needed workers to help in war industries and alleviate manpower shortages in agriculture. Some Barbadians also went to Britain as volunteers in the armed forces.

After the war large-scale emigration began once more. Many people, like Siebert Allman, went to Britain on the Sponsored Workers Scheme. British companies and government agencies including the London Transport Executive and the British Hotel and Restaurant Association sent recruiters to Barbados, and people from all over the island, including St. Lucy, traveled to Bridgetown to be interviewed. If they measured up, as most did, they were assigned a job, trained, and transported to England. Many women went to Britain to become nurses or work in light industry in cities like Manchester, Liverpool, and Birmingham. The Barbados government provided some people with travel loans. Between 1955 and 1961 nineteen thousand Barbadians left for Britain, nearly forty-five hundred as "assisted migrants."

In the 1960s the emigration tide shifted to Canada and the United States, which had eased their immigration restrictions, at the same time that Britain, through the Commonwealth Immigration Act (1962), was closing its doors to immigration. Although U.S. and Canadian policies favored skilled workers and professionals, some unskilled workers managed to obtain "labor certification" to become domestic workers and seasonal agricultural laborers. One of our neighbors in Josey Hill went to the United States six times during the 1960s to pick fruit in the Northeast. Another villager cut sugarcane in Florida for five years. Emigration continues today. Student household surveys in five St. Lucy villages in 1994 and 1996 found that nearly one-fifth of household heads had lived abroad and that a quarter of the households currently had one or more children living abroad. According to both our own and our students' interviews with teachers and students over the years, the majority of St. Lucy secondary students would like to emigrate to the United States after graduation to find work or further their education.

The influence of emigration is felt as soon as people leave. Families at home must readjust; young children often move in with a granny or aunt. Emigrants soon begin sending home "remittances" as well as goods and news from North America, England, and elsewhere. Roosevelt Griffith, profiled in chapter 4, managed to save a large part of his income and return home to build a wall house. In 1991 remittances to Barbados amounted to $11,716,000 BDS. Men living on their own sometimes send back as much as half their pay to their mothers or wives. Many people in St. Lucy still receive cartons of clothes and other goods at Christmas each year. An older villager remembers that, even if the carton contained only hand-me-downs or clothes bought secondhand, "no matter how old, from America, it look new." Barbadians abroad also help family members when they emigrate or visit. When villagers we know visit their relatives abroad. the cost of their plane ticket is often reimbursed on arrival. With the foreign currency villagers buy clothing and household goods to bring home.

Most people who emigrate intend to stay only a few years and then return. "On the way over to England," remembers Roy Campbell, who grew up in the village of Rockfield, "my thinking was that I'd be away no more than five years. I had a goal of saving a certain amount of money and then coming back to Barbados and getting a little house." A good indication of most Bajans' strong attachment to home and of their intention to return is the fact that they have one of the lowest naturalization rates of any foreign-born immigrant group in the United States.

When Bajans return home they become agents of change. Their influence starts when they send back money to their relatives to hire a contractor to build a house. Most return with substantial capital from their savings and the sale of overseas assets, sometimes a house and car, which they invest in housing at home. In St. Lucy the most substantial wall houses have been built by returnees, the earliest with "Panama money." Today returnee housing is almost invariably large and of high quality, setting a standard to which others in the parish aspire. Early returnees also introduced material innovations. Those who came back from Panama, for example, are credited with introducing better household sanitation and window screens. North American returnees have brought back wall-to-wall carpeting. Today, however, because of the pervasive influence of television and film, there is little new in the way of material objects that returnees can introduce that villagers are not already familiar with.

Returnees do, nevertheless, continue to be an important source of information. In the words of Valenza Griffith, who lived in England:

> When I was a child the people that came back from overseas were accepted back into the community [Coles Cave, St. Lucy]. We were eager to learn things from them—what the houses were like, what the education was like, do they write like us. . . . Today people know a lot more about America and England than they did in my time. But some people still asked me some weird questions [when I returned in 1973], like if you get false teeth for free in

England or if they really bury three and four people in the same grave or if people's toes drop off in England from the cold.

In an earlier survey of Barbadian returnees, one of us found that nearly half of those who took jobs at home believed that they had been able to introduce changes at their workplace based on knowledge they had acquired abroad. An American-trained certified public accountant, for example, introduced the electronic processing of financial accounts to a Bridgetown firm. A nurse trained in England introduced new techniques for monitoring babies before birth. A former rector of the St. Lucy Parish Church instituted policies he learned in England that expanded his parishioners' participation in church services. In some fields major innovations can be attributed to the influence of return migrants. A movement to deinstitutionalize childcare in Barbados came from returnees working in the Ministry of Social Services who had become familiar with new approaches while working in Canada. While most of these changes have taken place outside the parish, they still have an indirect affect on many villagers' lives.

Some returnees, of course, have a direct impact on the parish. Siebert and Aileen Allman opened a small general store in the village of Sutherland. Another St. Lucy couple shipped three buses home from England and set up a mini-bus service. Although such enterprises typically do not employ many people, they do provide needed services and contribute to the smooth running of the parish economy and the convenience of its residents.

Villagers who have lived abroad return with acquired values: an appreciation for promptness and efficiency, familiarity with a faster pace, and more materialistic goals. They are also considered more "worldly" than those who have never gone away. Some evidence suggests that returnees heighten other villagers' political awareness and racial consciousness. Returnees tell family and friends about the racial remarks and incidents they experienced while living abroad. Not only did Siebert Allman experience racism while working on the buses in England; he and Aileen were turned away from an apartment in Canada even though the landlord had told them over the telephone that it was available. Writer George Lamming, in *The Castle of My Skin*, contrasts the protagonist's own naive lack of awareness with the racial consciousness acquired by his friend Trumper while in the United States: "If there was one thing I thank America for, she teach me who my race wus. . . . None o' you here on this islan' know what it mean to fin' race." Anthropologists Constance Sutton and Susan Makiesky believe that return migrants in the village they studied had greater influence on people's racial and political consciousness than either middle-class Barbadians or student radicals. The emigration experience, for many people, also strengthens a regional identification with other West Indians whom they have lived with in London and New York.

The influence that returnees have at the local level, however, is much less than it could be. Many returnees encounter jealousy and resistance to their new ideas. Some of Valenza Griffith's ideas were rejected by her fellow nurses:

> The standard of nursing in England is completely different. . . . Up there you are exposed to more equipment and teaching than here, and you have more different kinds of cases there. But you can't apply what you learned up there without being criticized. They'd [fellow nurses] soon tell you, "You should've stayed up there."

A civil servant who had worked in England believes his colleagues ignored his ideas "because . . . they feel threatened. They don't want to admit that maybe you have the answer, especially when you've only been on the job half as long." A teacher recalls the way her colleagues would "push up their faces" (skeptically grimace) at her suggestions. Another frustrated returnee explains: "We [returnees] have the same ideas as North Americans who live here. The difference is that people will listen to what the foreigner has to say but not to their own kind. They'll say, 'Who the hell is he to tell us what to do? He's only Barbadian like us.'"

One difficulty in assessing the influence returnees have, either at the national or local level, is trying to disentangle their role as agents of change from the many other external influences, such as television and tourism, that bombard people each day. In the aggregate we believe that emigration introduces many new ideas and has been a significant force for change. Certainly, migrants who return to Barbados come back as changed individuals. If nothing else, those villagers who interact with them are bound to observe and perhaps to absorb, even if reluctantly, some of their new attitudes and ways.

Today many Bajans travel abroad themselves for pleasure and to visit family and friends. In 1993, for example, U.S. Emigration issued nonimmigrant visas to twenty-five thousand Barbadians, or nearly 10 percent of the population, so they could visit the United States. Other popular destinations include Canada and England and, to a lesser extent, South America and other Caribbean islands. Barbadians also take advantage of airline promotions and inexpensive package trips to go to Puerto Rico, Miami, St. Martin, and Margarita Island, off the coast of Venezuela, on short shopping trips. Most take long shopping lists from family and friends along and return with bags packed with clothing, fabric, linens, and small appliances purchased at a fraction of what they cost at home. Street vendors who sell on Swan Street in Bridgetown may travel as often as six times a year to purchase popular clothing items such as designer jeans. School groups from St. Lucy visit Puerto Rico, Venezuela, and Disney World. Although fundraisers help defray the costs, many parish children cannot afford to go. Despite all this travel, some people seldom leave the parish—one elderly man we know claims never to have been to Bridgetown—and most have never left the island. This difference captures a very real feature of the parish, which is the growing gap in experience among people. It was not so long ago that most people worked on the same plantations, lived in the same modest houses, and shared the same experiences. Today this is no longer true.

13. Virtually Vietnamese

Kim-an Lieberman

Interdisciplinary cultural studies scholar Kim-an Lieberman, examines the role of the Internet in defining Vietnamese identity. After the 1975 diaspora, Vietnamese outside of Vietnam created virtual national identities. She documents the communities and websites used as a "switchboard" for activists who aim to influence the future of Vietnam. She suggests that globally dispersed Vietnamese people are imagining new communities for themselves and using technology to create a postmodern cyberspatial Vietnam—diverse, global, chaotic, and heavily media-driven. Most of this activity is not in Vietnam, whose government does promote the "online club" but outside it.

We are in the epoch of simultaneity: we are in the epoch of juxtaposition, the epoch of the near and far, of the side-by-side, of the dispersed.

> —Michel Foucault, "Of Other Spaces"

Beyond the impossible, we are the possible.

> —Hoang Viet Cuong, Coalition of Vietnamese National Parties Homepage

THE REPUBLIC OF VIETNAM: "EVERYWHERE AND NOWHERE"

The fall of Saigon to Hò Chí Minh's communist army in 1975 triggered an exodus of over two million Vietnamese who disagreed with or feared for their lives under the new regime. They scattered across the globe, resettling in Australia, France, the United States, and many other countries. Support for a Vietnamese democracy, however, remained strong. With the 1989 unification of Germany and the subsequent dissolution of communism in Eastern Europe, political change in Vietnam seemed increasingly tenable. Vietnamese nationalists, although

189

dispersed, began forming several democracy movements. Their common goal: a free Vietnam. Among the most efficient and effective tools in their cause has been, and continues to be, the Internet.

As David Lamb points out, "anyone with a computer and $20 for subscription fees to a service provider can become a dissident activist these days."[1] Dorothy Dunning echoes, "The Internet is clearly changing the landscape of political discourse and advocacy."[2] Unlike older forms of public discourse, the large majority of Internet space still lacks an overt power structure. There are no editors, critics, sponsors or other authority figures mediating access. Not only do authors get unlimited air time, but they have a ready-made audience of millions. Publication is immediate, worldwide, and (beyond access to a computer) independent of material or social status; the transfer of information is instantaneous and simultaneous. With a vastly wider and faster range of transmission than photocopied manifestos, short-wave radio, or public access television, the Internet has become a essential grassroots medium for expressing dissent, even altering the very nature of civil war. Peter Eng notes, "In fighting Burma's brutal military government Lwin Moe used to wear combat fatigues, wield an AK-47 rifle and roam the jungles with Regiment 201 of the All Burma Students Democratic Front. Today, in business jackets and from an office in neighboring Thailand, he still fights the same enemy but a very different type of war. His weapons now are two 233 MHz desktop computers. His battle ground is Cyberspace."[3] Moe much prefers the computer because "We can fight without bloodshed. We can send statements to the entire world and we can send a virus to the [government] machine."[4] Another Burmese opposition group, with only "a single computer powered by a 286 chip," applied for a grant to buy additional computers "and now has become a potent anti-government force. At times it has crippled the government's e-mail system with a flood of junk messages."[5] China's communist government is contending with its own self-proclaimed "hacktivists."[6] In Indonesia, protesters used "literally hundreds of e-mail lists" to rally support for an underground movement that successfully ended President Kemusu Suharto's thirty-two-year rule.[7] Other world regions with volatile political climates, such as east central Europe and northern Africa, have found themselves battling conflict on land as well as in cyberspace.[8]

Overseas Vietnamese have also harnessed online free speech for political ends. The Internet has become a springboard for their dissent from Vietnam's current government. "Accurate information," asserts one organization, "must be one of the most effective and peaceful weapons to conduct the struggle for democracy and freedom against that worst tyranny in the history of Vietnam."[9] Claims another, "by utilizing the Internet for information and suggestions from people around the world, [we] may also have invented a new way of fighting for Human Rights, Freedom and Democracy for Vietnam."[10] Self-directed, uncensored, and globally broadcast, online media such as webpages and e-mail are the perfect complements to Vietnamese political activism—especially since the activists cannot easily gather together on physical ground. Journalist David Case explains that "for years, [overseas Vietnamese] have been separated from Vietnam and one another by the vast geography of the globe. The Internet has changed that, bringing them as close as the nearest modem." He concludes that "Next century, Vietnam's battles will be fought in cyberspace."[11]

There are over two dozen websites devoted entirely to Vietnamese anticommunist activism. Among them: homepages for the fifty-year-old Việt Nam Quốc Dân Đảng (Vietnamese

Nationalist Party, known as "Việt Quốc" for short);[12] the southern California—based Đoàn Thanh Niên Phan Bội Châu (Youth For Democracy Group);[13] and the Đại Việt Cách Mạng Đáng (Vietnam Revolution Party) with its battle cry of "humanism, democracy, prosperity."[14] The outspoken Phong Tráo Thống Nhất Dân Tộc và Xây Dụng Dân Chú (Movement to United the People and Build Democracy) uses its Internet space to announce that "*blind* adherence to Marxist doctrine led to an totalitarian state at the expense of the health and welfare of the [Vietnamese] people. Communism has now proven to be [a] miserable failure."[15] Other online declarations detail specific steps toward the reestablishment of a Vietnamese Democratic Republic, ranging from the self-titled Government of Free Vietnam's "A Program to Save the Nation and Build the Nation"—a series of "whereas" and "because" statements that reads strikingly like Abraham Lincoln's Emancipation Proclamation[16]—to the Free Vietnam Alliance's step-by-step outline for "the Democratization Process," with different directives for the leadership of the Vietnamese Communist Party and its "progressive" members, Vietnamese in Vietnam and overseas, and "all democratic forces."[17] A handful of websites even propose restoration of the Nguyen Dynasty's monarchical descendents (within a democratic structure, of course) as remedy to communism.[18]

The Internet has become the central switchboard for Vietnamese activists exchanging and disseminating information. Many organizations, including the Vietnam Human Rights Network (Mạng Luói Nhân Quyền) and the International Committee for Freedom (Cao Trào Nhân Bán), use the Internet to monitor political violence and persecution in Vietnam.[19] Others—like the recently retired Vietnam Insight, maintained throughout the 1990s by an activist who worked from her home in suburban San Jose[20]—function as a general clearinghouse of news articles "carrying the voice of opposition against the oppressive regime in Vietnam to the outside world."[21] All are accessible from any country that is linked to the Internet; their authors might come from the United States or Germany; their host computers might be located in New Zealand or Taiwan. "The Internet and e-mail are fantastic for crossing borders," says Doan Viet Hoat, a prominent Vietnamese dissident, because "no dictator could stop it."[22] As webpage author Lý Thanh Bình proclaims, "This new political party will be everywhere and nowhere."[23]

Even if not political in purpose, the webpages for many Vietnamese communities and associations include their own anticommunist mission statements or reference other sites with corresponding agendas. A recent posting on the general-interest Vietnamese American web portal Kicon Vietspace provides a direct link to the Committee For Religious Freedom in Vietnam, along with information about the organization's upcoming protest against the new China-Vietnam border agreement.[24] The international Vietnamese Professionals Society—a forum hoping "to facilitate the exchange of professional information, the interaction between Vietnamese and non-Vietnamese professionals, and between groups of Vietnamese of different professions"—lists among its primary goals "to contribute to . . . the formation of a democratic Vietnam" and avers that "its members oppose all activities that benefit the dictatorial regime."[25] Vietnamese university student groups often use the Internet to vocalize political opinions: in October 1997, UCLA's Vietnamese Student Union homepage highlighted its protest of an on-campus performance by Hanoi's Thăng Long Water Puppet Troupe, a movement spread by e-mail to Vietnamese student associations at Berkeley and elsewhere.[26] Likewise, the soc.culture.vietnamese Usenet newsgroup, easily accessible through web-based services like DejaNews, has become an active arena for anticommunist debate and information exchange. One posting lists the "top websites" of "free Vietnamese people all over the world," informing interested readers about their online options for activism and information.[27]

Taking advantage of the web as multimedia, Vietnamese online express their political opinions visually as well as textually. Anticommunist icons, sounds, and speech abound in Vietnamese Internet space. The Việt Quốc webpage, for instance, depicts the "Mourning Soldier" statue that stood in South Vietnam's National Military Cemetery until dismantled at the end of the war by Communist forces.[28] Online maps of Vietnam often have "Saigon" prominently labeled where "Hồ Chí Minh City" should be.[29] Real-time audio technology enables politically minded broadcasts like Radio Free Vietnam and Vietnamese Public Radio to reach a global audience.[30] Perhaps most boldly, the yellow and red striped flag of the Việt Nam Cộng Hoà (Republic of Vietnam), displaced in 1975 by the Communists' five-point star, still waves—literally, through the use of animated graphics—on a website proudly claiming to represent the late South Vietnamese armed forces.[31] Adorning the large majority of political and even nonpartisan Vietnamese webpages, the decommissioned Republican flag has become a commonplace motif online.[32] The education reference page for the ABC Interactive World Factbook includes former South Vietnam in its "Flags of all Countries" section, "By Popular Demand."[33] There is even a website whose sole purpose is "Protection of the Flag of the Republic," waving its own flag graphic to a rousing MIDI-synthesizer rendition of the South Vietnamese national anthem.[34] As this last site explains, its fanfare of sight and sound is deliberately meant to capture attention: "We do know our flag does not exist on the international map, that is why we have to protect and keep [it] alive. . . ."[35] Technically, the Republic of Vietnam fell with Saigon, but in many senses it has been resurrected on the Internet.

This essay is an exploration of how the Internet both enables as well as shapes Vietnamese democratic activism. I am especially interested in the Internet as a site of imagination and empowerment, of possibility for change—and how that environment can affect the formation of individual identity. With cyberspace standing as proxy for the unobtainable space of Vietnam, how do those of the Vietnamese diaspora define themselves and their nationality? How does Vietnam itself respond? I look closely at the online manifestations of common national markers: language, history, and homeland. This is all uncharted territory; my hope is that future researchers will further explore these issues. We all know that the Internet is changing the way that we shop, work, communicate. How is it changing the way that we envision ourselves in political and geographic space?

IMAGINING THINGS

It may be dictator-proof, but an idealized online manifestation of Vietnam still has its complications. After all, the efficacy of a political movement without central leaders or tangible presence is questionable. Especially when its opponents are an all-too-real and powerful communist government firmly ensconced in the homeland, online activists are vulnerable to the accusation that their democratic alternative is (and has always been) a fantasy. How do you prove the validity of social structure, of actual and significant achievement, in a physical unreality located "everywhere and nowhere"? For Vietnamese activists on the Internet, the answer has been to take conscious control of the imagined ideal. This alone is a source of empowerment: the ability to determine the way that the Vietnamese democratic community conceives itself. As Guobin Yang writes of a parallel online movement among overseas Chinese, "Their success story is a story of connection: they provide points of entry and connection for a dispersed population."[36]

The process of imagining community, to borrow Benedict Anderson's term, is a pivotal hinge for "entry and connection." Vietnamese activists build national and political allegiance by remaining cognizant of the larger context in which they operate—using the literal network of the Internet to reach their symbolic network of compatriots. Like Anderson's newspaper reader, who is "well aware that the ceremony he performs is being replicated simultaneously by thousands (or millions) of others of whose existence he is confident, yet of whose identity he has not the slightest notion,"[37] the Việt Quốc party explicitly recognizes its widespread but anonymous audience: "The primary objective of this homepage is to provide those who read English with profound insights into the true situation in Vietnam and the conflict between the communists and non-communists. . . . With such better knowledge, we hope the readers would lend their strong support to the right causes of our Vietnamese non-communist bloc."[38] Similarly, the Government of Free Vietnam invokes "the Holy Spirit of the Fatherland, our glorious Ancestors . . . our heroes . . . seventy million compatriots, inside the country and abroad."[39] If we start with Anderson's definition of the newspaper as "an 'extreme form' of the book, a book sold on a colossal scale, but of ephemeral popularity,"[40] then the Internet takes it one step further, an "extreme form" of the newspaper which achieves an even greater scale, and is not even ephemeral but instantaneous.

As "extreme" newspapers, webpages and e-mail help project national identity. The subjects of Anderson's study, however, arrive at their nationalism through a relatively passive and ambient awareness of neighbors. The Vietnamese online community, as a product of diasporic experience, must actively manufacture its sense of interconnection. As John Rex explains, "A diaspora is said to exist when an *ethnie* or nation suffers some kind of traumatic event which leads to the dispersal of its members, who nonetheless, continue to aspire to return to the homeland."[41] Just like Anderson's newspaper nation, the dispersed nation is a concept fabricated by self-identifying members. The role of imagination in diasporic nationalism, however, is differently inflected. Anderson places the crux of imagination in community formation: "It is *imagined* because the members of even the smallest nation will never know most of their fellow-members, meet them, or even hear of them, yet in the minds of each lives the image of their communion."[42] The diaspora, by contrast, are a globally disbanded network of former neighbors, a collective that has ostensibly fallen apart: "two million Vietnamese had to escape by any means possible, scattering all over the world."[43] It is a patchwork of cross-continental span that embraces but cannot effectively unite its members. What they have in common, I suggest, is the image of their *separation*.

In place of communion, the diaspora construct what James Clifford calls "a history of dispersal, myths/memories of the homeland, alienation in the host (bad host?) country, desire for eventual return, ongoing support of the homeland, and a collective identity importantly defined by this relationship."[44] The diasporic framework shifts emphasis from imagined community to imagined origin, from notions of fellow newspaper-readers to "myths/memories of the homeland."[45] Online, Vietnamese activists take control of this act of imagining. The home-land is made mythic and memorable on the Internet through the active and collaborative presentation of personal anecdotes, photo montages, nostalgic or epic histories. On the Vietnamese Boatpeople Connection webpage, former refugee Binh D. Dao collects "Untold Stories" of "perilous escapes to freedom that no one could have imagined," valorizing the anecdotes as a vital act of remembering: "I decided to set up this website, hoping that many fortunate survivors would be willing to share their stories. I know many stories are just too painful to recall. I just hope that you would somehow find the courage to share. Now that it is a thing of the past, only its legacy remains . . ."[46] Tuan Nguyen's effusive webpage, "Vietnam: The Land of Hope and Prosperity," also solicits collective participation in the act of construction: "Welcome all. Together we are going to discover the beauty of our homeland." Nguyen then goes on to figure Vietnam in mythic proportions, "a precious stone which can never be shat-tered. Each struggle of this lovely land is like a polishing, and after each polishing it becomes clearer and brighter. . . . When the wave of democracy washes over Vietnam, it will polish down all the flaws and the Vietnam Jade will become ten times brighter and more refined."[47]

Awareness of imagining is key to the Vietnamese activists' agenda. Even if they no longer reside in the Vietnamese nation, they can still claim national allegiance to a Vietnam that has been deliberately idealized through memories of the past or hopes for the future. Edward Said posits that "there is no doubt that imaginative geography and history help the mind to inten-sify its own sense of itself"; it is precisely recognition of this "imaginative geography and his-tory" upon which Said's argument about orientalism as the crystallization of occidental identity hinges.[48] For the diaspora, who remain by definition politically and geographically marginal-ized, imagination has everything to do with identity—and the Internet helps them to extend their imaginative grasp. Ananda Mitra notes that "the determinate moment in the process of voicing on the Internet is the moment of creating the utterance and not so much the moment at which the utterance is heard. This perspective is particularly important for marginal groups who might not have had the opportunity to express themselves in their own authentic voice until the Internet was available. In making that possibility available, the Internet empowers the marginal in ways that no other media technology has been able to do before. . . . [and] makes that empowerment particularly significant since many such traditionally powerless voices can now connect with each other to empower each other."[49] If not immediately effecting the desired political change, Vietnamese online expression does something equally important: it enables Vietnamese expatriates as authors of their own collectively imagined identity.

Monique T. D. Truong, in one of the only existing studies of Vietnamese American iden-tity by a Vietnamese American, writes that "For the majority of Americans, Vietnam as a self-defined country never existed."[50] Instead, Vietnam signifies a war, an era, a landmark in American (but not Vietnamese American) historical and social consciousness. "Vietnamese Americans" are consequently stereotyped as boat people, ambiguous enemy-victims, martyrs from the "other side"—marked by war, not cultural heritage. The general conception of Vietnamese American life and identity remains one wholly divested of individual choice: "Immigrants *choose to come* to a new life, whereas refugees *are forced to flee*—often for their lives. Vietnamese refugees left their old life, not freely, but because they were persecuted or feared being persecuted on account of their ethnic, religious, or political affiliations; had they not felt threatened, they would not have left."[51] Paul James Rutledge echoes that "a significant factor in the Vietnamese flight from their homeland is the fact that they left as refugees and not as immigrants."[52] The distinction, of course, is shaky. Historically, the experiences of "immigrant" and "refugee" overlap; each decision to leave the homeland (Vietnam or otherwise) is almost always part choice, part crisis. There is no room in this model of emigration for those who *choose* to flee. As one disgruntled reader penciled into the margin of my library copy of Rutledge's *The Vietnamese Experience in America,* "even refugees have time to prepare."

A glance at the scholarship on Vietnamese diasporic identity in general indicates a significant lag between public perceptions and actual demographics. Thomas A. DuBois acknowledges the need for a new model, something that moves past the problematic litany of "refugees, migrants, immigrants, ethnics, and . . . racial minorities."[53] The refugee rubric, in particular, encourages "the tendency to view Southeast Asians as passive, immobilized, and pathetic."[54] While DuBois does not provide any immediate answers for the problems that arise from such categorization and stereotyping, he does point out the need for refocusing academic attention on "discursive models of the Southeast Asian as invented and reinvented by scholars, the general American populace, and Southeast Asians themselves."[55] DuBois's request simply underscores the extent to which individual choice has been defused. Including "Southeast Asians themselves" in a discourse about Southeast Asian identity should be axiomatic.

Not only has the ability of Southeast Asians to participate in scholarly discourse about themselves been underestimated, but the refugee model, flawed in the first place, is quickly becoming irrelevant. A second, post-1975 generation of overseas Vietnamese, predominantly born and raised in their "host" countries, is emerging as a separate voice. The term *refugee* simply does not apply to them, literally or figuratively. But the persisting problem in the creation of Vietnamese diasporic identity is not just inaccurate terminology: it is a lack of Vietnamese agency in shaping the entire discourse. In this light, I believe that online political activism becomes an important statement of self-determined Vietnamese American (and other overseas Vietnamese) identity. Mitra suggests that "diasporic communities are increasingly embracing the Internet system to produce a new sense of community where they can textually create images of their own national and tribal communities."[56] The Internet has become a crucial forum for the expression of ideas that before were suppressed either actively, in the case of communist censorship of Vietnamese democracy, or passively, in the case of Western stereotypes of Vietnamese identity.

ESTABLISHING A CARTOGRAPHY

Because all of this active imagining and self-determination ultimately passes through the filter of online communication, I would like to return to a more detailed consideration of the Internet itself. Both Anderson's imagined community and the Vietnamese diasporic nation still maintain specific physical and political ties to the tangible world, whether through daily actions (of reading a newspaper) or assertions (of feeling patriotic toward one's homeland). The Internet, by contrast, transcends bodily and geographic boundaries. It is imagination unharnessed; it is a public sphere where public authority does not intrude. People can do, say, and be whatever they want. Like the economically booming "Pacific Rim," the Internet is a fabricated space of promise, of opportunity, of modernity and change.[57] For the idealized democracy of Vietnamese diasporic activism, which exists in direct opposition to the spatial realities of a fragmented population and a communist-governed Vietnam, cyberspace seems a perfect fit.

Karim H. Karim notes that "the phenomenon of inter-continental diasporic communication has existed for centuries," exploiting almost every possible medium: mail, telegraph, telephone, fax, audio- and videotape, film, television, satellite. The Internet, however, "is particularly suited to the needs of diasporas" because of its unprecedented accessibility and global reach.[58] All webpages are created equal: the online world has unlimited room for divergent voices, and assigns everyone the same status. It is the global village, the information superhighway, "the new middle landscape, the garden in the machine, where democratic values can thrive in a sort of cyber-Jeffersonian renaissance."[59] Sherry Turkle suggests that cyberspace presents an escape from static and hierarchical paradigms of identity: "When people adopt an online persona, they cross a boundary into highly charged territory. Some feel an uncomfortable sense of fragmentation, some a sense of relief. Some sense the possibilities for self-discovery, even self-transformation."[60] Similarly, Shawn P. Wilbur sees "virtual community" as a revolutionary act of imagination: "With their eyes wide open and using the tools we have inherited . . . researchers may be able to carry forward the study of community in directions which we had not previously ever imagined."[61] The online explorer must be prepared not only to imagine self and community in a number of new ways, but also to uncover conclusions that fall outside that initial imagining. In a specifically ethnic context, this slippage even allows for release from racial markers: "If being Vietnamese today is not what you want to be, you could pick some other category."[62]

The boundless extremity of this freedom, however, can also give way to instability. In the absence of physical markers—when it is quite possible to misrepresent age, gender, ethnicity, or any other traditional touchstone of identity—how do you form genuine communities based on common experience? How do you keep disguised intruders out of spaces reserved for a specific group such as Asian Americans or women? Even if you suspect that someone is lying, by what authority can you demand the truth? These fears of misrepresentation expose the shaky underpinnings of online representation. The Internet is, at a basic level, a world of imagined interpersonal connections. This complicates a project like the Web-based spread of Vietnamese democratic activism, which depends so much on real individual identity in relation to an urgent collective cause. It presents a situation where foreknowledge of the mechanisms of imagination do not empower but paralyze: the same freedom that makes room for the authentic voice also allows for its possible impersonation and usurpation.[63]

Anxiety about multiplicity and duplicity is not unique to the Vietnamese online community, but is a symptom of the broader, technology-infused narrative of postmodernity: urban disarray, global diversity, media blitz, millennial anarchy. Robert Jay Lifton, in *The Protean Self: Human Resilience in an Age of Fragmentation,* writes, "We are becoming fluid and many-sided. Without quite realizing it, we have been evolving a sense of self appropriate to the restlessness and flux of our time. This mode of being differs radically from that of the past, and enables us to engage in continuous exploration and personal experiment. . . . The protean self emerges from confusion, from the widespread feeling that we are losing our psychological moorings. We feel ourselves buffeted about by unmanageable historical forces and social uncertainties."[64]

A similar sentiment, attributed more pointedly to technology, is echoed by Kenneth Gergen, who writes, "As a result of advances in radio, telephone, transportation, television, satellite transmission, computers, and more, we are exposed to an enormous barrage of social stimulation. Small and enduring communities . . . are being replaced by a vast and ever-expanding array of relationships . . . this massive increment in social stimulation—moving toward a state of saturation—sets the stage both for radical changes in our daily experiences of self and others. . . ."[65] Gergen writes about a "saturated" self, not able to support much more change, while Lifton envisions a "protean" self, adapting to new situations. In either case, there is a sense of fragmentation within the self and of distance from history, a breaking off from one's roots. The self is being reinvented, and perhaps overloaded, by "restlessness and flux," a "vast and ever-expanding array of relationships."

Internet culture, as ultimate pastiche, is a prime example of "restlessness and flux." It is certainly "vast and ever-expanding," and infamous for its unreliability: in any given day, hundreds of webpages undergo makeovers, relocate to new servers, or disappear completely. The web also makes a strong case for rootlessness; it is "outside of the human experiences of space and time."[66] It is geographically unbounded, a virtual space not subject to landlocked necessities. It is inherently ahistoric, because everything exists on the Internet simultaneously in an identical state of newness. In the face of so much disorder, writes critic Scott Bukathman, "There is an ongoing attempt to explore and cognitively map the new terminal spaces, to establish a cartography."[67] Even the jargon of the Internet suggests a desire for spatial orientation: people "navigate" the web, "visit" a webpage, use "links" and "frames" to organize information. The personal webpage, the starting point, is comfortably called "home." Physical terminology helps to anchor the shifting modalities of online existence in recognizable, familiar concepts. As Ananda Mitra and Rae Lynn Schwartz propose, "It is no longer possible to live within the metaphors of maps, movements, and nations, but it is important to move away from these signifiers to ones that address the more authentic lived experience of web-maps, hyperlinked-spaces, and cyber-communities. . . ."[68] Traditional notions of location and place, in other words, have been dramatically altered by the development of Internet culture; but basic human concerns with self-location and self-placement remain highly relevant nevertheless.

For Vietnamese online activists, the desire to "establish a cartography" has materialized in their webpages, which often connect political efforts to undeniably "real" phenomena. The Free Vietnam Alliance's homepage, for example, includes links to "Vietnam Time," which displays the current local time in "Hanoi-Saigon, Vietnam" in relation to current Greenwich Mean Time;[69] and to "Vietnam Weather," which brings up the current and extended forecast for multiple Vietnamese cities, complete with windspeed, visibility, and a satellite overview.[70] A more literally cartographic approach can be found on websites like the Vietnam Picture Gallery and Lien Hoa's Vietnam My Country. Both sites invite users to click anywhere on a map of Vietnam in order to produce a page of full-color photographs depicting the individual city of interest.[71] Through associating the map's representative outlines with vivid real-life images, these websites assert the tangibility and visibility of an online Vietnam. Similarly, Cuong Nguyen's Maps of Vietnam page exhibits an array of twenty-eight "various maps of Vietnam that I have collected," with no further explanation. Each mini-map in the grid can be clicked for "an enlarged fullscale image." Gathered together, Nguyen's twenty-eight maps insist that Vietnam is not simply an imagined place, dreamed up in the nebulous realm of cyberspace, but a land with physical shape and charted coordinates.

Many other websites conjure Vietnam through illustration. Vietnam's Knowledge Base offers sixteen postcard-quality "Images of Vietnam,"[72] while both Chi D. Nguyen's elegant viet-touch.com and Dang Anh Tuân's French-and-English Pays D'Eau (Land of Water) make extensive use of graphics to help outline Vietnamese culture and history.[73] Taking things one step further, the VietScape homepage is designed not only to display temporary pictures online, but to let the user actually affix a "Vietnam landscape" on the desktop of his computer screen: "With mouse over image, click mouse right button and select 'Set As Wallpaper' or 'Set This As Background Image.'" The mobile landscape, with point-and-click rapidity, brings "Vietnam" right into the user's own room. Additionally, Internet images help overseas Vietnamese to visualize one another. Extensive online archives of photographs and videos taken at anticommunist rallies, demonstrations, and speeches around the world allow individual members of the Vietnamese diaspora—no matter how isolated or far-flung—to experience the excitement of united political protest.[74] Like Nguyen's maps, these images help to confirm tangible Vietnamese realities. They refresh memories, revive cultural connections, and strengthen nationalist sentiment. Through online visualization of a commonly remembered homeland and a collectively mobilized cause, Vietnamese democratic activists promote their political survival.

In this capacity, anticommunist icons on the Internet become pivotal stand-ins for physical evidence. The waving Republican flag of South Vietnam, for instance, validates a political regime that today's communists demean as a "puppet government"; the relabeled map asserts the geographical reality of Saigon despite the official name change that effaced that city's existence in modern-day Vietnam. Pointedly defiant, one webpage displays a tattered, fragmentized image of Vietnam's "communist bloody flag"—just under a healthily waving Republican flag—with a list of "the exact location and date of any Vietnam communist flags which were brought down" in the United States. The graphics are strategically arranged on the screen to emphasize the contrast between the proudly hoisted, upright Republican banner and its flattened communist counterpart. Another webpage uses flashing red dots on a map to indicate the locations of recent uprisings against the communist government by Vietnamese citizens in Thái Bình and Xuân Lộc.[75] On its own site, Vietworld publishes a Virtual Memorial Wall of the names, occupations, and locations/circumstances of death for 898 of the political prisoners verified to have perished in Vietnam's "reeducation camps" after the war's end. The sheer length of this document, divided into nine sections "for your viewing convenience," speaks for itself.[76]

As its title indicates, the Vietworld Wall also makes deliberate reference to the Vietnam Veterans Memorial Wall in Washington, D.C. Introducing each section of the Vietworld is a picture of a candle held up to a black granite slab, in which the camp victims' names appear to be engraved—just as veterans' names are carved in the actual black granite of the D.C. monument. The Vietnam Oral History Project has a similar Cyber Wall displaying against a gray marble background the names of several South Vietnamese soldiers killed in battle.[77] Like the flashing maps and waving flags, these simulated monuments function as online forms of visible "proof." They locate Vietnamese diaspora within a physically tangible geographical and historical absolute—and, at the same time, undermine the communist-specific version of that geography and history. They stamp political messages with the iconic solemnity and solidity of names carved in stone.

VNI, VIQR, VISCII

Perhaps the most vivid illustration of the desire for concretized affirmation amid online flux has been the push to reproduce the Vietnamese language—for many overseas Vietnamese, the authentic voice—in a computerized environment. Because it has a Roman alphabet, Vietnamese can be approximated with American standard code for information interchange (ASCII) characters, the international Internet standard that comprises all the letters, numbers, and symbols found on a normal English-language keyboard. The diacritic marks that differentiate tonal variants and thus determine meaning for Vietnamese words cannot, however, be fully represented in ASCII text. Without the proper tonal designations, reading Vietnamese becomes an exercise in guesswork.

As a temporary solution, people posting Vietnamese-language messages in newsgroups and other computerized contexts devised the Vietnamese quoted-readable (VIQR) convention, which uses ASCII marks to connote diacritics.[78] Basically, the diacritics are represented with similar-looking keyboard symbols, typed after (instead of over or under) the letters themselves: *ế* becomes *e^'* and *ử* becomes *u+* in VIQR. The process is admittedly awkward, as the official example illustrates:

> *Vietnamese:* Tôi yêu tiếng nuớc tôi tú khi mới ra đời.
>
> *VIQR:* To^i ye^u tie^'ng nu + o +'c to^i tu + `khi mo + `i ra ddo + `i.

I should note that the official example is fortified with a heavy dose of nationalism. The opening line of a famous folksong by Vietnamese American composer Phạm Duy, it reads: "I have loved the language of my country since the first moment of my life."[79]

In 1989, the nonprofit Vietnamese-Standard Working Group (Viet-Std) was formed "to promote the standardization of Vietnamese character encoding and to monitor ongoing work of international bodies in this regard."[80] Viet-Std proposed the Vietnamese standard code for information interchange (VISCII), which made possible the keyboard entry of Vietnamese words with properly placed diacritics. Another nonprofit group, TriChlor Software, helped to make special computer programs for the composition and viewing of Vietnamese documents widely available.[81] With appropriate software and fonts installed, anyone could now write and read a webpage in neatly formatted Vietnamese. Viet-Std announced its accomplishments in a 1992 report: "It is our dream one day to be able to read, write, and exchange Vietnamese data of a common format on any machine, any platform, and to take advantage of all the processing tools that have been produced by the computing world. That dream, once a pure exercise in imagination, has today come many steps closer to realization."[82]

Unfortunately, several other people had the same idea. VISCII is perfectly viable, but it contends with a host of other Vietnamese-font options. The main competitors are VPS (from the Vietnamese Professionals Society[83]) and VNI (from a flashy for-profit software company by the same name[84]), but countless others exist: the latest version of VietKey typing software recognizes an astounding forty-four options.[85] As a result, one webpage might use VISCII conventions, while another might use VPS, and still another might offer a choice between VIQR and VNI. To vex matters, most of these fonts are incompatible, requiring additional software simply to convert from one to the next. The problem has become not *how* to put Vietnamese on the Internet, but *which* Vietnamese to use. New developments in typography software such as Unicode (which allows a single standard font, like Times New Roman, to support multiple languages[86]) and web font embedding (which allows the author to control exactly how a webpage will appear on the user's screen[87]) are helping to overcome some of these barriers by replacing ASCII with a new universal standard that happens to support Vietnamese-language type. Still, these improvements remain version-specific. That is, without the right software and fonts installed on both ends—for both author and user—a Vietnamese webpage is rendered unreadable.

The quandary would be easier to dismiss as a technological glitch were it not for the large resonance that Vietnamese nationalism has with the online restoration of the language. As Anderson indicates, the Vietnamese language has long been integral to Vietnamese national identity: "French and American imperialists governed, exploited, and killed Vietnamese over many years. But whatever else they made off with, the Vietnamese language stayed put."[88] Even before Western colonization, a thousand years of Chinese rule managed to influence but not replace the Vietnamese language. The word for written script—*quốc ngữ*—contains the Sino-Vietnamese radical *quốc*, or "nation," and literally means "national language." In this light, VNI language software is hailed by its supporters as "an honor for all Vietnamese people, and a major contribution to the Vietnamese community abroad";[89] its efforts "deserve being recorded on the pages of Vietnamese history,"[90] and it is deemed "something . . . valuable to the Vietnamese at home and abroad, Your good name VNI will be remembered generations after generations."[91] One user "was moved to the point of tears when I first saw Vietnamese writing appear on my monitor and from my printer."[92] Another expressed hope that "come some fine day, perhaps a day in the not-too-distant future, the work of VNI will constitute a truly significant contribution to the restoration of our homeland."[93] Meanwhile, given this context, it is unsurprising that the Vietnamese communist government chose to develop its own national typing system, TCVN (also known, suggestively, as "ABC"). Equally unsurprising is the fact that TCVN, the universal standard within Vietnam, is rarely used outside of the country.[94]

If language is a conduit for national sentiment—literally, in terms of person-to-person communication, and figuratively, as an emblem of commonality—then the electronic labyrinth of Vietnamese-language software frustrates any move toward a unified front for those working online. Instead of "restoration," the proliferation of Vietnamese(s) results in a deeper splintering and separateness. Instead of a single "national language," there are suddenly several dozen incompatible versions. This conscious attempt to pin down a shared reality produces only uncomfortable instability and a breakdown in communication. Vietnamese and all its cultural meanings are crudely reduced to a "standard code for information interchange." At the same time, the myriad versions of computerized Vietnamese also enable a form of democratic choice. Like the separate development of Vietnam's official TCVN system, the decision of members of the Vietnamese diaspora *not* to use that particular make of "language" on their webpages—and to offer, instead, forty-four different options—becomes a fundamental statement of political position and dissent.

VIETNAM: "THE GREAT LEAP FORWARD INTO CYBERSPACE"

Amid the plans and efforts of Vietnamese overseas activists, the Socialist Republic of Vietnam itself is facing a critical dilemma: what to do about the Internet? Cyberspace, as a fundamentally unmediated forum, presents a direct threat to a one-party regime wishing to keep tabs on the flow of imported media and cultural exposure; the busy "hacktivists" of Burma, China, and Indonesia provide object lessons. At the same time, Internet-based communication is arguably the single most significant part of modern business and industrial growth, and a country already struggling economically cannot afford to get left behind. Vietnam's approach to the Internet, consequently, has been "an acute contradiction. On the one hand, it is eager to facilitate knowledge of business nature. . . . On the other hand, Vietnam cannot drop its obsession to maintain control over information both within the country and with the outside world."[95] Alternately, as the Hanoi-based *Vietnam Investment Review* phrases it, "The problem is control, or more precisely, how to integrate with the rest of the world without suffering the ills, such as moral ambiguity, alienation, consumerism, and homogenisation of culture."[96] Ironically, many of Vietnam's misgivings about the Internet stem directly from the strong online presence of the Vietnamese diaspora.

Politics aside, globalization (and Westernization) of culture is a concern for many countries, not just Vietnam, and is a process intimately tied to advances in modern technology. As Vu Dinh Cu notes, "Traditional arts are flooded and sometimes swept away by a powerful wave of Western movies, videotapes, CDs. Folklore is seemingly dead or dying, theaters are empty of any audience. . . . the money cult reigns, extreme individualism and egoism are manifest, serious damages occur to community institutions, the three-generation family (children, parents, grandparents) is breaking down, and the inter-generation gap is widening."[97] International media, mass production, and widespread consumerism—the same postmodern conditions that generate Gergen's "saturated" or Lifton's "protean" self—are major issues confronting any culture that attempts to participate in the modern marketplace. Vietnam's concerns are echoed by other members of the Association of South East Asian Nations (ASEAN), as expressed in a 1996 agreement: "[T]he trans-border nature of the Internet would open individual countries to external influences and [this] affirmed the importance of having safeguards against easy access to sites which ran counter to our cherished values, traditions and culture."[98] ASEAN member Singapore addressed this problem by using firewall software that blocks access to certain politically or culturally objectionable websites.[99] Malaysia, on the other hand, has decided to make the Internet an integral part of its "cherished values": prepaid cards are available to access the Internet from public kiosks,[100] and in the further interest of industry, Prime Minister Dato Mahatir announced a commitment to "developing the necessary [online] infrastructure" and "not censoring the Net."[101] Vietnam is still ironing out its own approach—vacillating all the while between Singapore's caution and Malaysia's enthusiasm.

Even among ASEAN nations, Vietnam has been particularly slow to accept online technology. In 1992, the Viện Công Nghệ Thông Tin, or Institute of Information Technology (IOIT), began tentatively "researching its Internet options."[102] Two years later, the Vietnam Academic Research Educational Network (VAREnet) was established for the exchange of academic and scientific information. Assisted by the Australian National University, VAREnet established a rudimentary e-mail system, using only nine telephone lines; messages were received via Australia in five daily batches and then hand delivered around the city.[103] VAREnet next teamed with a Canadian sponsor to create Netnam, a Hanoi-based computer network providing e-mail, bulletin board, and informational database services to businesses and other government-approved organizations in Vietnam.[104] Until November 1997, Netnam would remain the only point of contact between Vietnam and the Internet. Faster and larger than the original VAREnet, Netnam managed to attract several hundred subscribers. Still, it was a highly unreliable method of communication, approved for use by a very limited audience. To address the government's concerns about their "control over information," Netnam's system administrators routinely censored messages before sending them out.[105]

Moving beyond Netnam was inevitable, however, with the Internet playing an increasingly crucial role in economics, politics, education, and social interaction worldwide. At the end of 1997, Vietnam finally decided "to open up to the Internet and take the great leap forward into Cyberspace."[106] After months of "near-weekly proclamations in the country's official press herald[ing] the imminent arrival of the Internet, amid much ballyhoo about how it will help propel Vietnam into the new millennium,"[107] the Vietnamese government granted licenses to four in-country, state-regulated Internet service providers: Vietnam Data Communication (VDC), Saigon Postel, Finance Promoting and Technology (FPT), and the Institute of Information Technology (IOIT/Netnam).[108] The "great leap forward" was heralded as a new age of Internet freedoms, a virtual perestroika; November 19 was officially declared Vietnam Internet Day.[109] There was even a formal introduction, as Vietnam unveiled its "first public website" to the rest of the world. Written almost exclusively in English, Vietnam Online targeted an audience of non-Vietnamese tourists, workers, and investors as "a comprehensive site covering the ins and outs of life and doing business in Vietnam." Still, Vietnam Online was not all together "public": though free of charge, visitors were asked to sign up for a username and password so that their presence could be monitored.[110] Again, information control remained a priority.

Vietnam Online was the first of many projected advances: instantaneous e-mail, access to the "real Internet," first-rate educational and economic benefits for Vietnamese citizens.[111] These advances, however, have yet to materialize fully. A number of factors continue to hinder development. First, the luxury of Internet access is more than most Vietnamese can afford. A personal computer is beyond the reach of the typical family, and the financial barrier is aggravated by Vietnam's prohibitive telecommunications costs (which remain among the highest in the world).[112] Users also have to contend with an outdated and congested network. The entire country has a bandwidth of sixty megabits per second—a respectable speed for a single desktop computer, but not much when divvied up nationwide—and connections often drop or freeze without warning.[113] Despite regular government-mandated reductions to Internet access charges and the addition of a fifth service provider (Vietel), Vietnam's online population remains extremely low. There are only 200,000 registered users, representing a negligible 0.2 percent of the country's eighty million inhabitants.[114]

For those willing and able to deal with the drawbacks, the government's insistence on "control over information" remains an added obstacle to forward movement. While "certain organisations and corporations" enjoy online privileges, "regular users will have to wait for more cautious trials, and the step-by-step process that comes with access to outside information from

Vietnam."[115] Personal or private homepages are not allowed; Vietnamese webpages are all government, corporate, or academic. E-mail accounts are often shared by entire businesses, limiting their use to work-related transactions, while the accounts themselves remain subject to regular search and censorship.[116] Citizens are only allowed to access "culturally acceptable" sites,[117] and are blocked from using e-mail accounts, newsgroups, or networks which originate outside Vietnam.[118] The consequences of not following government restrictions on Internet usage can be harsh: large monetary fines, denial of online service, seizure of computer equipment, and even imprisonment.[119]

The government's hard-line policy is aimed, in large part, at foiling the efforts of the community of democratic Vietnamese activists, which continue to flourish online. Vietnam's reluctance to embrace "outside information" undoubtedly references the Free Vietnam Alliance webpage and the CyberWall of political victims, the tracts calling for democracy in Vietnam and the point-by-point condemnations of the Vietnamese Communist Party. Even the 1997 decision to go online was steeped in explicit distrust of Vietnamese diaspora on the Internet. Concurrent with the "great leap forward" press release,

> The *Nhan Dan* Communist Party daily [newspaper] . . . blasted Voice of America radio, saying it had called on Vietnamese living abroad and opposed to communism to send information on the Internet which could be harmful to the regime.
>
> "It's clear that someone with their black plot is deliberately blocking our peoples' steps towards building and defending the country," it said in a commentary.
>
> It added that the Internet was a double-edged sword for any country, including the United States.[120]

To fight back, *Nhan Dan* launched its own procommunist website in June 1998, aimed specifically at overseas Vietnamese.[121] An April 2002 meeting of the Committee for Overseas Vietnamese in Hanoi had a parallel discussion about "the need to upgrade transmission equipment, improve the quality of T.V. and radio programmes, and diversify the content of electronic publications" in order to reach those Vietnamese living abroad and, presumably, to communicate the government's viewpoints more effectively to them.[122] Asserts one Ministry of Culture and Information official, "The information must not distort the truth"[123]—that is, the Communist Party version of the "truth."

Attacking the problem of unwanted information on an even broader level, Vietnam (like neighbors Singapore and China) has chosen to surround itself with "a restrictive firewall used to block access to select websites deemed or viewed as a 'social evil.' "[124] All Internet transactions pass through the firewall's filtering software, which blocks out "politically, religiously or sexually offensive" material. The government routinely adds to its list of censored web addresses—including, of course, most anticommunist sites by overseas Vietnamese.[125] To see the firewall in action, *Wall Street Journal* reporter Stan Sesser attempted to access freeviet.org directly from a computer in Hồ Chí Minh City: "When I typed in the address, a box came up asking me for an ID and an authorization code."[126] This "Internet Iron Curtain," as it has been called,[127] is not infallible, however—as Sesser discovered when he was able to access FreeViet after all, fooling the firewall by using an indirect link on a third-party website.[128] Pham Ngoc Lan, who runs the webpage for another overseas Vietnamese organization on the government's blacklist, claims that "temporary holes" in the firewall occasionally allow his friends in Vietnam to visit his site.[129] The Libertarian website Revolution, meanwhile, "extends a hearty welcome to any Vietnamese citizens who have thwarted their government in reaching this page."[130]

As one Vietnamese official states, "Control through the firewall is no longer effective. . . . If anyone who has a wish to get over the wall, they will. It is just a technical measure. If we put all our future hopes on the firewall, we will fail."[131] Concrete evidence of firewall breaching appears in the increasing reluctance of Vietnamese youth to accept the status quo: "We want personal freedom, we want to be able to achieve our full potential without the mistakes of incompetent leaders. CNN and the Internet tell us that is possible."[132] Inside the firewall, things are not serene, either. Political dissidents within Vietnam have discovered that the Internet can be a powerful resource and soapbox, and "a disturbing new phenomenon" of renegade websites and online transmissions has been plaguing the country's network.[133] Nor has the Communist Party itself escaped the online-aided spread of internal criticism: "e-mail and Internet [internal dissident] texts fly around the world so that increases the heat. . . . the broad dissemination . . . adds to the amount of angst the party feels, [and] puts them under more pressure so therefore they have to respond."[134]

Within Vietnam, circumventing official constraints on Internet accounts has ironically been facilitated by the government's tight grip on online access fees. The high cost of maintaining a personal computer and e-mail account has led to a boom in Internet cafés, where the Vietnamese public at large can cheaply (and often anonymously) log onto the web.[135] Also, because accounts are usually shared by several people, administrators cannot easily regulate use by an unauthorized outsider or trace the author of an offensive e-mail—generating what Dang Hoang-Giang describes as a "kind of Wild West behavior among the user community."[136] The very act of constructing firewalls is, furthermore, economically counterproductive. By blocking certain kinds of computer communications, the firewall frustrates attempts at developing software, running ordinary office applications, and launching cooperative business ventures—hindering Vietnam's bid for the lucrative technology market and scaring off potential partners from overseas.[137] The constant monitoring of Internet transactions also slows down the nation's already sluggish network, causing occasional system-wide crashes.[138]

The bumpiness of Vietnam's attempts at moderating online access seems to be a consequence of a backfired policing. At the same time, it attests to the inexorable overlap between the Internet and free speech. As it links to the global online network, Vietnam is agreeing to join a discussion that, until now, it has essentially dismissed. There are no sure safeguards to prevent overseas Vietnamese activists—like the Burmese insurrectionists in Thailand—from challenging, attacking, or sabotaging the Socialist Republic of Vietnam's online presence. Furthermore, Vietnam is entering a forum that has significant meaning for the structure of the country in terms of political reality as well as the citizen's imagination; for the role of representation and language in the construction of national consciousness; and for the formation of Vietnamese identity in relation to the rest of the world. The power to negotiate these issues of national and cultural strength, as overseas Vietnamese have demonstrated through their patriotic interconnection online, is no longer restricted by geography.

Meanwhile, the reluctance of Vietnam and other nondemocratic countries to join the online club (or, in China's recent curtailment of Hong Kong Internet activity, to take a member away) remains hotly debated within the Internet community—a group dominated, naturally, by countries with a strong investment in unimpeded information exchange. One Asian journalist declares that Vietnam's Internet policy "could only draw laughter from foreign reporters, who would point to its contradictory nature. For what meaning could a controlled Internet have? After all, it is meant to allow users to freely surf through waves of information."[139] Another paints a mocking analogy: "It is said that there is a big, fat and lazy Dinosaur sitting on Vietnam's Information Highway that will bite everyone daring to pass it. If the Government cannot solve this problem, it will forever be sitting on and trying to hatch what may eventually turn out to be a fossilized egg.[140] For the same reason that political dissidence and individual expression thrive on the web, governments wishing to "hatch" a streamlined cultural approach to the Internet are constantly patching holes in their firewalls. Whether or not they achieve their goals within Vietnam proper, Vietnamese democratic activists are making significant impact with their online presence. They have managed, through the creation of a strong Internet community with its own take on being "Vietnamese," to affect strategically the ways in which Vietnam will conduct and evaluate itself in an international context.

What I am interested to see, and call for future researchers to explore, is the reciprocal effect of Vietnam's online presence on Vietnamese overseas. The country, until recently nonexistent on the Internet, has been the organizing factor and determining memory around which the diasporic Vietnamese online community defines itself. Anderson argues that the imagined community is made possible because "a fundamental change was taking place in modes of apprehending the world, which, more than anything else, made it possible to 'think' the nation."[141] How does this new fundamental change—the addition of Vietnam to the Internet—impact the "thinking" of Vietnamese diasporic nationalism? The successful construction of the Vietnamese activist network has been largely dependent upon Vietnam's absence from the web. What does it mean to have the communist side of the debate fully represented on the web, on equal par with the democratic? Does this shift the focus of dissident webpages, or alter the tenets of the activist cause? How does the nature of authentication and spatiality change as the mythic homeland itself becomes a physical entity on the Internet? Hopefully, these new lines of communication between Vietnam and its former citizens will further a better appreciation, on both sides, of the different ways in which individuals and communities can imagine their national identities.

NOTES

Because many Vietnamese names and terms are not published with the proper diacritics, I only provide tonal marks when they are printed in the source. All of the online information was current and accessible as of May 12, 2002, unless otherwise specified; where possible, I also indicate posting dates.

1. David Lamb, "The Right to Surf in Vietnam," *Los Angeles Times,* October 6, 1997, home edition, D3.

2. Dorothy E. Dunning, "Activism, Hacktivism, and Cyberterrorism: The Internet As a Tool for Influencing Foreign Policy," Nautilus Institute, December 10, 1999, online at <http://www.nautilus.org/info-policy/workshop/papers/denning.html>.

3. Peter Eng, "A New Kind of Cyberwar—in Burma, Thailand, Indonesia, Vietnam: Bloodless Conflict," *Columbia Journalism Review* 37 no. 3 (1998): 20.

4. Ibid.

5. Lamb, "The Right to Surf," D3.

6. Maggie Farley, "Dissidents Hack Holes in China's New Wall" *Los Angeles Times,* January 5, 1999, record edition, 1. For a more detailed look at the "hacktivism" phenomenon worldwide, see Julie L. C. Thomas, "Ethics of Hacktivism," SANS Institute, January 12, 2001, online at <http://rr.sans.org/hackers/hacktivism2.php>.

7. Eng, "Cyberwar," 20. See also Bertil Linter and Ashley Craddock, "Indonesia's Net War," *Wired News* (May 29, 1998), online at <http://www.wired.com/news/topstories/0,1287,12609,00.html>.

8. Laura B. Lengel, "New Voices, New Media Technologies: Opportunity and Access to the Internet in East Central Europe," *Convergence* 4, no. 2 (1998): 27–30, online at <http://www.v2.nl/~arns/Projects/Converge/Cleng.html>; and Laura Lengel and Daniel P. Fedak, "The Politicization of Cybernetic Discourse: Discourse Conflict and the Internet in North Africa," (c. 1998), online at <http://www.vptech.demon.co.uk/lengell/research/africa2.htm>. Dunning's work is also helpful here.

9. "Introduction," Việt Quốc Home Page, <http://www.vietquoc.com/INTRODUC.HTM>.

10. Khanh K. Chau, "Austin Texas: VN Refugees Protest—Human Rights for VietNam," April 12, 1999, online at <http://www.ampact.net/vietnetworks/chinhtri/Austinprotest.htm>.

11. David Case, "Big Brother Is Alive and Well in Vietnam—and He Really Hates the Web," *Wired,* (November 1997), online at <http://hotwired.lycos.com/collections/connectivity/5.11_vietnam1.html>.

12. Việt Quốc Home Page, <http://www.vietquoc.com>.

13. DTN Phan Bội Châu, <http://members.aol.com/dtnpbc>.

14. DVCMD Main Page, <http://www.daiviet.org>.

15. Nguyen Viet Thang, "Manifesto," PTTNDT (July 16, 1992), online at <http://www.pttndt.org>.

16. Government of Free Vietnam, "Chúong Trình Cứu Nuóc & Xây Dụng Đât Nuóc" (A Program to Save the Nation and Build the Nation) (April 30, 1995), online at <http://www.vntd.org/vietnamese/chuong_trinh_cndn/ctcndn1.htm>. My comments are based upon the English-language translation posted on the Government of Free Vietnam website in November 1999; currently, the document is available

only in Vietnamese. A new English-language website, however, is slated for launch in May 2002.

17. Free Vietnam Alliance, "A Proposal to Build a Democratic Society in Vietnam," (November 16, 1991), online at <http://www.fva.org/document/propose.htm> and "Roles of the Vietnamese from Different Strata in the Democratization Process," at <http://www.fva.org/document/prop4.htm>.

18. See the Website of the Vietnamese Constitutional Monarchist League, <http://www.geocities.com/vietmonarchy/home.html> or Imperial Vietnam: A Website for the Restoration of the Nguyen Dynasty, <http://www.geocities.com/imperialvietnam/mainpage.html>.

19. Vietnam Human Rights Network (Mạng Lưới Nhân Quyền), online at <http://www.vnhrnet.org>; International Committee for Freedom (Cao Trào Nhân Bản), online at <http://www.ctnb.org>. Many organizations also track human rights in Vietnam as a function of their global activism. See, for example, the Vietnam sections on the Human Rights Network's United Nations "For the Record" System, online at <http://www.hri.ca/fortherecord2001/vol3/vietnam.htm>, or Amnesty International's website, <http://web.amnesty.org/ai.nsf/COUNTRIES/VIET%20NAM>.

20. Tim Karr, "Dial-In Diasporas: Firewalls and Filters Fail to Halt Vinsight.org Penetration into Opinion-Sensitive Vietnam," *WorldPaper Online* (April 2000), <http://www.worldpaper.com/2000/April00/karr.html>. Vietnam Insight, which was established in 1992 by Chan Tran and remained one of the most important and well-known Vietnamese democratic activist websites throughout the 1990s, was formerly posted at <www.vinsight.org>. As of April 2002, however, it was no longer available.

21. See note 20; this mission statement, quoted from the original Vietnam Insight homepage, still appears on many sites that continue to reference the now-defunct site—including the Yahoo! web directory, <http://dir.yahoo.com/Regional/Countries/Vietnam/News_and_Media>.

22. "'Frustrations Are High': Dissident Doan Viet Hoat Speaks His Mind," *Asia Week* (January 29, 1999) online at <http://www.asiaweek.com/asiaweek/99/0129/nat7.html>.

23. Ly Thanh Bình, "A Declaration of Freedom for Viet-Nam," Viet-Nam Freedom Party website, <http://home.navisoft.com/vfp/statemt.htm>; no longer available as of May 2002.

24. Kicon Vietspace (April 2002), online at <http://vietspace.kicon.com>; Committee For Religious Freedom in Vietnam (Ủy Ban Tự Do Tôn Giáo Cho Vietnam), online at <http://www.crfvn.org>.

25. Vietnamese Professionals Society, "Mission Statement and Goals" (January 1, 2002), online at <http://www.vps.org/article.php3?id_article=191>.

26. The webpages that supported this cause no longer exist. Some coverage of the protest, however, can still be found on the UCLA student newspaper website. See Jonathan Pham, "Controversial Water Puppet Show Spreads Communist Propaganda," *Daily Bruin Online* (October 16, 1997), <http://www.dailybruin .ucla.edu/ DB/issues/97/10.16/view.pham.html>; and Tram Linh Ho, "Vietnam Needs A Change," *Daily Bruin Online* (October 16, 1997), <http://www.daily-bruin.ucla.edu/ DB/issues/97/10.16/view.ho.html>.

27. Lý Thanh Bình, "Top Vietnam's Government: Politics Websites on Yahoo! (none from CSVN)," (October 24, 1997), online at <news:soc.culture.vietnamese>.

28. "The Wandering Statue," Việt Quốc Home Page, <http://www.vietquoc.com/ thngtiec.htm>.

29. See, for example, the "Vietnam Clickable Map" in Hoàng Khai Nhan's Vietnam Picture Gallery, online at <http://www.saigonline.com/hkn/queviet/main/index .html> or Cuong Jake Tran's homepage, <http://www.geocities.com/Athens/Crete/ 4888>. Tran underlines the point with a message to his readers: "Notice that some provinces' names here are the names were used to be used [*sic*] in Vietnam before 1975. Thank you!"

30. Radio Free Vietnam (Đài Phát Thanh Việt Nam Tự Do) is based in Westminster, California, and is online at <http://www.rfvn.com>; Vietnamese Public Radio (VPR/Đài Tiếng Nói Việt Nam Hái Ngoại) is based in Falls Church, Virginia, and online at <http://www.vietnamradio.com>. For a list of other Vietnamese-language radio broadcasts available on the Web, see *Kicon Vietspace,* online at <http://www .kicon.com>.

31. Army of the Republic of Vietnam (ARVN), or Quân Lực Việt Nam Cộng Hoà (QLVCH), online at <http://www.vnet.org/qlvnch>. The animated gif (graphic image file) is called "cobay," short for "co bay" or "flying flag."

32. To give an idea of how widespread and varied the uses of Republican flag graphics have become on the web, I present a small sampling:

    • ARVN Army Ranger, <http://www.bdqvn.org>

    • Federation of Overseas Free Vietnamese Communities (Cộng Đồng Nguời Việt Quốc Gia Hái Ngoại), <http://kicon.com/freevietnam>

    • *Gọi Dân (Call to the People)* radio program, <http://www.goidan.com>

    • Liên Hội Nguời Việt Quốc Gia Bắc California (Coalition of Nationalist Vietnamese Organizations of Northern California), <http://www.lienhoi.com>

    • Liên Minh Dân Chú Việt Nam (Alliance For Democracy in Vietnam), <http:// www.lmdcvn.org>

    • Tan Le, Vietnam's Knowledge Base, <http://www.geocities.com/Tokyo/5673/ index.html>

    • Tuan Nguyen, VIETNAM: Land of Hope and Prosperity, <http://www.plum-site.com/ vietnam>

    • Vietnamese American Business Association, "*Sống Trên Dất Mỹ (Living in America)* radio program, <http://songtrendatmy.net>

- Vietnamese National Military Academy Alumni, Association, <http://www.vobi-vietnam.org>

33. Information Technology Associates, "Vietnam through Yugoslavia," (May 1, 1996) at the Flags of All Countries website, <http://www.theodora.com/flags_20.html>.

34. Úy Ban Báo Vê Quôc Kỳ Viêt Nam Cộng Hoà (Committee for Protection of the Flag of the Republic of Vietnam), online at <http://chaocovnch.8m.com>. To hear the anthem, click on the first link at the bottom of the page ("National Anthem—Digital Sound"), or go directly to <http://chaocovnch.8m.com/ chao_Quocky.htm>.

35. Committee for Protection of the Flag of the Republic of Vietnam, "Why Do We Have To Protect Our Flag?" online at <http://chaocovnch.8m.com/ dear_young _patriotism.htm>.

36. Guobin Yang, "Information Technology, Virtual Chinese Diaspora, and Transnational Public Sphere," (April 23, 2002) Nautilus Institute, Virtual Diasporas website, <http://www.nautilus.org/virtual-diasporas/paper/Yang.html>.

37. Benedict Anderson, *Imagined Communities: Reflections on the Origin and Spread of Nationalism* (London: Verso, 1991), 35.

38. "Introduction," *Việt Quốc* home page.

39. Government of Free Vietnam, "Chuong Trình Cúu Nuóc."

40. Anderson, *Imagined Communities,* 34.

41. John Rex, "The Nature of Ethnicity in the Project of Migration," in *The Ethnicity Reader: Nationalism, Multiculturalism and Migration,* ed. Montserrat Guibernau and John Rex (Cambridge: Polity Press, 1997), 274.

42. Anderson, *Imagined Communities,* 6.

43. Ngo T. Duc, speech at Stanford University, (April 27, 1995), online at <http://www.fva.org/0595/speech.html>.

44. James Clifford, "Diasporas," in Guibernau and Rex, eds., *The Ethnicity Reader,* 284.

45. Stuart Hall addresses the issue of the "presence/absence" of the original country as "a necessary part of the [national] imaginary"; see Hall, "Cultural Identity and Diaspora," in *Identity: Community, Culture, Difference* (London: Lawrence, 1990), 222–37.

46. "Vietnamese Boatpeople Stories," Vietnamese Boatpeople Connection website, <http://www.boatpeople.com/stories>.

47. Tuan Nguyen, "Vietnam: The Land of Hope and Prosperity," online at <http://www.plumsite.com/vietnam/hope.htm>.

48. Edward Said, *Orientalism* (New York: Vintage, 1978), 55.

49. Ananda Mitra, "Creating Immigrant Identities in Cybernetic Space," paper presented at the Media Performance and Practice across Cultures Conference at

University of Wisconsin-Madison, (March 14–17, 2002), online at <http://poly-glot.lss.wisc.edu/ mpi/conference/mitra.htm>.

50. Monique T. D. Truong, "Vietnamese American Literature," *An Interethnic Companion to Asian American Literature,* ed. King-Kok Cheung (Cambridge: Cambridge University Press, 1997), 220.

51. James M. Freeman, *Hearts of Sorrow: Vietnamese-American Lives* (Stanford: Stanford University Press, 1989), 11.

52. Paul James Rutledge, *The Vietnamese Experience in America* (Bloomington: Indiana University Press, 1992), 9.

53. Thomas A. DuBois, "Constructions Construed: The Representation of Southeast Asian Refugees in Academic, Popular, and Adolescent Discourse," *Amerasia Journal* 19, no. 3 (1993): 1–25. Note, however, that DuBois still favors the term *refugee,* at least insofar as the title indicates.

54. Ibid., 5.

55. Ibid., 21.

56. Ananda Mitra, "Nations and the Internet: The Case of a National Newsgroup, 'soc.cult.indian,'*Convergence* 2, no. 1 (1996), abstract online at <http://www .luton.ac.uk/convergence/volumetwo/numberone/abstracts.shtml>. Amit S. Rai explores a parallel point in "India On-line: Electronic Bulletin Boards and the Construction of a Diasporic Hindu Identity," *Diaspora 4,* no. 1 (1995): 31–57.

57. For a discussion of the imagined space of the Pacific Rim, see Arik Dirlik, "Introducing the Pacific" and Donald M. Nonini, "On the Outs on the Rim: An Ethnographic Grounding of the 'Asia-Pacific' Imaginary" in *What Is In a Rim? Critical Perspectives on the Pacific Region Idea,* ed. Arik Dirlik (Boulder, CO: Westview, 1993).

58. Karim H. Karim, "Diasporas and Their Communication Networks: Exploring the Broader Context of Transnational Narrowcasting," (April 23, 2002) Nautilus Institute, Virtual Diasporas website, <http://www.nautilus.org/virtual-diaspo-ras/paper/Karim.html>.

59. Shawn P. Wilbur, "An Archaeology of Cyberspaces: Virtuality, Community, Identity," in *Internet Culture,* ed. David Porter (London: Routledge, 1997), 14.

60. Sherry Turkle, "Who Am We?" *Wired,* (January 1996), 198.

61. Wilbur, "Archaeology," 20.

62. Daniel C. Tsang, "Notes on Queer 'N' Asian Virtual Sex," in *Asian American Sexualities: Dimensions of the Gay and Lesbian Experience,* ed. Russell Leong (New York: Routledge, 1996), 156.

63. While somewhat overwrought, many of the essays in *Resisting the Virtual Life: The Culture and Politics of Information,* ed. James Brook and Iain A. Boal (San

Francisco: City Lights, 1995), are also concerned with these same issues of the Internet as potentially dangerous or destabilizing to individual identity.

64. Robert Jay Lifton, *The Protean Self: Human Resilience in an Age of Fragmentation* (New York: Basic Books, 1993), 1.

65. Kenneth J. Gergen, *The Saturated Self: Dilemmas of Identity in Contemporary Life* (New York: Basic Books, 1991), xi.

66. Scott Bukathman, *Terminal Identity: The Virtual Subject in Postmodern Science Fiction* (Durham, NC: Duke University Press, 1993), 2.

67. Ibid., 117.

68. Ananda Mitra and Rae Lynn Schwartz, "From Cyber Space to Cybernetic Space: Rethinking the Relationship between Real and Virtual Spaces," *Journal of Computer-Mediated Communication 7*, no. 1 (2001), online at <http://www.ascusc.org/jcmc/vol7/issue1/mitra.html>.

69. "Vietnam Time," Free Vietnam Alliance, online at <http://www.fva.org>; link to "Local Time in Hanoi-Saigon, Vietnam," online at <http://www.hilink.com.au/times/bin/time.sh?offset=0700&loc=Hanoi-Saigon,+Vietnam>.

70. "Vietnam Weather," Free Vietnam Alliance, online at <http://www.fva.org>; link to "Yahoo! Weather by WeatherNews Inc., Weather: Asia: Vietnam," online at <http://weather.yahoo.com/regional/Vietnam.html>. As of May 2002, this link as listed on the Free Vietnam Alliance is actually outdated: the correct URL is <http://weather.yahoo.com/regional/VMXX.html>.

71. "Vietnam Clickable Map"; Lien Hoa, "mapvn.gif," Vietnam My Country website, <http://disc.cba.uh.edu/~lienhoa>.

72. Tan Le, "Images of Vietnam," Vietnam's Knowledge Base website, <http://www.geocities.com/Tokyo/5673/images.htm>.

73. Chi D. Nguyen, VIET NAM (Vietnam) website, <http://www.viettouch.com>; Dang Anh Tuân, Pays D'Eau (Land of Water) website, <http://www.limsi.fr/Recherche/ CIG/menu.html>.

74. For example, see the Free Vietnam Alliance website's "Pictures," <http://www.fva.org/imgindex.html> or Kicon Vietscape's "Flag Protest in Little Saigon," <http://kicon.com/flagprotest>.

75. "Lửa Thái Bình & Xuân Lộc" (Thái Bình & Xuân Lộc Uprisings), online at <http://ampact.net/ uybanyemtrodongbaoquocnoi>. The political message is incontrovertible: clicking anywhere on the map automatically launches a RealAudio music file of the South Vietnamese national anthem. For more background, see the news clips on THAIBINH'S Home Page, <http://www.geocities.com/CapitolHill/ Lobby/4417>.

76. "Re-education Camps Memorial Wall," *VietWorld* (April 24, 1999), online at <http://www.vietworld.com/Holocaust/index.html>.

77. "The Cyber Wall," Vietnam Oral History Project website, <http://www.viet.org>. Most of the names also act as hyperlinks to information about the individual soldier's rank and date/place of death.

78. See "The VIQR Convention," *Non Sông Magazine* (October 23, 1996) online at <http://www.nonsong.org/viqr.html>; or the Vietnamese-Standard Working Group's official "Viet-Std Bilingual Report," (September 1992), online at <http://www.viet-std.org>. VIQR bears resemblance to the common online methods of using abbreviations or smiley faces to express the cadences of natural conversation. For further discussion of ASCII chat language, see Elizabeth Reid, "Virtual Worlds: Culture and Imagination," in *CyberSociety: Computer-Mediated Communication and Community,* ed. Steven G. Jones (Thousand Oaks, CA: Sage, 1995), 164–83.

79. "The VIQR Convention"; my translation. The song is called "Tình Ca" ("Love Song"); written in 1953, it presents a patriotic and romanticized vision of Vietnam with tacit disapproval of the country's split into Northern and Southern halves.

80. "The Vietnamese Standardization Working Group," (October 23, 1996), Vietnamese-Standard Working Group website, <http://www.vietstd.org/document/vietstd.htm>; no longer available as of April 2002.

81. TriChlor Organization website, <http://www.vnet.org/trichlor>.

82. "Viet-Std Bilingual Report."

83. Vietnamese Professionals Society website, <http://www.vps.org>.

84. VNI Software Company website, <http://www.vnisoft.com>.

85. Đặng Minh Tuấn, *VietKey 2000,* build 10727 (Hanoi: Vietkey Group, 2001).

86. Unicode Home Page, <http://www.unicode.org>. See also *Non Sông* magazine's "Unicode FAQs," online at <http://www.nonsong.org/Unicode>, for a specific discussion of how Unicode enables Vietnamese-language type.

87. Steve Mulder, "Embedding Fonts Tutorial" at the Webmonkey website, <http://hotwired.lycos.com/webmonkey/design/fonts/tutorials/tutorial2.html>, provides a helpful overview and discussion of embedded web fonts.

88. Anderson, *Imagined Communities,* 148.

89. Cao Anh Nguyet, "Comments," VNI Software Company website, <http://www.vnisoft.com/english/comments.htm>.

90. Nguyen Thanh Long, "Comments," VNI Software Company.

91. Le Ai Ly, "Comments," VNI Software Company.

92. Truong Tan Loc, "Comments," VNI Software Company.

93. Brother Nguyen Van An, "Comments," VNI Software Company.

94. TCVN, which stands for "Tiêu Chuẩn Việt Nam" or "Vietnam standard," refers to a series of several thousand benchmark regulations issued by the state's Ministry of Science, Technology and Environment—ranging from industrial safety requirements to the technical specifications for an electric rice cooker (TCVN 5393-91).

More information can be found on the official TCVN website, <http://www.tcvn.gov.vn>. Starting in July 2002, however, Vietnam began using Unicode as its official typing system.

95. Dang Hoang-Giang, "Internet in Vietnam: From a Laborious Birth into an Uncertain Future," *Informatik Forum* 1 (1999), online at <http://www.interasia.org/vietnam/dang-hoang-giang.html>. Another helpful overview is John S. Quarterman's anecdotal "Internet in Vietnam," *Matrix News* 8, no. 2 (1998), online at <http://www.mids.org/mn/802/vn.html>.

96. "Surfers Stand By for the First Wave," in "Internet: A Special Vietnam Investment Review Advertising Feature," *Vietnam Investment Review,* June 9–15, 1997, 13.

97. Vu Dinh Cu, "I.T. in Vietnam: Opportunities and Challenges," Interasia Organization, at Le Viet Nam, aujourd'hui website, <http://perso.wanadoo.fr/patrick.guenin/cantho/internet/dinh.htm>. This particular article is not dated, but since it mentions Vietnam's involvement with the Internet, we can safely assume that it was written in the late 1990s.

98. ASEAN Statement, quoted in Joel Deane, "Asia and the Internet: Why Are Vietnam, Singapore and China Practicing Cybercensorship?" (June 30, 1997) ZD-Net Products website, <http://www5.zdnet.com/products/content/articles/199706/np.asia>; no longer available as of May 2002. Dang, "Internet in Vietnam," also discusses the impact of the 1996 ASEAN agreement, which was signed by all member countries except for the Philippines.

99. Deane, "Asia and the Internet." Singapore is using proxy servers, which control what users can access from inside the firewall but not what they receive from external parties (via e-mail, newsgroups, etc.). For more information on the elements and construction of a network firewall, see the Firewalls FAQ website, <http://www.faqs.org/faqs/firewalls-faq>.

100. Lamb, "The Right to Surf," D3.

101. Deane, "Asia and the Internet."

102. Nguyen Tri Man and Sam Korsmoe, "Linking Up to the World," *Vietnam Economic Times Online* (March 13, 1997); the *Vietnam Economic Times* archives for 1996–2000, originally stored at <www.batin.com.vn>, are no longer available. More recent back issues, from September 2001 to the present, can be found on the *Vietnam Economy* website, <http://www.vneconomy.com.vn>.

103. Dang, "Internet in Vietnam."

104. Netnam website, <http://www.netnam.vn>. As the possibilities for Vietnamese Internet access have improved, the service has expanded to support home users as well.

105. In my own experience with Netnam during the summer of 1997, about 50 percent of my incoming and outgoing messages were either "lost" or delayed by several days.

106. "What's Ahead on Vietnam's Web: Vietnam Online—A Sneak Preview," in "Internet: A Special Vietnam Investment Review Advertising Feature," 13.

107. Case, "Big Brother."

108. "Four ISPs Begin Operations in Vietnam," *New York Times* (December 13, 1997), at VietGATE Internet News from Vietnam, online at <http://www.vietgate .net/news>; "Internet Users in Vietnam on the Rise to 15,000," *AsiaBizTech* (December 9, 1998), at Le Viet Nam, aujourd'hui website, <http://perso.wanadoo .fr/patrick.guenin/cantho/internet/itnews.htm>.

109. "Net, Toilets Slow to Reach Vietnam," *Wired News* (November 18, 1997), online at <http://www.wired.com/news/politics/0,1283,8622,00.html>.

110. "Welcome Page," Vietnam Online, <http://www.vietnamonline.net>; no longer available as of May 2002. The site stopped requiring user registration after a few years of operation.

111. "Surfers Stand By."

112. Michelle Castillo, "Telecommunications Infrastructure," *Information Technology Landscape in Vietnam,* MBA report, American University, c. 2001, online at <http://american.edu/carmel/mc5916a/telecommunications.htm>.

113. "Vietnam Catches Up" (April 2, 2002), Asia.internet.com, <http://asia.internet .com/asia-news/article/0,3916,161_1001841,00.html>. I base this observation on personal experience as well. While traveling throughout Vietnam in April 2002, I rarely managed to find a stable Internet connection.

114. "Software and Internet Promise New Economy: Despite Internet Censorship, IT Imperative Drives Nation," *Washington Times* International Reports: Vietnam 2002, online at <http://www.internationalreports.net/asiapacific/vietnam/2002/soft-ware.html>. Compare Vietnam's 0.2 percent to regional averages: 3 percent of Chinese, 7 percent of Thais, 9 percent of Malaysians, and 30 percent of Singaporeans are online. At the other end of the spectrum, 45 percent of Canadians and 53 percent of Americans use the Internet—as does 54 percent of Hong Kong ("Geographics: The World's Online Populations" *CyberAtlas* (March 21, 2002), online at <http://cyberatlas.internet.com/big_picture/geographics/article/0,,5911 _151151,00.html>).

115. "Surfers Stand By."

116. Dang, "Internet in Vietnam."

117. "Four ISPs."

118. Dang, "Internet in Vietnam."

119. See Adam Creed, "Vietnam Govt Readies New Internet Rules," *Newsbytes* (August 30, 2001), online at <http://www.newsbytes.com/news/01/169564.html>; Reporters San Frontières, "Two Dissidents Arrested for Publishing Documents on the Internet" (March 15, 2002), online at <http://www.rsf.org/article .php3?id_article=575>.

120. Reuters News Service, "Vietnam Sets Mid-November for Full Internet Access" (October 13, 1997), at University of Saskatchewan Vietnamese Students' Association website, <http://duke.usask.ca/~ss_vsa/news16.html>.

121. Nhân Dân website, <http://www.nhandan.org.vn>.

122. "Society," *Voice of Vietnam News* (April 12, 2002), online at <http://www.vov.org.vn/2002_04?12/english/xahoi.htm>; no longer available as of May 2002.

123. Kristin Huckshorn, "Hanoi, Eager for Links with World, Still Suspicious of Internet," *San Jose Mercury News* (June 1, 1998), at Internet, Vietnam website, <http://www.hf.ntnu.no/anv/HjemmesiderIFAS/Olafstoff/Internet,Vietnam.html>.

124. "Software and Internet Promise New Economy."

125. Mark McDonald, "Vietnam Heavily Filters Content, but Firewalls Are Leaking," *Mercury News* (August 12, 2001), online at <http://www.landfield.com/isn/mail-archive/2001/Aug/0087.html>.

126. Stan Sesser, "Internet Cafes Flourish in Vietnam, Presenting a Puzzle about Policy," *Wall Street Journal Interactive* (January 18, 2000), online at <http://interactive.wsj.com/articles/ SB948137265699680614.htm>.

127. "Vietnam: Asian's Next IT Success Story?" (November 2, 2001) Global Sources Computer Products website, <http://www.globalsources.com/MAGAZINE/CP/0112/PVIET.HTM>.

128. Sesser, "Internet Cafes." Increasingly, third-party websites that allow users to duck firewalls (like www.anonymizer.com, which Sesser used in this instance) are themselves being targeted for censorship by the Vietnamese authorities.

129. McDonald, "Vietnam Heavily Filters Content." Pham runs *Thông Luận* <http://www.thongluan.org>, an online newsletter for the international Vietnamese activist group Rally for Democracy and Pluralism.

130. Addendum to "Vietnam Prepares to Join the Internet," *Revolution* (1996), online at <http://www.boogieonline.com/revolution/express/techno/internet/vietnam.html>.

131. Do Quy Doan, qtd. in McDonald, "Vietnam Heavily Filters Content."

132. Huw Watkin, "Restless Youth Yearn for Change" (July 21, 1999) Vietnam Insight website, at <http://www.vinsight.org/1999news/0721.htm>; no longer available as of April 2002. Also helpful is Tim Larimer's article "Disquiet among the Quiet," which discusses the growing discontent among Vietnamese youth as well as the Vietnamese public at large; *Time Asia* (January 18, 1999), online <http://www.time.com/time/asia/asia/magazine/1999/990118/vietnam_dissidentsl.html>.

133. McDonald, "Vietnam Heavily Filters Content."

134. Andy Solomon, "ANALYSIS—Mixed Signals From Hanoi General's Ouster," (January 13, 1999); originally at Vietnam Insight, <http://www.vinsight.org/1999news/0113.htm>; no longer available as of April 2002.

135. Sesser, "Internet Cafes." See also Mary Kelly, "Internet News: Getting Wired in Vietnam," (November 2000) Vietnamese-American Chamber of Commerce Hawaii website, <http://www.vacch.org/ecom_112200.htm>.

136. Dang, "Internet in Vietnam."

137. Ibid. See also "What's the Rush? Vietnam Reacts Slowly to Technology Wave," *Far Eastern Economic Review* (July 15, 1999), online at <http://perso.wanadoo.fr/ patrick.guenin/ cantho/internet/itnews.htm>. For a Vietnamese perspective on the software industry, see the Research Vietnam website, <http://www.researchviet-nam.com>.

138. Huckshorn, "Hanoi"; and McDonald, "Vietnam Heavily Filters Content."

139. Yomiuri Shimbun, "Vietnam Tries to Have It Both Ways," *Daily Yomiuri* (December 3, 1997); originally at Vietnam Insight, <http://www.vinsight.org/1997news/1203 .htm>; no longer available as of April 2002.

140. Dao Yen, "Can Vietnam Hatch The e-Commerce Golden Egg?" *E-Commerce News* (August 21, 2001) online at <http://www.internetnews.com/ec-news/arti-cle/0,,4_869671,00.html>.

141. Anderson, *Imagined Communities,* 22.

14. Democracy and Terror in the Era of Jihad vs. McWorld

Benjamin R. Barber

The post-9/11 world brought our global interdependencies into sharp relief. Americans struggled to understand why such attacks occurred and grappled with how such acts of terror would reshape the future. Benjamin Barber is a political scientist and spokesman for the progressive position, in which democracy and the prerequisites of citizenship are foremost concerns. He examines the broader context for terrorism and the ideological divisions that create "wild capitalism" and "international desparados," pitting both what he terms McWorld and Jihad against democratization. In his argument, neither the behavior of individualistic capitalists, or groups of militant fundamentalists promote global citizenship or responsible democracy. He ends his essay asking how governments, in a transnational age, can define and provide for the common good.

A week after the trauma of the first large-scale assault on the American homeland, more successful than even its scheming perpetrators could possibly have hoped for, President George Bush joined the abruptly renewed combat with Jihadic terrorists by deploying the rhetoric of retributive justice: 'We will bring the terrorists to justice,' he said gravely to a joint session of Congress, 'or we will bring justice to the terrorists'. The language of justice was surely the appropriate context for the American response, but it will remain appropriate only if the compass of its meaning is extended from retributive to distributive justice.

The collision between the forces of disintegral tribalism and reactionary fundamentalism I called Jihad (Islam was not the issue) and the forces of integrative modernization and aggressive economic and cultural globalization (the US was not alone responsible) I called McWorld in my *Jihad vs. McWorld*[1] has been brutally exacerbated by the dialectical interdependence of these two seemingly oppositional sets of forces. In that critical examination of the relationship between globalization and fundamentalism, I warned that democracy, caught between a clash of movements each of which for its own reasons seemed indifferent to freedom's fate, might suffer grievously. It is now apparent, as the US successfully concludes the first phase of a military offensive against Jihad (understood not as Islam but as militant fundamentalism), that democracy rather than terrorism may still become another victim of the battle being waged.

Only the globalization of civic and democratic institutions is likely to offer a way out of the global war between modernity and its aggrieved critics. Democracy responds both to Jihad and to McWorld. It responds directly to the resentments and spiritual unease of those for whom the trivialization and homogenization of values is an affront to cultural diversity and spiritual and moral seriousness. However, it also answers the complaints of those mired in poverty and despair as a consequence of unregulated global markets and of a capitalism run wild because it has been uprooted from the humanizing constraints of the democratic nation state. By extending the compass of democracy to the global market sector, it can promise to those wishing to join the modern world and take advantage of its economic blessings, opportunities for accountability, participation and governance; by securing cultural diversity and a place for worship and faith insulated from the shallow orthodoxies of McWorld's cultural monism, it can address the anxieties of those who fear secularist materialism and are fiercely committed to preserving their cultural and religious distinctiveness. The outcome of the cruel battle between Jihad and McWorld, which will be won only if democracy is the victor, will depend upon the capacity of moderns to make the world safe for women and men in search of both justice and faith.

A DEMOCRATIC FRONT

If democracy is to be the instrument by which the world avoids the stark choice between the sterile cultural monism of McWorld and the raging cultural fundamentalism of Jihad, neither of which services diversity or civic liberty, then the US, the UK and their allies will have to open a crucial second civic and democratic front aimed not against terrorism *per se* but against the anarchism and social chaos—the economic reductionism and its commercializing homogeneity—that have created the climate of despair and hopelessness which terrorism has so effectively exploited. A second democratic front will be advanced not only in the name of retributive justice and secularist interests, but in the name of distributive justice and religious pluralism.

The democratic front in the war on terrorism is not a battle to dissuade terrorists from their campaigns of annihilation. Their deeds are unspeakable, and their purposes can neither be rationalized nor negotiated. When they hijacked innocents and turned civilian aircraft into lethal weapons, these self-proclaimed 'martyrs' of faith in truth subjected others to a compulsory martyrdom indistinguishable from mass murder. The terrorists offer no terms and can be given none in exchange. When Jihad turns nihilistic, bringing it to justice can only take the form of extirpation—root, trunk and branch. Eliminating terrorists will depend on professional military intelligence and diplomatic resources whose deployment will leave the greater number of citizens in the US and throughout the world sitting on the sidelines, anxious spectators to a battle in which they cannot participate, a battle in which the nausea that accompanies fear will dull the appetite for revenge. The second front, however, engages every citizen with a stake in democracy and social justice, whether within nation states or in the relations between them. It transforms anxious and passive spectators into resolute and engaged participants—

the perfect antidote to fear, as activated passengers on commercial flights have recently learned as they participate in subduing would-be terrorists and bombers.

Because an outraged and wounded American nation demands it, and because terrorists bent on annihilation will not yield to blandishments or inducements, the first military front must be prosecuted. Terrorists are looking not for bargains but for oblivion. Yet it will be the successful prosecution of a second civic front in the war rather than the strictly military campaign that will determine the outcome in the long term. It, too, in President Bush's words, will be a war for justice, but a war defined by a new commitment to distributive justice: a readjudication of north-south responsibilities, a redefinition of the obligations of global capital as it faces the claims of global justice and comity, a repositioning of democratic institutions as they follow markets from the domestic to the international sector, a new recognition of the place and requirements of faith in an aggressively secular market society. The war against Jihad will not, in other words, succeed unless McWorld is also addressed.

To democratize globalism and render McWorld less homogenizing and trivializing to religion and its accompanying ethical and spiritual values will, to be sure, do nothing to appease the terrorists, who are scarcely students of globalization's contractual insufficiencies. Jihadic warriors offer no quarter, whether they are the children of Islam, of Christianity or of some found blood tribalism; they should be given none. These Jihadic warriors detest modernity—the secular, scientific, rational and commercial civilization created by the Enlightenment as it is defined by both in its virtues (freedom, democracy, tolerance and diversity) and its vices (inequality, hegemony, cultural imperialism and materialism). What can enemies of the modern do but seek to recover the dead past by annihilating the living present?

Terrorists then cannot themselves be the object of democratic struggle. They swim in a sea of tacit popular support and resentful acquiescence, however, and these waters—roiling with anger and resentment—prove buoyant to ideologies of violence and mayhem. Americans were themselves first enraged and then deeply puzzled by scenes from Islamic cities where ordinary men, women and children who could hardly be counted as terrorists, nonetheless manifested a kind of perverse jubilation in contemplating the wanton slaughter of American innocents. How could anyone cheer such acts? Yet an environment of despairing rage exists in too many places in the Third World, and also in too many Third World neighbourhoods of First World cities, enabling terrorism by endowing it with a kind of a quasi-legitimacy it does not deserve. It is not terrorism itself but this facilitating environment against which the second-front battle is directed. Its constituents are not terrorists, for they are themselves terrified by modernity and its costs, and as a consequence vulnerable to ameliorative actions if those who embrace democracy can find the will to take such actions. What they seek is justice, not vengeance. Their quarrel is not with modernity but with the aggressive neo-liberal ideology that has been prosecuted in its name in pursuit of a global market society more conducive to profits for some than justice for all. They are not even particularly anti-American: rather, they suspect that what Americans understand as prudent unilateralism is really a form of arrogant imperialism, what Americans take to be a kind of cynical aloofness is really self-absorbed isolationism and what Americans think of as pragmatic alliances with tyrannical rulers in Muslim nations such as Egypt, Saudi Arabia and Pakistan are really a betrayal of the democratic principles in which Americans claim to believe.

A WAR WITHIN CIVILIZATION

Hyperbolic commentators such as Samuel Huntington have described the current divide in the world as a global clash of civilizations, and warn of a cultural war between democracy and Islam, perhaps even between 'the West and the rest'. However, this is to ape the messianic rhetoric of Osama bin Laden—who called for precisely such a war. The difference between bin Laden's al-Qaeda terrorists and the poverty-stricken Third World constituents he tries to call to arms, however, is the difference between radical Jihadic fundamentalists and ordinary men and women concerned to feed their children and nurture their religious communities. Fundamentalists can be found among every religious sect and represent a tiny, aggravated minority whose ideology contradicts the very religions in whose names they act. The remarkable comments of the American fundamentalist preacher Jerry Falwell interpreting the attacks on New York and Washington as the wrath of God being vented on abortionists, homosexuals and the American Civil Liberties Union no more defines Protestantism than the Taliban defines Islam. The struggle of Jihad against McWorld is not a clash of civilizations but a dialectical expression of tensions built into a single global civilization as it emerges against a backdrop of traditional ethnic and religious divisions, many of which are actually created by McWorld and its infotainment industries and technological innovations. Bin Laden without modern media would have been an unknown desert rat. Terrorism without its reliance on credit cards, global financial systems, modern technology and the internet would have been reduced to throwing stones at local sheiks. What we face is not a war of civilizations, but a war within civilization, a struggle that expresses the ambivalence within each culture as it faces a global, networked, material future and wonders whether cultural and national autonomy can be retained; the ambivalence within each individual juggling the obvious benefits of modernity with its equally obvious costs.

From Seattle and Prague to Stockholm and Genoa, street demonstrators were protesting the costs of this civilizational globalization long before September 11, 2001. Yet, although President Chirac of France acknowledged after the dissident violence of Genoa months before the attacks in New York and Washington that 100,000 protesters do not take to the streets unless something is amiss, they have mostly been written off as anarchists or know-nothings. More media attention has been paid to their theatrics than to the deep problems those theatrics are intended to highlight. After September 11, some critics even tried to lump the anti-globalization protesters in with the terrorists, casting them as irresponsible destabilizers of world order. But the protesters are the children of McWorld and their objections are not Jihadic but merely democratic. Their grievances concern not world order but world disorder, and if the mostly young demonstrators are a little foolish in their politics, a little naive in their analyses and a little short on viable solutions, they understand with a sophistication their leaders apparently lack that globalization's current architecture breeds anarchy, nihilism and violence. They know too that the greater number of those in the Third World who seem to welcome American suffering are at worst reluctant adversaries whose principal aim is to make clear that they too suffer from violence, even if it is less visible and destroys with greater stealth and over a longer period of time than the murderous schemes of the terrorists. They do not want to belittle American suffering but to use its horrors to draw attention to their own. How many of these 'enemies of McWorld', given the chance, would prefer to enjoy modernity and its blessings if they were not so often the victims of modernity's unevenly distributed costs? How many are really fanatic communists and how many are merely instinctive guardians of fairness who resent not capitalism's productivity but only the claim that in the absence of global regulation and the democratic rule of law, capitalism can possibly serve them. It is finally hypocrisy rather than democracy that is the target of their rage.

For those living in the Second and Third Worlds to the south of the US, Europe and Japan, globalization too often looks like an imperious strategy of a predominantly American economic behemoth; what we understand as the opportunities to secure liberty and prosperity at home too often seem to them but a rationalization for exploitation and oppression in the international sphere; what we call the international order is too often for them an international disorder. Our neo-liberal antagonism to all political regulation in the global sector, to all institutions of legal and political oversight, to all attempts at democratizing globalization and institutionalizing economic justice looks to them like brute indifference to their welfare and their claims for justice. Western beneficiaries of McWorld celebrate market ideology with its commitment to the privatization of all things public and the commercialization of all things private, and consequently insist on total freedom from government interference in the global economic sector (*laissez-faire*). Yet total freedom from interference—the rule of private power over public goods—is another name for anarchy. And terror is merely one of the many contagious diseases that anarchy spawns.

What was evident to those who, before September 11, suffered the economic consequences of an undemocratic international anarchy beyond the reach of democratic sovereignty was that while many in the First World benefited from free markets in capital, labour and goods, these same anarchic markets left ordinary people in the Third World largely unprotected. What has become apparent to the rest of us after September 11 is that that same deregulated disorder from which financial and trade institutions imagine they benefit is the very disorder on which terrorism depends. Markets and globalized financial institutions, whether multinational corporations or individual currency speculators, are deeply averse to oversight of nation states. McWorld seeks to overcome sovereignty and makes its impact global. Jihad, too, makes war on sovereignty, using the interdependence of transportation, communication and other modern technological systems to render borders porous and sovereign oversight irrelevant. Just as jobs defy borders, haemorrhaging from one country to another in a wage race to the bottom; just as safety, health and environmental standards lack an international benchmark against which states and regions might organize their employment; so too anarchistic terrorists with loyalty to no state and accountable to no people range freely across the world, knowing no borders can detain them, no united global opinion can isolate them, no international police or juridical institutions can interdict them. The argument laid out in what follows then proposes that both Jihad and McWorld undermine the sovereignty of nation states, dismantling the democratic institutions that have been their finest achievement without discovering ways to extend democracy either downwards to the subnational religious and ethnic entities that now lay claim to people's loyalty or upwards to the international sector in which McWorld's pop culture and commercial markets operate without sovereign restraints.

Ironically, it is the terrorists and not the leaders of the US who acknowledge and exploit the actual interdependence that characterizes human relations in the twenty-first century. Theirs, however, is a perverse and malevolent interdependence, one in which they have learned to use McWorld's weight jujitsu-style against its massive power. Yet even as it fosters an anarchic absence of sovereignty at the global level, the US has resisted the slightest compromise of its national sovereignty at home. The US has complained bitterly in recent years about the prospect of surrendering a scintilla of its own sovereignty, whether to NATO commanders, to supra-national institutions such as the International Criminal Tribunal, or to international treaties such as those banning landmines or regulating fossil fuels (in response to global warming). Even today as the US successfully prosecutes a military campaign against terrorism surrounded by a prudently constructed coalition, it has made clear that it prefers 'coalitions' to 'alliances' because it wants to be free to target objectives, to develop strategy and to wage war exactly as it wishes. It still shies away from 'nation building' and other strategies that might entangle it in the web of interdependence.

Yet terrorism has already made a mockery of sovereignty. What was the hijacking of air-liners, the calamitous razing of the Twin Towers of the World Trade Center, the brash attack on the Pentagon, but a profound obliteration of American sovereignty? Terrorism is the neg-ative and depraved form of that interdependence which in its positive and beneficial form we too often refuse to acknowledge. As if still in the nineteenth century, the US has persuaded itself that its options today are to preserve an ancient and blissfully secure independence that puts Americans in charge of American destiny, or to yield to a perverted and compulsory interdependence that puts foreigners and alien international bodies like the United Nations or the World Court in charge of American destiny. In truth, however, Americans have not enjoyed a real independence since sometime before the great wars of the twentieth century; certainly not since the advent of AIDS and the West Nile virus, of global warming and an ever more porous ozone layer, of a job 'mobility' that has decimated America's industrial econ-omy and of restive speculators who have made 'capital flight' a more 'sovereign' reality that any conceivable government oversight. Interdependence is not some foreign adversary against which citizens need to muster resistance, it is a domestic reality that has already compromised the efficacy of citizenship in scores of unacknowledged and uncharted ways.

It was the interdependence of the US with the world and the interdependence of shared economic and technological systems everywhere on which the Jihadic warriors counted when they brought terror to the American homeland. They not only hijacked America's air trans-portation system, turning its airplanes into deadly missiles; they provoked the nation into closing it down entirely for nearly a week. They not only destroyed the cathedral of American capitalism at the World Trade Center, they forced capitalism to shut down its markets and they shocked the country into deep recession of which the stock market in freefall was only a leading indicator. How can any nation claim independence under these conditions?

In the world before McWorld, there was genuine independence for democratic sovereign nations, and sovereignty represented a just claim by autonomous peoples to autonomous con-trol over their lives. In Andrew Jackson's premodern, rural America where communities existed in isolation, where there was no national system of transportation or communication, system-atic terror was simply not an option: there was no system. There was no way to bring America to its knees because in a crucial sense America did not exist, not at least as a collectivity of inter-dependent regions with a single interest—not until after the Civil War and the Industrial Revolution that followed it. Today there is so much systemic interactivity, so highly integrated a global network, so finely tuned an integral communications technology, that it has become as easy to paralyse as to use the multiple systems and networks. Hence, the decision that would-be sovereign peoples face today it not the felicitous choice between secure independence and an unwanted interdependence, it is only the sobering choice between, on the one hand, a relatively legitimate and democratic and useful interdependence which, however, is still to be constructed and which leaves sovereignty in tatters; and, on the other hand, a radically illegitimate and undemocratic interdependence on the terms of criminals, anarchists and terrorists, an interdependence that is already here and which will triumph in the absence of a democratizing political will.

In short, we can allow either McWorld and Jihad—Hollywood cowboys and international desperadoes—to set the terms of our interdependence; or we can leave those terms to transnational treaties, new global democratic bodies and a new creative common will. We can have our interactivity dictated to us by violence and anarchy or we can construct it on the model of our own democratic aspirations. We can have a democratic and useful interdependence on whatever common ground we can persuade others to stand on, or we can stand on the brink of anarchy and try to prevent criminals and terrorists from pushing us into the abyss.

It will be hard for defenders of modernity—whether of McWorld's markets or democracy's citizenship—to have it both ways. Terrorism turns out to be a depraved version of globalization no less vigorous in its pursuit of its own special interests than are global markets, no less wedded to anarchist disorder than are speculators, no less averse to violence when it serves terrorists' ends than marketers are averse to inequality and injustice when they represent the 'costs of doing business'. It is their instinctive reading of this equation that turns poor people into cheering mobs when Americans experience grievous losses. It is their perception of overwhelming hypocrisy that leads them to exult what we would wish them to grieve.

In his address to Congress, President Bush said 'you are with us or you are with the terrorists'. Americans may appreciate the impulse to divide the world into good and evil (even though it smacks of the Manicheanism for which Americans excoriate their fundamentalist adversaries), but enemies of the US (and more than a few of its friends) are likely to find this discourse misleading if not hubristic—for a US that comprehends the realities of interdependence and wishes to devise a democratic architecture to contain its disorder cannot ask others to join it or 'suffer the consequences'. It is not for the world to join the US: McWorld already operates on this premise and the premise is precisely the problem; certainly anything but a key to the solution. It is rather for the US to join the world on whatever terms it can negotiate on an equal footing with the world. Whether a product of arrogance or prudence, the demand that the world join the US simply will not secure results. It defies the very interdependence to which it is addressed. It assumes a sovereign autonomy the US does not and cannot enjoy.

THE US AND ANARCHIC GLOBAL CAPITALISM

In the last ten years the US has intensified its commitment to a political culture of unilateralism and faux autonomy that reinforces rather than attenuates the effects of McWorld. There is hardly a multilateral treaty of significance to which the US has shown itself willing to subscribe in recent times—whether the Kyoto Protocol on global warming, or the ban on land-mines or the comprehensive test ban treaty. Indeed, after a month or two of diplomacy with President Putin of Russia, President Bush simply walked away from the Anti-Ballistic Missile Treaty in order to be able to develop and deploy his missile defence shield. There is hardly a single international institution that has not been questioned, undermined or abandoned out-right by the US in the name of its 'need' to protect its sovereign interests. Only the compet-ing need to gather a coalition to underwrite its anti-terrorist military strike compelled the American government finally to pay its UN dues and to commit to modest amounts of sim-ple humanitarian aid that should have been a function of normalcy. The US still spends a smaller percentage of its GNP on foreign aid—less than 0.01 per cent—than any other developed nation in the world. Other nations spend double that, and the goal of the United Nations is that the figure should reach 0.07 percent.

The Bretton Woods institutions, such as the International Monetary Fund and the World Trade Organization (heir to the General Agreement on Tariffs and Trade) could be of real suc-cour in the effort to construct a more democratic globalism, were they to be put to the kinds of developmental and democratic purposes for which they were originally designed in post-war Europe. Instead they have been cast by the democratic governments that control them as undemocratic instruments of private interest—seeming tools of banks, corporations and investors (which to an untoward degree also control the policies of the international financial institu-tions' member governments). Anarchism in the global sector is no accident: it has been assid-uously cultivated.

Yet what is terrorism but a depraved version of this global anarchism—one which, for all its depravity, is as vigorous and self-justifying as global markets? It, too, profits from the arro-gant pretence of claims to national sovereignty. It, too, benefits by the absence of interna-tional executive police and juridical institutions. It, too, exploits global anarchy to ferment national anarchy and the further weakening of the capacity of nations to control their own des-tinies, either apart or together. In late nineteenth-century America when the federal govern-ment was markedly weaker than it is today, America looked locally rather like social relations look today globally. Lawlessness came easy, both to the robber barons of growing capitalist metropolises and the robber desperadoes of the western prairies. Then, too, the outlaws pros-pered in the suites as well as in the streets.

The global sector today seems driven by the same anarchy in which burgeoning forces of what our own bankers have called wild capitalism spread both their productivity, which we welcome, and their injustices, which we try to ignore. Wild capitalism is not alone: alongside it rage reactionary forces of wild terrorism. Against capitalism's modern message, Jihadic fun-damentalism spreads its anti-modern message, sowing fear and nurturing chaos, hoping to bring democracy no less than capitalism to its knees. The war between Jihad and McWorld takes no prisoners. It cannot serve democracy, however it turns out.

The democratic project is to globalize democracy as we have globalized the economy; to democratize the globalism that has been so efficiently marketized. The issue is no longer utopian longing for global democracy against the siren call of consumerism or the passionate war cries of Jihad; it is the securing of safety. Following September 11, global governance has become a sober mandate of political realism.[2]

However, it will not be easy for America to overcome the reassuring myth of national independence and innocence with which it has lived so comfortably for 200 years. Before it traded in the currency of McWorld that made it the global merchandiser, America had invented a simpler story about itself. In the Puritan myth of the City on the Hill, in the Enlightenment conceit of a *tabula rasa* on which a new people would inscribe a fresh history, Americans embraced Tom Paine's quaint and revolutionary notion that on the new continent humankind could literally go back and start over again as if at the beginning of the world. Europe's cruel torments, the ancient prejudices and religious persecutions would be left behind. Safeguarded by two immense oceans, at home on a bountiful and empty continent (the red man was part of the new world's flora and fauna), Americans would devise a new experimental science of government, establish a new constitution fortified by rights and, with the innocence of newborn peoples, write a new history. Slavery, a great civil war, two world conflagrations, totalitarian regimes abroad could not dissuade America from its precious self-definition. Even as the oceans became mere streams that could be crossed in an instant by invisible adversaries, even as the pressures of an impinging world grew too complex to yield to simplicity, America imagined it might, with its vaunted technology, re-create virtual oceans, deploying a magic missile shield that would ward off foreign evil.

Was America ever really a safe haven island in the tainted streams of world history? Was it ever any more innocent than the children of every nation are innocent? Human nature is everywhere morally ambivalent, the better angels cooing into one ear, their demonic cousins crowing into the other. Americans seem to know no evil, even when they do it. To others the claim to innocence is an assertion of hypocrisy—among the deadliest of sins for Muslims and others who watch the US demonize others and forgive itself.

If ever such an age of innocence existed in the US, terrorism brought it to a close. How could the myth of independence survive September 11? The Declaration of Independence that announced a new coming, a new kind of society, had achieved its task of nation building by the end of America's first century. To build the new world that is now required calls for a new Declaration of Interdependence, a declaration recognizing the interdependence of a human race that can no longer survive in fragments—whether the pieces are called nations or tribes, peoples or markets. There are no oceans wide enough to protect a nation from a tainted atmosphere or a spreading plague, no walls high enough to defend a people against a corrupt ideology or a vengeful prophet, no security strict enough to keep a determined martyr from his sacrificial rounds. Nor is any nation ever again likely to experience untroubled prosperity and plenty unless others are given the same opportunity; suffering, too, has been democratized and those most likely to experience it will find a way to compel those most remote from it to share the pain. If there cannot be an equity of justice there will be an equity of injustice; if all cannot partake in plenty, impoverishment—both material and spiritual—will be the common lot. That is the hard lesson of interdependence.

In a certain sense, to declare interdependence is merely to acknowledge what is already a reality. It is to embrace willingly and constructively a fate terrorists would like to force on sovereign nations. Their message is: 'Your sons want to live, ours are ready to die.' The democratic response must be: 'We will create a world in which the seductions of death hold no allure because the bounties of life are accessible to everyone.'

In the wake of two centuries of either quiescent isolationism or aggressive unilateralism, with only a few wartime pauses for coalition building and consultation, the US is inexperienced in the hard work of creative interdependence and international partnership. When the US discerns problems in international treaties (the Kyoto Protocol on global warming, the landmine ban, the International Criminal Court) and it cannot negotiate its way in; it has made a habit of simply walking out. When international institutions like UNESCO and the United Nations and international conferences like the Durban Racism meeting resonate with hostility, it withdraws in an arrogant pique instead of participating with a view to make its influence felt. The missile shield with its attendant requirement that the US abandon the ABM Treaty is a typically unilateral and hubristic instance of the United States' inclination to go it alone. The shield (actually a tactic to permit continued interventions without fear of retaliation) is technologically infeasible. More importantly, when terrorists cannot be kept off domestic flights and individual 'sleepers' engage in biological and chemical warfare from within, intercepting multiple warheads and their multiplying decoys without a hitch, even if it one day becomes possible, is irrelevant. The missile shield once again isolates the US from a world it ought to participate in changing.

Ronald Reagan imagined a virtual bubble that would keep the nation safe from foreign nightmares, but the nightmares reached American shores in the bright light of morning and there is no shield against terror except a confrontation with its complex global genealogy. It is a peculiarly American conviction that technology can take the place of human ingenuity and action in warding off trouble. Smart bombs are given preference over smart people, missiles that 'think' take the place of policy makers who think; electronic listening posts replace culturally and linguistically adept human agents. Technology is the last redoubt of the vanishing independence of the US, the means by which it aspires to keep alive the fading dream of sovereign autonomy. Yet technology itself, like the science from which it arises, is a product of transnational communities and is a better symbol of interdependence than independence. McWorld itself, with its reliance on global communications technology, teaches that lesson.

THE GLOBAL DEMOCRATIC DEFICIT

When the US finally turns from its mythic independence and acknowledges the real world of interdependence, it will face an irony it helped create: the international institutions available to those who wish to make interdependence a tool of democracy and comity are few and far between. McWorld is everywhere, CivWorld is nowhere. But Nike and McDonald's and Coke and MTV can contribute nothing to the search for democratic alternatives to criminal terrorism. In the melancholy dialectic between them, they inadvertently contribute to its causes.

The encompassing practices of globalization nurtured by McWorld have in fact created a radical asymmetry: they have managed to globalize markets in goods, labour, currencies and information without globalizing the civic and democratic institutions that have historically comprised the free market's indispensable context. Put simply, capitalism has been removed from the institutional 'box' of laws and regulations that has (quite literally) domesticated it and given its sometimes harsh practices a human face. To understand why taking capitalism 'out of the box' has been so calamitous, we need to recall that the history of capitalism and free markets has been one of synergy with democratic institutions. Free economies have grown up within and been fostered and contained and controlled by democratic states. Democracy has been a precondition for free markets—not, as economists try to argue today, the other way round. The freedom of the market that has helped sustain freedom in politics and a spirit of competition in the political domain has been nurtured in turn by democratic institutions. Contract law and regulation as well as cooperative civic relations have attenuated capitalism's Darwinism and contained its irregularities, its contradictions, and its tendencies towards self-destruction around monopoly and the eradication of competition. On the global plane today, the historical symmetry that paired democracy and capitalism has gone missing. We have globalized the marketplace willy-nilly because markets can bleed through porous national boundaries and are not constrained by the logic of sovereignty; but we have not even begun to globalize democracy, which—precisely because it is political and is defined by sovereignty—is 'trapped' inside the nation-state box.

The resulting global asymmetry, in which both states and markets serve only the interests of markets, damages not only a well-functioning democratic civic order, but also a well-functioning international economic order. The continuing spread of the new globalization has only deepened the asymmetry between private vices and public goods. McWorld in tandem with the global market economy has globalized many of our vices and almost none of our virtues. It has globalized crime, the rogue weapons trade, and drugs, pornography and the trade in women and children made possible by 'porn tourism'. Indeed, the most egregious globalization has been the globalization of the exploitation and abuse of children in war, pornography, poverty and sex tourism. This aspect of globalization entails that slow suffering, the deliberately paced violence, that has created so fertile a ground for recruiting terrorists. Indeed, it is terrorism itself along with its propaganda that has been most effectively globalized—sometimes (ironically) using the modern technologies of the world wide web and the worldwide media to promote ideologies hostile both to technology and to anything smacking of the worldwide or the modern. Following September 11 and up until that last glimpse of his gaunt and hunted face at the end of 2001, Osama bin Laden was a regular on the channels of McWorld (including their new Arab language competitors). McWorld's conduits were used for the attack on McWorld.

Globalization has been complete in the private sector then, but lacks anything resembling a civic envelope. Thus it cannot support the values and institutions associated with civic culture, religion and the family; nor can it enjoy their potentially softening, domesticating and civilizing impact on raw market transactions. No wonder Pope John Paul said in his Apostolic Exhortation on the Mission of the Roman Catholic Church in the Americas: 'If globalization is ruled merely by the laws of the market applied to suit the powerful, the consequences cannot but be negative.'[3] One expects the Pope to moralize in this fashion. More startling is a similar message from another more powerful pope of the secular world, who wrote recently:

> You hear talk about a new financial order, about an international bankruptcy law, about transparency, and more . . . but you don't hear a word about people. . . . Two billion people live on less than two dollars a day. . . . We live in a world that gradually is getting worse and worse and worse. It is not hopeless, but we must do something about it now.[4]

The moralist here is the hardheaded James Wolfensohn, president of the World Bank, who has begun to replace the Bank's traditional energy and industrialization projects thought to favour the interests of foreign investors with environmental and health projects aimed at the interests of the populations being directly served.

International institutions already exist, of course, that might serve as building blocks for a global democratic box into which the economy could safely be put. The international financial institutions conceived at Bretton Woods after the Second World War to oversee the reconstruction of the shattered European and Asian economies were intended originally to function as regulatory agencies to assure peaceful, stable and democratic redevelopment under the watchful eye of the victorious allied powers. Although the World Bank and the IMF (and later the GATT and the WTO that grew out of it in 1995) were ostensibly forged as instruments of democratic sovereign nations designed to guide and regulate private sector interests in the name of public sector reconstruction, over a period of time they became instruments of the very private sector interests they were meant to channel and to keep in check. Those who today call for their elimination in the name of transparency, accountability and democracy might be surprised to learn that these norms were once regarded as among the postwar financial order's primary objectives. Given the role that the modern institutions representing this order play as potential pieces in a global regulatory infrastructure, one way to begin the process of global democratization would be to redemocratize them and subordinate them to the will of democratic peoples.

Globalization does not, of course, occur in a vacuum. Its corrosive impact on democratic governance and our inability to put international financial institutions that are nominally already at the service of democracy to real democratic use is augmented by a cognate ideology of privatization that is prevalent both in the international scene and within the countries whose economies are being globalized. McWorld is accompanied by this ideology of privatization—what Europeans often call neo-liberalism, and what George Soros has labelled market fundamentalism (an appropriate implicit comparison to Jihadic fundamentalism)—is an ideology that saps democracy by attacking government and its culture of public power. By arguing that markets can do everything government once did better than government, and with more freedom for citizens, privatization within nation states opens the way for a deregulation of markets that in turn facilitates the globalization of the economy. It softens up citizens to accept the decline of political institutions and tries to persuade them that they will be better off—more 'free'—when their collective democratic voice is stilled, when they think of themselves not as public citizens but private consumers. Consumers are poor substitutes for citizens, however, as corporate CEOs are poor substitutes for statesmen.

On the fateful morning of September 11, 2001, no American or German or free Afghan called Bill Gates or Michael Eisner to ask for assistance in dealing with terrorism. Long-neglected public institutions reacquired overnight their democratic legitimacy and their role as defenders of public goods. Can this renewed legitimacy be employed on behalf of international institutions dedicated to public rather than private goods? If it can, new forms of civic interdependence can be quickly established. The ideology of privatization has always confounded private and public modes of choosing. Consumer choice is always and necessarily private and personal choice. Private choices, autonomous or not, cannot affect public outcomes. Democratic governance is not just about choosing, it is about public choosing, about dealing with the social consequences of private choices and behaviour. In the global sector this is crucial, because only public and democratic decisions can establish social justice and equity. Private markets cannot, not because they are capitalist but because they are private. In Rousseau's language, through participation in the general will, global citizens can regulate the private wills of global consumers and global corporations.

Rousseau understands the vital difference between public and private liberty, a difference that may go to the heart of Pope John Paul's complaint that 'the human race is facing forms of slavery which are new and more subtle than those of the past, and for far too many people, freedom remains a word without meaning'. To think that shopping is what freedom means is to embrace the slavery against which the Pope warns (though of course the Pope is a thoroughly unmodern man, if not yet a Jihadic warrior).

There are many things governments cannot do very well but there are many others things that *only* governments can do, such as regulate, protect and sometimes subsidize and redistribute—not because it does them particularly well or even 'better' than the market, but because they are public things for which only 'we' (the public) can be held accountable. These *res publica* include education, culture, incarceration, transportation, defence, health care and, yes, the human genome. They include the war on terrorism. And they include the construction of a fair and equitable international order that offers every people (and every person) equal access and equal opportunity. Put simply, the struggle against Jihad (which is itself a holy 'struggle' against us) can succeed only if it is also a struggle on behalf of genuine transnational public goods against the private interests manifest in McWorld.

Capitalism is an extraordinarily productive system. There is no better way to organize human labour for productivity than mobilizing a billion private wills motivated by self-interest. It fails miserably at distribution, however, which is necessarily the object of our public institutions, motivated by the search for common ground and a way to overcome the private conflicts and private inequalities that arise out of private production. Domestically, most nation states have struck the balance: that is the meaning of democratic capitalism. Internationally, there is only a raging asymmetry that is the first and last cause of that anarchism in which terror flourishes and terrorists make their perverse arguments about death to young men and women who have lost hope in the possibilities of life.

The war between Jihad and McWorld cannot be won. Only a struggle of democracy against not only Jihad but also against McWorld can achieve a just victory for the planet. A just, diverse, democratic world will put commerce and consumerism back in its place and make space for religion; it will combat the terrors of Jihad not by making war on it but by creating a world in which the practice of religion is as secure as the practice of consumption and in which the defence of cultural values is not in tension with liberty but part of how liberty is defined. Terror feeds off the parasitic dialectics of Jihad and McWorld. In a democratic world order, there will be no need for militant Jihad because belief will have a significant place; and there will be no advantage to McWorld because cultural variety will confront it on every television station and at every mall, the world over. When Jihad and McWorld have vanished as primary categories, terror may not wholly disappear (it is lodged in a small but impregnable crevice in the dark regions of the human soul), but it will become irrelevant to the hopes and aspirations of women and men who will have learned to love life too much to confuse religion with the courtship of death.

NOTES

1. Benjamin R. Barber, *Jihad vs. McWorld* (New York: Ballentine Books, 1996).

2. For an account of the new democratic realism see Benjamin R. Barber, 'Terrorism and the New Democratic Realism', *The Nation,* January 4, 2002.

3. Pope John Paul's Apostolic Exhortation, cited in the *New York Times,* January 24,1999.

4. James D. Wolfensohn, president of the World Bank, cited by Jim Hoagland, 'Richer and Poorer', *Washington Post* National Weekly Edition, May 3, 1999, p. 5

15. Two Cheers for Colonialism

Dinesh D'Souza

When there is one social phenomenon, there are at least two interpretations. Some argue that current academia is too liberal without looking at the other side. "Liberal" scholars have been accused of biasing readers. This article shows how the "conservative" scholars recall the impacts of colonization. The "liberal side" tends to emphasize how colonialism, the early phase of globalization, destroys the fundamental social fabric of non-Western societies. The "conservative side" argues that Western culture has contributed to colonized people. D'Souza contends that Western capitalism and democracy, brought by British colonialism, liberated the Indian people who were shackled with traditions of caste system, human bondage, and oppression. Probably, many American anthropologists would not agree with the author on all points. However, our readers need to understand multiple perspectives, and develop critical, analytical skills in understanding global social and cultural issues without prejudgment.

Colonialism has gotten a bad name in recent decades. Anticolonialism was one of the dominant political currents of the 20th century, as dozens of European colonies in Asia and Africa became free. Today we are still living with the aftermath of colonialism. Apologists for terrorism, including Osama bin Laden, argue that terrorist acts are an understandable attempt on the part of subjugated non-Western peoples to lash out against their longtime Western oppressors. Activists at last year's World Conference on Racism, including the Rev. Jesse Jackson, have called on the West to pay reparations for slavery and colonialism to minorities and natives of the third world.

These justifications of violence, and calls for monetary compensation, rely on a large body of scholarship that has been produced in the Western academy. That scholarship, which goes by the name of anticolonial studies, postcolonial studies, or subaltern studies, is now an intellectual school in itself, and it exercises a powerful influence on the humanities and social sciences. Its leading Western scholars include Edward Said, Gayatri Spivak, Walter Rodney, and

Samir Amin. Their arguments are supported by the ideas of third-world intellectuals like Wole Soyinka, Chinweizu, Ashis Nandy, and, perhaps most influential of all, Frantz Fanon.

The assault against colonialism and its legacy has many dimensions, but at its core it is a theory of oppression that relies on three premises: First, colonialism and imperialism are distinctively Western evils that were inflicted on the non-Western world. Second, as a consequence of colonialism, the West became rich and the colonies became impoverished; in short, the West succeeded at the expense of the colonies. Third, the descendants of colonialism are worse off than they would be had colonialism never occurred.

In a widely used text, *How Europe Underdeveloped Africa,* the Marxist scholar Walter Rodney accuses European colonialism of "draining African wealth and making it impossible to develop more rapidly the resources of the continent." The African writer Chinweizu strikes a similar note in his influential book *The West and the Rest of Us.* He offers the following explanation for African poverty: "White hordes have sallied forth from their Western homelands to assault, loot, occupy, rule, and exploit the world. Even now the fury of their expansionist assault on the rest of us has not abated." In his classic work *The Wretched of the Earth,* Fanon writes, "European opulence has been founded on slavery. The well-being and progress of Europe have been built up with the sweat and the dead bodies of Negroes, Arabs, Indians, and the yellow races."

Those notions are pervasive and emotionally appealing. By suggesting that the West became dominant because it is oppressive, they provide an explanation for Western global dominance without encouraging white racial arrogance. They relieve the third world of blame for its wretchedness. Moreover, they imply politically egalitarian policy solutions: The West is in possession of the "stolen goods" of other cultures, and it has a moral and legal obligation to make some form of repayment. I was raised to believe in such things, and among most third-world intellectuals they are articles of faith. The only problem is that they are not true.

There is nothing uniquely Western about colonialism. My native country of India, for example, was ruled by the British for more than two centuries, and many of my fellow Indians are still smarting about that. What they often forget, however, is that before the British came, the Indians had been invaded and conquered by the Persians, the Afghans, Alexander the Great, the Mongols, the Arabs, and the Turks. Depending on how you count, the British were preceded by at least six colonial powers that invaded and occupied India since ancient times. Indeed, ancient India was itself settled by the Aryan people, who came from the north and subjugated the dark-skinned indigenous people.

Those who identify colonialism and empire only with the West either have no sense of history or have forgotten about the Egyptian empire, the Persian empire, the Macedonian empire, the Islamic empire, the Mongol empire, the Chinese empire, and the Aztec and Inca empires in the Americas. Shouldn't the Arabs be paying reparations for their destruction of the Byzantine and Persian empires? Come to think of it, shouldn't the Byzantine and Persian people be paying reparations to the descendants of the people they subjugated? And while we're at it, shouldn't the Muslims reimburse the Spaniards for their 700-year rule?

As the example of Islamic Spain suggests, the people of the West have participated in the game of conquest not only as the perpetrators, but also as the victims. Ancient Greece, for example, was conquered by Rome, and the Roman Empire itself was destroyed by invasions of Huns, Vandals, Lombards, and Visigoths from northern Europe. America, as we all know, was itself a colony of England before its war of independence; England, before that, had been subdued and ruled by Normans from France. Those of us living today are taking on a large project if we are going to settle on a rule of social justice based on figuring out whose ancestors did what to whom.

The West did not become rich and powerful through colonial oppression. It makes no sense to claim that the West grew rich and strong by conquering other countries and taking their stuff. How did the West manage to do that? In the late Middle Ages, say 1500, the West was by no means the world's most affluent or most powerful civilization. Indeed, those of China and of the Arab-Islamic world exceeded the West in wealth, in knowledge, in exploration, in learning, and in military power. So how did the West gain so rapidly in economic, political, and military power that, by the 19th century, it was able to conquer virtually all of the other civilizations? That question demands to be answered, and the oppression theorists have never provided an adequate explanation.

Moreover, the West could not have reached its current stage of wealth and influence by stealing from other cultures, for the simple reason that there wasn't very much to take. "Oh yes there was," the retort often comes. "The Europeans stole the raw material to build their civilization. They took rubber from Malaya, cocoa from West Africa, and tea from India." But as the economic historian P. T. Bauer points out, before British rule, there *were* no rubber trees in Malaya, no cocoa trees in West Africa, no tea in India. The British brought the rubber tree to Malaya from South America. They brought tea to India from China. And they taught the Africans to grow cocoa, a crop the native people had never heard of. None of this is to deny that when the colonialists could exploit native resources, they did. But that larceny cannot possibly account for the enormous gap in economic, political, and military power that opened up between the West and the rest of the world.

What, then, is the source of that power? The reason the West became so affluent and dominant in the modern era is that it invented three institutions: science, democracy, and capitalism. All those institutions are based on universal impulses and aspirations, but those aspirations were given a unique expression in Western civilization.

Consider science. It is based on a shared human trait: the desire to know. People in every culture have tried to learn about the world. Thus the Chinese recorded the eclipses, the Mayans developed a calendar, the Hindus discovered the number zero, and so on. But science—which requires experiments, laboratories, induction, verification, and what one scholar has called "the invention of invention," the scientific method—that is a Western institution. Similarly, tribal participation is universal, but democracy—which involves free elections, peaceful transitions of power, and separation of powers—is a Western idea. Finally, the impulse to trade is universal, and there is nothing Western about the use of money, but capitalism—which requires property rights, contracts, courts to enforce them, limited-liability corporations, stock exchanges, patents, insurance, double-entry bookkeeping—this ensemble of practices was developed in the West.

It is the dynamic interaction among these three Western institutions—science, democracy, and capitalism—that has produced the great wealth, strength, and success of Western civilization. An example of this interaction is technology, which arises out of the marriage between science and capitalism. Science provides the knowledge that leads to invention, and capital-ism supplies the mechanism by which the invention is transmitted to the larger society, as well as the economic incentive for inventors to continue to make new things.

Now we can understand better why the West was able, between the 16th and 19th cen-turies, to subdue the rest of the world and bend it to its will. Indian elephants and Zulu spears were no match for British rifles and cannonballs. Colonialism and imperialism are not the cause of the West's success; they are the result of that success. The wealth and power of European nations made them arrogant and stimulated their appetite for global conquest. Colonial pos-sessions added to the prestige, and to a much lesser degree the wealth, of Europe. But the pri-mary cause of Western affluence and power is internal—the institutions of science, democracy, and capitalism acting together. Consequently, it is simply wrong to maintain that the rest of the world is poor because the West is rich, or that the West grew rich off stolen goods from Asia, Africa, and Latin America. The West created its own wealth, and still does.

The descendants of colonialism are better off than they would be if colonialism had never happened. I would like to illustrate this point through a personal example. While I was a young boy, growing up in India, I noticed that my grandfather, who had lived under British colo-nialism, was instinctively and habitually antiwhite. He wasn't just against the English; he was generally against white people. I realized that I did not share his antiwhite animus. That puz-zled me: Why did he and I feel so differently?

Only years later, after a great deal of reflection and a fair amount of study, did the answer finally hit me. The reason for our difference of perception was that colonialism had been pretty bad for him, but pretty good for me. Another way to put it was that colonialism had injured those who lived under it, but paradoxically it proved beneficial to their descendants. Much as it chagrins me to admit it—and much as it will outrage many third-world intellectuals for me to say it—my life would have been much worse had the British never ruled India.

How is that possible? Virtually everything that I am, what I do, and my deepest beliefs, all are the product of a worldview that was brought to India by colonialism. I am a writer, and I write in English. My ability to do this, and to reach a broad market, is entirely thanks to the British. My understanding of technology, which allows me, like so many Indians, to function successfully in the modern world, was largely the product of a Western education that came to India as a result of the British. So also my beliefs in freedom of expression, in self-government, in equality of rights under the law, and in the universal principle of human dig-nity—they are all the products of Western civilization.

I am not suggesting that it was the intention of the colonialists to give all those wonder-ful gifts to the Indians. Colonialism was not based on philanthropy; it was a form of conquest and rule. The British came to India to govern, and they were not primarily interested in the development of the natives, whom they viewed as picturesque savages. It is impossible to measure, or overlook, the pain and humiliation that the British inflicted during their long period of occupation. Understandably, the Indians chafed under that yoke. Toward the end of the British reign in India, Mahatma Gandhi was asked, "What do you think of Western civi-lization?" He replied, I think it would be a good idea."

Despite their suspect motives and bad behavior, however, the British needed a certain amount of infrastructure to effectively govern India. So they built roads, shipping docks, railway tracks, irrigation systems, and government buildings. Then they realized that they needed courts of law to adjudicate disputes that went beyond local systems of dispensing justice. And so the British legal system was introduced, with all its procedural novelties, like "innocent until proven guilty." The British also had to educate the Indians, in order to communicate with them and to train them to be civil servants in the empire. Thus Indian children were exposed to Shakespeare, Dickens, Hobbes, and Locke. In that way the Indians began to encounter words and ideas that were unmentioned in their ancestral culture: "liberty," "sovereignty," "rights," and so on.

That brings me to the greatest benefit that the British provided to the Indians: They taught them the language of freedom. Once again, it was not the objective of the colonial rulers to encourage rebellion. But by exposing Indians to the ideas of the West, they did. The Indian leaders were the product of Western civilization. Gandhi studied in England and South Africa; Nehru was a product of Harrow and Cambridge. That exposure was not entirely to the good; Nehru, for example, who became India's first prime minister after independence, was highly influenced by Fabian socialism through the teachings of Harold Laski. The result was that India had a mismanaged socialist economy for a generation. But my broader point is that the champions of Indian independence acquired the principles, the language, and even the strategies of liberation from the civilization of their oppressors. This was true not just of India but also of other Asian and African countries that broke free of the European yoke.

My conclusion is that *against their intentions,* the colonialists brought things to India that have immeasurably enriched the lives of the descendants of colonialism. It is doubtful that non-Western countries would have acquired those good things by themselves. It was the British who, applying a universal notion of human rights, in the early 19th century abolished the ancient Indian institution of suttee—the custom of tossing widows on their husbands' funeral pyres. There is no reason to believe that the Indians, who had practiced suttee for centuries, would have reached such a conclusion on their own. Imagine an African or Indian king encountering the works of Locke or Madison and saying, "You know, I think those fellows have a good point. I should relinquish my power and let my people decide whether they want me or someone else to rule." Somehow, I don't see that as likely.

Colonialism was the transmission belt that brought to Asia, Africa, and South America the blessings of Western civilization. Many of those cultures continue to have serious problems of tyranny, tribal and religious conflict, poverty, and underdevelopment, but that is not due to an excess of Western influence; rather, it is due to the fact that those countries are insufficiently Westernized. Sub-Saharan Africa, which is probably in the worst position, has been described by U.N. Secretary General Kofi Annan as "a cocktail of disasters." That is not because colonialism in Africa lasted so long, but because it lasted a mere half-century. It was too short a time to permit Western institutions to take firm root. Consequently, after their independence, most African nations have retreated into a kind of tribal barbarism that can be remedied only with more Western influence, not less. Africa needs more Western capital, more technology, more rule of law, and more individual freedom.

The academy needs to shed its irrational prejudice against colonialism. By providing a more balanced perspective, scholars can help to show the foolishness of policies like reparations as well as justifications of terrorism that are based on anticolonial myths. None of this is to say that colonialism by itself was a good thing, only that bad institutions sometimes produce good results. Colonialism, I freely acknowledge, was a harsh regime for those who lived under it. My grandfather would have a hard time giving even one cheer for colonialism. As for me, I cannot manage three, but I am quite willing to grant two. So here they are: two cheers for colonialism! Maybe you will now see why I am not going to be sending an invoice for reparations to Tony Blair.

Dinesh D'Souza is a fellow at the Hoover Institution at Stanford University and the author of What's So Great About America, *published by Regnery.*

16. What Real Globalization Would Mean

David Graeber

Globalization, global village, and emerging global culture are the most common terms used by scholars and the media. But do we know what this phenomena means? Graeber considers this idea carefully and urges us to consider what globalization would mean from a variety of perspectives. He argues that the wealthy capitalists' interpretation of globalization, the free market, is unchecked capital flight. He posits that more restriction of immigration from poor nations to wealthy nations maintains the lower prices of labor in poor nations. What would seem to be a common sense understanding of globalization changes radically as different people experience and interpret it.

In the wake of the massive protests at the IMF/World Bank meetings in Washington, pundits have been painting demonstrators the same way they did the protesters at Seattle: as enemies of "globalization"—and, by implication, benighted souls trying to duck the tide of history. Speaking as someone who stood on the barricades in D.C., I can attest that, from the protesters' perspective, *the truth is precisely the other way around.* If "globalization" means the unfettered movement of people, products, and ideas, then we're the ones in favor of it. You didn't see any banners denouncing "globalization" in Washington; what you saw were denunciations of "*corporate* globalization"—a system, embodied in organizations like the IMF, the WTO, and the World Bank, which is as much about imposing and maintaining forms of protectionism as about eliminating them.

Consider for a moment what real globalization—the genuine unification of our planet— might entail.

FREE IMMIGRATION

The globe today is divided up by invisible walls called "borders," maintained by hundreds of thousands of soldiers and police. As a result, if you happen to be a farmer born in a country which is mostly desert, it is illegal to simply move to one where there are adequate supplies of water. If you have the bad luck to be born in a country with no decent school system, it is illegal to move someplace where there is one. As a result, most people in the world today feel like prisoners. Real globalization would begin to take these barriers apart. *Proponents of corporate globalization demand exactly the opposite.* They want to maintain the invisible walls, and keep the poor trapped behind them, so as to allow Nike and The Gap to reap the profits of their desperation.

The Global Rule of Law

Real globalization would also mean creating the backbone of worldwide legal institutions: for instance, permanent tribunals to prosecute war criminals, enforce labor rights, and protect the global ecosystem. But it's the protesters who are pushing for such institutions; it's the U.S. government, that great proponent of corporate globalization, which is doggedly clinging to outmoded notions of national sovereignty in order to resist it.

The Free Movement of Knowledge, Cultural Products and Ideas

As economists like Dean Baker note, *the single most significant form of protectionism in the world today is our gargantuan system of patents and copyrights.* If we had a genuinely free global marketplace, whoever could manufacture the best computer chip for the cheapest price would be free to do so: whether they live in Chicago, Latvia, or Bangladesh. Prices everywhere would plummet, and some of the money freed up could easily be redirected towards publicly funded research. Instead, the U.S. government, which systematically violated English patent laws when we were the ones trying to industrialize in the nineteenth century, is now, like other proponents of corporate globalization, trying to prevent others from doing the same—even going so far as to threaten a trade war with China to preserve Warner Brothers' right to charge workers who make sixteen cents a day, $15.95 for a Michael Jackson CD, or trying to tighten patent restrictions on pharmaceutical production to prevent Indian companies from continuing to manufacture medicine that Indian people can actually afford. Real globalization would loosen such forms of protectionism, or even eliminate them.

This is not the only measure by which the protesters are actually greater supporters of free trade than their opponents.

Uniform Standards for Products and Licensing

Governments and business organizations have spent decades creating uniform international product standards. A screw or a lug wrench made in Mexico or the Philippines is now likely to fit an engine made in America. If it wasn't for this painstaking groundwork, it would have been impossible for American factories to so freely relocate to such countries. However, there has been no similar effort to create uniform standards in professional services: for instance, qualifications to practice law, medicine, or accountancy. As a result, sheet metal workers in St. Louis have to compete with their counterparts in Tijuana, but lawyers, CPAs, and insurance claims adjusters there do not. If they did, the public would save billions, but a lot of prosperous and influential people would get upset. *Corporate* globalizers want to protect the professional classes from international competition. *Real* globalizers would demand that everyone play by the same rules.

Market Principles in Banking

One near universal demand among the protesters in Washington was forgiveness for Third World debt. Really, this is just a demand to apply normal market discipline to international bankers. When a banker makes a loan, he is supposed to be taking a risk. That's what entitles him to collect high rates of interest. If a banker were to lend a million dollars to Al Capone to build the world's largest toothpick factory, and he skipped off with the cash, we'd say that banker was a fool and deserved to swallow his losses. If that same banker lends a million dollars to a Third World dictator, he need never do so, because he knows the IMF will always be there to squeeze the money out of the dictator's former victims. (If millions of children have to go hungry as a result, so be it.) Once again, as long as it is Citibank's interest that's at stake, corporate globalizers are happy to insist on the sacred principle of national sovereignty.

It is time be honest.

The real argument is not between those who are for globalization and those who are against it. It never was.

The real argument is not about whether to reduce the barriers; it's about which barriers to reduce, and how far, and for whose benefit.

Real globalization means reducing restrictions on everyone. *Corporate* globalization means reducing restrictions on those who are already rich and powerful, and strengthening the walls which imprison the poorest and most vulnerable. It is plainly immoral. That's why so many thousands of America's young people having been mobilizing to protest it, and demanding a form of globalization which will actually benefit the vast majority of people with whom we share this earth.

David Graeber is an assistant professor of anthropology at Yale University. He is author of the books Towards an Anthropological Theory of Value *and* Fragments of an Anarchist Anthropology.